PEOPLE, TASKS, & GOALS

STUDIES IN CHRISTIAN LEADERSHIP
AN INDEPENDENT-STUDY TEXTBOOK

"modified and printed for the Global Training Network of Teen Challenge International"

by Billie Davis

Developed in Cooperation with the ICI University Staff

Instructional Development Specialist:
David D. Duncan

Illustrator: Rick Allen

Global Training Network
PO Box 890
Locust Grove, VA 22508

First Edition 1983
Second Edition 1997 8/97 3M LR

© 1997　　　　　　　　　　　　　　　　　　S6261E-90
All Rights Reserved
ICI University　　　　　　　　　　　　ISBN 1-56390-029-7

Table of Contents

	Page
Course Introduction	5

UNIT ONE: PEOPLE *What leaders are like and how they relate to other people*

Lesson

1 People Who Lead and Follow	14
2 Leaders Appreciate People	40
3 Leaders Grow and Help Others Grow	66

UNIT TWO: TASKS *What leaders do and how they guide others in the work*

4 Leaders Plan and Organize	94
5 Leaders Communicate	120
6 Leaders Solve Problems and Make Decisions	146

UNIT THREE: GOALS *How leaders establish objectives and work with people to achieve the goals of the church*

7 Leaders Accept Responsibility	178
8 Leaders Work Toward Objectives	202
9 Leaders Are Motivated and Motivate Others	226
Appendices	258
Glossary	272
Answers to Self-Tests	282
Unit Student Reports	289
Answer Sheets	303

GLOBAL TRAINING NETWORK TRAINING PROGRAM

This is one of the many courses being offered by GTN to help prepare people to work with people who have life controlling problems and are wanting to work in a faith-based drug and alcohol rehabilitation setting. Each one of our courses is designed to meet your needs as you prepare for the work ahead.

There are several modules to our program:

- Biblical Knowledge
- Counseling Ministry
- Health Education
- Ministry Service
- Business Administration
- Personnal Growth

Each one of these targets areas of needs that must be addressed in preparation to serve. All of these have been prepared in a self-teaching format.

Course Introduction

Most learning comes to us in two ways: from patterns and from principles. In this course you will study leadership in both these ways. You will examine the patterns, or examples, provided by several of God's chosen leaders. You will be guided in an analysis of the principles which made their leadership effective. You will have opportunities for Bible study, using a fresh perspective—the theme of leadership. Also, you will learn the most advanced theories of human development and leadership and see how to apply these theories in harmony with Christian faith and practice.

The central truth in this course is that leadership is God's method and God's tool for working out His plan and His purpose for earth and people. The course is organized into three units to emphasize the three major factors in leadership: the PEOPLE (both leaders and those who are led), the TASKS which must be accomplished, and the GOALS which are to be achieved. Good leadership requires balanced attention to the three factors. Therefore the three major leadership qualities which the course will help you to develop are: EMPATHY, to help you work with people; COMPETENCE, to help you do the tasks effectively; and a sense of mission or CALLING, to help you achieve the objectives and goals.

Course Description

People, Tasks, and Goals: Studies In Christian Leadership is a course that presents the biblical foundations of leadership. It introduces the student to the theory and practice of leadership and guides him in the application of both biblical and theoretical principles. The material is appropriate for both beginning and experienced layleaders and ministers, as well as for those who wish to train others in Christian leadership. The main emphasis is upon development of gifts and capacities and interpersonal relationships among leaders and followers.

Course Objectives

When you finish this course you should be able to:

1. Explain the biblical concept of leadership, and give examples.
2. Explain the people, tasks, and goals model of Christian leadership.
3. Recognize and evaluate leadership gifts and capacities in yourself and others.
4. Demonstrate specific leadership skills, competencies, and attitudes, and help to develop these in others.
5. Accept and appreciate your roles and responsibilities in relation to other leaders and followers in the attainment of Christian goals.

Textbooks

You will use *People, Tasks, and Goals: Studies in Christian Leadership* by Billie Davis as both the textbook and study guide for the course. The Bible is the only other textbook required. The Scriptures in this course, unless otherwise noted, are from the New International Version, 1978 edition.

Study Time

How much time you actually need to study each lesson depends in part on your knowledge of the subject and the strength of your study skills before you begin the course. The time you spend also depends on the extent to which you follow directions and develop skills necessary for independent study. Plan your study schedule so that you spend enough time to reach the objectives stated by the author of the course and your personal objectives as well.

Lesson Organization and Study Pattern

Each lesson includes: 1) lesson title, 2) opening statement, 3) lesson outline, 4) lesson objectives, 5) learning activities, 6) key words, 7) lesson development including study questions, 8) self-test (at the end of the lesson development), 9) answers to the study questions.

Course Introduction 7

The lesson outline and objectives will give you an overview of the subject, help you to focus your attention on the most important points as you study, and tell you what you should learn.

Most of the study questions in the lesson development can be answered in spaces provided in this study guide. Longer answers should be written in a notebook. As you write the answers in your notebook, be sure to record the number and title of the lesson. This will help you in your review for the unit student report.

Do not look ahead at the answers until you have given your answer. If you give your own answers, you will remember what you study much better. After you have answered the study questions, check your answers with those given at the end of the lesson. Then correct those you did not answer correctly. The answers are not given in the usual numerical order so that you will not accidentally see the answer to the next question.

These study questions are very important. They will help you to remember the main ideas presented in the lesson and to apply the principles you have learned.

How to Answer Questions

There are different kinds of study questions and self-test questions in this study guide. Below are samples of several types and how to answer them. Specific instructions will be given for other types of questions that may occur.

A *MULTIPLE-CHOICE* question or item asks you to choose an answer from the ones that are given.

Example

1 The Bible has a total of
a) 100 books.
b) 66 books.
c) 27 books.

The correct answer is *b) 66 books.* In your study guide, make a circle around *b)* as shown here:

1 The Bible has a total of a
a) 100 books.
(b) 66 books.
c) 27 books.

(For some multiple-choice items, more than one answer will be correct. In that case, you would circle the letter in front of each correct answer.)

A *TRUE-FALSE* question or item asks you to choose which of several statements are TRUE.

Example

2 Which statements below are TRUE?
a The Bible has a total of 120 books.
(b) The Bible is a message for believers today.
c All of the Bible authors wrote in the Hebrew language.
(d) The Holy Spirit inspired the writers of the Bible.

Statements **b** and **d** are true. You would make a circle around these two letters to show your choices, as you see above.

A *MATCHING* question or item asks you to match things that go together, such as names with descriptions, or Bible books with their authors.

Example

3 Write the number for the leader's name in front of each phrase that describes something he did.

..1.. **a** Received the Law at Mt. Sinai   1) Moses

..2.. **b** Led the Israelites across Jordan   2) Joshua

..2.. **c** Marched around Jericho

..1.. **d** Lived in Pharaoh's court

Phrases **a** and **d** refer to Moses, and phrases **b** and **c** refer to Joshua. You would write **1** beside **a** and **d**, and **2** beside b and **c**, as you see above.

Ways to Study this Course

If you study this GTN course by yourself, all of your work can be completed by mail. Although GTN has designed this course for you to study on your own, you may also study it in a group or class. If you do this, the instructor may give you added instructions besides those in the course. If so, be sure to follow his instructions.

Possibly you are interested in using the course in a home Bible study group, in a class at church, or in a Bible school You will find both the subject content and study methods excellent for these purposes.

Unit Student Reports

At the end of the book you will find the Unit Student Report and Answer Sheets. Follow the directions included in the course and in the unit student reports. You should complete and send your answer sheets to your instructor for his correction and suggestions regarding your work. If you are not studying with an GTN office you will still benefit by answering the questions in the Student Report.

Certificate

Upon the successful completion of the course and the final grading of the unit answer sheets by your GTN instructor, you will receive your Certificate of Award.

Author of This Course

Billie Davis, Ed.D., has both training and experience in the fields of administration and management of church, school, and government organizations. She has degrees in sociology and education. She retired as associate professor of Behavioral Sciences, at Evangel College, in Springfield, Missouri, USA. She has written much material for Christian teachers and leaders, in two languages, and has conducted training seminars in many countries. She is an ordained minister in Christian service and is married to a minister.

Your GTN Instructor

Your GTN instructor will be happy to help you in any way possible. If you have any questions about the course or the unit student reports, please feel free to ask him. If several people want to study this course together, ask about special arrangements for group study.

God bless you as you begin to study *People, Tasks, and Goals, Studies in Christian Leadership*. May it enrich your life and Christian service and help you fulfill more effectively your part in the body of Christ.

for your notes

Unit 1
PEOPLE
WHAT LEADERS ARE LIKE AND HOW THEY RELATE TO OTHER PEOPLE

Lesson 1
People Who Lead and Follow

"I am happy to announce that we have selected a youth leader," said the pastor. "I want our work to be improved. There are many young people to reach. I can't do it alone, and now God has provided us an excellent helper. This is Mr. Pedro Gonzales."

Pedro was smiling as he walked briskly to the front of the room. "Thank you," he responded. "I feel that God has led me into this position. I ask your prayers that I will be a good leader."

This was a great moment for Pedro. He was born into a Christian family and had served the Lord since childhood. He had believed that someday God would place him in a position of leadership. "I will be a leader," he said to his older brothers one day. "It may be that sometime the members of my own family will be among those who follow me."

His brothers laughed at him. "What a great leader you'll make!" they said mockingly. Even his parents warned him. "Don't get big ideas, son," his father said.

But now his dreams were coming true. He was chosen above his brothers and others in the church. "I will show my brothers," he said in his heart. "I will show everyone what a good leader I can be. I will plan carefully and give clear instructions to all the young people. I will see that things are done right, and the Lord's work will prosper."

"I feel that God has led me ..."

What do you think of Pedro? Does he understand the meaning of leadership? Will he be a good leader? In this lesson we will look at the example of one of God's chosen leaders. It will help us discuss these questions. It will help us begin our study of what Christian leaders are like and how they work with people to accomplish the purposes of God.

lesson outline

Leadership in God's Plan
A Biblical Model–Joseph
Leadership Characteristics

lesson objectives

When you finish this lesson you should be able to:

- Describe the place of leadership in the plan of God.
- List characteristics typical of persons who are successful in positions of leadership.
- Recognize examples of leadership characteristics in biblical material and in life situations.

learning activities

1. Carefully read the preliminary section in this independent-study textbook. You will find examples of the kinds of study questions used in this textbook and how to answer each one.

2. Read carefully the opening pages of this lesson and the outline which is given. Read also the objectives, both the lesson objectives which are listed at the beginning of the lesson and the enabling objectives which are given throughout the lesson. These objectives tell you what you should be able to do after you have studied the lesson. The study questions and the self-test are based on them.

3. Before you begin the lesson, find the meaning of each word in the glossary at the end of this study guide. In a specialized study such as leadership, some words have meanings slightly different from those in common use; therefore, it is important that you refer to the glossary.

4. Read the lesson and do the exercises in the lesson development. Be sure to read Bible portions as you are instructed. This is necessary to gain a full understanding of the lesson material. Write answers to questions in this study guide where space is provided. Write longer answers in a notebook. You will get more out of the course if you make it a practice to put something of your own into writing before you look ahead to the answers. Check your answers with those given at the end of the lesson.

5. Take the self-test at the end of the lesson. Check your answers carefully with those provided at the back of this study guide.

key words

Understanding the key words we have listed at the beginning of each lesson will help you as you study. You will find key words listed in alphabetical order and defined in the glossary at the back of this independent-study textbook. If you are in doubt about the meaning of any of the words on the list, you may look them up now or when you come across them in your reading.

Please take time to learn the definitions of any new words, since they add to a complete understanding of this course.

administration	empowered	perpetuation
attitudes	exemplary	principle
authority	ministry	responsibility
behaviors	operations	responsible
capabilities	oppressive	specific
characteristics	organizations	traits

lesson development

LEADERSHIP IN GOD'S PLAN

Before we return to Pedro Gonzales, let's consider the basic question of why we are interested in the subject of leadership. Why are there leaders? If you think about it you begin to realize that some kind of leadership exists wherever two or more persons are doing something together. "You take that end and I'll take this end," you may say as you and another person begin to lift a heavy box or a piece of lumber. The other person cooperates with your suggestion, and suddenly you are the leader. As family members work together leadership becomes necessary. In the field and on the job there are leaders. At school and in church people lead and follow. Why is this so? What reason can you give?

1 Circle the letter in front of the completion you think is best for this sentence: The main reason leadership is needed is to
a) organize people into groups.
b) put capable people in control of others.
c) accomplish a purpose.

Leadership Defined

Objective 1. *Explain what is meant by the expression: the plan of God.*

Leadership is needed to accomplish a purpose—to get something done. The idea of Christian leadership exists because God has a purpose. There is something He wants done. He wants to express His love and mercy to all the peoples of the earth, and he wants to be loved and worshipped by them. God has a definite plan by which He will do this. So, when we speak of the *plan of God*, we mean that God has a certain, specific way of accomplishing His purpose. His will is not done in a random way, by chance. God has a plan. He knows in advance what His purpose is and how He will move to achieve it.

An important part of God's plan is that His work will be done by people, guided and empowered by the Holy Spirit God chooses people, and gives them specific tasks to do, in order to accomplish His purpose.

2 Match the statement on the left with the one on the right which best describes the situation.

.... **a** The leader urges everyone to bring visitors to church.   1) The leader has a plan.

.... **b** The leader says, "Our goal is 200 in attendance next week."   2) The leader has no plan.

.... **c** The leader gives each worker a list of persons to be visited this week.   3) The leader has a purpose.

3 Circle the letter in front of *each* correct ending for this sentence: When we say God has a plan we mean
a) God always works in the same way.
b) God has a specific way to accomplish His purpose.
c) God does His work without involving people.
d) God knows in advance what He will do.

Evidences of Leadership

Objective 2. *Recognize evidence that leadership is included in God's plan.*

Historical Accounts

There is no doubt that the concept or principle of leadership is included in God's plan. We know this from our study of the biblical accounts of God's relationship with mankind. When we read in the Bible the descriptions of events we find that there is no incident in which God is known to carry out His purpose by giving identical or similar instructions to every person who is to be affected by a message or a plan of action. God's method is to work through individuals; they share with others and involve others in accordance with what they have received from the Lord. God requires of certain persons that they be responsible for seeing that His plans are put into action. The result of this is that the responsible individuals take leadership positions, and, in many cases, organize groups which they guide toward the goal indicated by the Lord. Therefore, we can say that one evidence that leadership is included in God's plan is the evidence of *historical accounts*. Several of these accounts are given in this course.

Direct Calls and Instructions

In a number of the biblical accounts the actual call of God is recorded. God tells certain individuals that they are chosen to carry out His plans. In some cases He gives them detailed instructions. So another evidence of the need for leadership in God's plan is the evidence of *direct calls and instructions*. One example is the call of the apostle Paul, which we will examine in Lesson 3.

Gifts of Ministry

Bible writers, inspired by the Holy Spirit, state that God *gives* to the church persons to fill specific positions. These persons are called apostles, prophets, evangelists, pastors, and teachers (Ephesians 4:11-16; Romans 12:6-8). Such persons certainly hold leadership positions. And, in addition, God gives to the church abilities and operations which require leadership, such as the gift of administration or leadership and the gift of helping. Bible scholars refer to such persons and operations as *gifts of ministry*. These spiritual gifts are evidence of the importance of leadership in the plan of God.

Qualifications and Responsibilities

Another evidence that God's plan includes leadership is that detailed lists and descriptions of leadership *qualifications and responsibilities* are given in the Bible. In the Old Testament we find details concerning priests and kings. In the New Testament the qualifications for church leaders are clearly stated. The apostles showed great concern that persons in leadership positions be qualified spiritually, morally, and mentally.

Later in the course we will consider in greater detail the call of God, spiritual gifts, and biblical qualifications for leadership. We will study scriptural examples. We mention these matters now only as evidence that leadership is included in God's plan.

The church organizations with which most of us are familiar have been established on the basis of man's belief that God calls leaders and guides them for the purpose of accomplishing His plan on earth. The existence of the organized church, and many types of Christian ministries throughout the world, is evidence that God uses leaders.

4 Here are some brief quotations from the Bible. Read them thoughtfully. If you wish a more complete understanding, you may find them in the Bible and read the entire portions. Then match each quotation with a type of evidence from the list below.

.... **a** "Go and make disciples of all nations" (Matthew 28:19).

.... **b** "He Moses] chose capable men ... and made them leaders of the people" (Exodus 18:25).

.... **c** "A deacon ... must manage his children and his household well" (1 Timothy 3:12).

.... **d** "It was he who gave some to be apostles, some to be prophets, some to be evangelists, and some to be pastors and teachers" Ephesians 4:11).

.... **e** "Be shepherds of God's flock that is under your care" (1 Peter 5:2).

.... **f** "Joshua ... chose ... his best ... men and sent them out ..." (Joshua 8:3).

1) Historical account
2) Gifts of ministry
3) Direct calls and instructions
4) Qualifications and responsibilities

A BIBLICAL MODEL—JOSEPH

Objective 3. *Identify leadership principles in the experiences of Joseph.*

A local church, with a congregation of people and a place of worship, usually is the result of the leadership of one or a few persons. As such persons experience the calling and direction of God, they work to win souls and train Christians. The development and perpetuation of such activities require further leadership.

Now we can return to Pedro Gonzales. His story indicated that the pastor was a local church leader such as we have described. As this pastor worked to accomplish God's purpose, he realized that a helper was needed. That is how it came about that Pedro was placed into a position of leadership.

You notice that Pedro was to be a youth leader. At the same time, he was to work under the leadership of his pastor. Remember this principle, for we will study it later: Most Christian leadership is *middle leadership*. Most Christian leaders follow other leaders, and all follow the Lord.

Look back and review Pedro's thoughts and actions when he was presented as a leader. He felt that he was being led by God, and he requested prayer. Also, he declared that he would plan carefully and give clear instructions. He wanted the work of the Lord to prosper.

All this sounds very good. But do you see any problem in the way he was thinking? What about pride? Did he seem a little inclined to be proud of his position and boast of it? Did he seem perhaps too eager to use his authority to giving instructions to others? How should a Christian respond when he is given a position of leadership?

We can find help in answering such questions as we read Bible accounts of leadership experiences. One of the most complete and detailed of these is the life story of Joseph. Certainly this story is more than a historical record. God has preserved it for us, also, as a superb study in human behavior and leadership principles.

Even though you feel that you know the story well, you should take time now to review it, as our discussion will be from a viewpoint which may be new to you. The complete account is found in the book of Genesis, chapters 37, 39A8. Key portions for our study of leadership are: chapters 37, 39–42; 41:1-25; 43:1, 15, 24–31; 45:1-15. This may seem like a long reading assignment, but you will find it interesting as well as worthwhile.

Next we will examine a summary of the story. We will notice in it some of Joseph's characteristics and try to answer for ourselves the question: What kind of person was Joseph? In order to do this, we will consider three basic types of characteristics. These are: personal qualities, thoughts and feelings, and actions. Success as a leader relates to all of these.

When you read books on leadership you may find that the personal qualities of a leader are called *leadership traits*, the thoughts and feelings of a leader are called *leadership attitudes*, and the actions of a leader are called *leadership behaviors*. In this study we will use the word *characteristics* to include all of these. Nevertheless, it will be to your advantage to understand each of these terms, so we will use them from time to time throughout the course.

5 To help you identify traits, attitudes, and behaviors, read these sentences concerning Pedro Gonzales, and match each with the correct term given at the right.

.... **a** Pedro smiled and walked briskly.

.... **b** Pedro believed he would be a good leader.

.... **c** Pedro was a devoted Christian.

.... **d** Pedro was confident.

.... **e** Pedro gave clear instructions.

1) Trait
2) Attitude
3) Behavior

Joseph—A Leader in Slavery

"So you think you'll be the big boss, do you? And actually rule over us!" It was with words like these, spoken in tones of ridicule, that Joseph was answered when he told his dreams to his brothers. He dreamed he would be a great leader. His brothers had a belief which is wrong but is shared by many people. They believed that the main purpose of leadership is to give one person power over others—to boss people.

The Bible account of Joseph's experiences leads us to know that this is not God's idea of leadership. Joseph may have had some pride in his heart as he told his dreams, but nothing in his life suggests that he was boastful or oppressive to others. Probably his feeling concerning the dreams was more like wonder and amazement, which he shared openly with his family. He seems to have had a sense of being chosen by God for some purpose. We believe this, because in later years he reminded his brothers that it was God's plan to place him in a position of leadership, not for his own honor, but to accomplish God's purpose for many other people.

Probably Joseph did not fully understand this in his youth, but evidently he did accept without question the fact that God was leading him. The Bible record repeats several times the words: *The Lord was with Joseph*. Surely Joseph was aware of this, and his actions are evidence that he felt confident of God's guidance.

6 Do you see already in the experience of Joseph an example of God's methods? Why does God choose leaders? Write your answer here.

When Joseph's jealous brothers sold him as a slave, he was taken to Egypt and bought by a government official. In a short time he was put into a position of leadership. This is an example of the principle of *middle leadership*, isn't it? Joseph was a slave and had to follow orders from his master. At the same time, the master needed a helper in order to get all his work accomplished. So he chose Joseph as a middle leader, with assigned areas of responsibility. Joseph was put in charge of everything in the household and business of his master. That meant he had to manage property, money, and people. The Bible says that the Lord gave Joseph success in all that he did. This indicates to us that he was noticed by his master. It indicates, also, that Joseph made it known that God was the source of his success. The fact that the Lord was with him did not mean that his work was easy, but rather that God gave him strength to do it. It did not mean that God kept him from having problems, either. Rather, God gave him wisdom, courage, and faith so that he was able to solve problems.

Major problems began when his master's wife tried to tempt him with sexual advances. He refused her absolutely, saying, "I will not take advantage of my position of authority. I will not betray my master who has put me in a place of trust and responsibility. I will not sin against God who has blessed me."

So we see that Joseph respected his master, and even more, the Word and the will of God. But the woman persisted and became angry with Joseph because he rejected her. Finally, she accused him falsely and caused him to be put into prison.

7 Joseph's story shows us that a person in a lowly position can, at the same time, be an effective leader. Circle the letter in front of two statements which give the most important reasons for his success.
a) He required complete obedience from those under him.
b) He respected the authority of those over him.
c) He acted in accordance with God's will.
d) He believed that God would make his work easy.

Joseph—A Leader In Prison

Now it must have seemed to Joseph that his dreams of leadership would never come true. He had done his best, and those he served had turned against him. It is evidence of his true leadership character that he did not say, "What's the use? People are like that. You just can't trust anyone!"

Joseph was intelligent and very much aware that he had been mistreated. Nevertheless, he continued to have faith in God, and, most remarkable for our study of leadership, he continued to work efficiently and relate well to people on various social levels. Even life in prison could not keep the God-given dream from its influence upon the life of Joseph. Again his leadership capabilities became evident. The Bible gives no details, but says simply that the Lord was with Joseph and gave him success, and the warden put Joseph in charge of the other prisoners and all prison business.

How did the warden know that the Lord was with Joseph? What do you suppose a person could do in prison to show that he has God-given leadership ability? What did the warden see? Keep these questions in mind. Later, when we compare the story of Joseph with what we find in books on leadership we will understand that Joseph demonstrated several of the characteristics typical of successful leaders.

While Joseph was in prison two members of the king's staff—the chief baker and the cupbearer—were convicted of crimes. Since Joseph was in charge, they were under his supervision. One day he noticed that they looked dejected. Joseph was interested in them. He was concerned when they appeared to have troubles. "Why are you sad?" he asked them. They explained that they had had dreams which bothered them. Joseph did not hesitate to take control of the situation. "God can give us the meaning of your dreams," he declared. This showed again his complete confidence in the Lord and in his own relationship with the Lord.

God gave Joseph the true interpretation of the dreams, and he explained them to the men. For the cupbearer the dream meant release and restoration to his place with the king. Then Joseph wisely took advantage of an opportunity which seemed to be supplied by God. He told the man of his own situation. "When you go before the king," he asked, "please tell him about me, and request him to consider my case."

"All right," the cupbearer replied. But when he was released he forgot about Joseph. Once more a person failed to live up to Joseph's expectations.

Two years later the king had disturbing dreams. He began to inquire if anyone could interpret them. Then finally, the cupbearer did remember his experience in the prison. He told the king about Joseph. Joseph was brought from the prison to face the king, and again, giving all the credit and honor to the Lord, he told the interpretation of the dreams.

8 God used the dream of another prisoner in His plan to have Joseph released from prison. How did Joseph learn about the dream? Circle the letter in front of the correct answer.
a) Joseph told the prisoners to come to him for advice.
b) Joseph went to the prisoners and asked them why they were sad.

9 What does your answer to the last question tell you about the character of Joseph? Circle the letter in front of the correct answer.
a) He was interested in other people.
b) He expected other people to recognize his position.

Joseph—A Leader in Triumph

"The dreams mean that a famine is coming," Joseph told the king. "This land will have seven years of very good crops and abundant harvests. There will be more food than is needed. Then seven years of famine will come, when all crops will fail. There will be starvation, not only here, but in the lands all around us. It would be a good idea for you to set up a plan for storing food during the good years. Then there will be food during the seven bad years."

People Who Lead and Follow 27

The king was impressed with Joseph and his words of wisdom. "I will put you in charge," he said. "You work out the plan you have described and put it into operation." So Joseph was released from his prison sentence and placed in a position of leadership next to the king himself. He made the plans and saw that food was collected and stored.

The results were just as the Lord had revealed to Joseph. When the famine came, food distribution was begun and the people were saved from starvation. Many came from the surrounding countries to buy food. Joseph's position became more and, more powerful, and he was given the highest honor and respect

One day, as Joseph was supervising the selling of grain to those who had come from other countries, he saw his own brothers coming to buy food. They did not recognize him, for in the rich clothing of his office he was a very different person from the youth they had sold into slavery. But Joseph recognized them. And they bowed down before him, in respect as to a king. His dream of being a leader over them had come true at last.

We see in the Bible account that Joseph did not boast of his position nor try to get revenge for the way his brothers had treated him. He used the opportunity to help them learn some lessons, but did it with kindness, not for his own honor, but to strengthen them. Finally, he was not ashamed to let them see his emotion. He wept with gladness and love for his family.

Most important of all to his success as a leader chosen by God was that he recognized, in the time of his greatest power and victory, that he was an instrument used by God to bring benefits to others and to accomplish a divine purpose.

10 Read Genesis 45:4-13 again. It is the custom of some leaders to remind people of their past mistakes and scold them for faults and errors. Did Joseph scold his brothers? Explain briefly.

LEADERSHIP CHARACTERISTICS

Objective 4. *Name some characteristics which are shown by studies to be typical of leaders, and recognize examples and descriptions of these.*

No one who has made a careful study of the subject of leadership would try to describe the "typical leader." Studies show that some successful leaders have one set of characteristics and some have another. Hundreds of pages have been written on the subject. One book on leadership lists 339 references concerning characteristics of leaders. Writers of other books have declared that leadership cannot be understood in terms of characteristics, so there is no use for any discussion of the subject

It is our belief that no set of traits, attitudes, and behaviors can, in itself, describe a successful leader. However, we see considerable value in making a brief study of leadership characteristics. We have begun this already in our study of Joseph. We found that his traits (the sort of person he was), his attitudes (the way he thought and felt), and his behaviors (the way he acted) all combined to make him a successful leader. For example, we know from the words of Pharaoh that Joseph was wise and discerning, or discreet (Genesis 41:39). Also, we know that he was patient, since he waited many years without losing confidence that God would work out His plan. We could say, then, that wisdom and patience are two traits of a good leader. This does not mean that every person who is wise and patient will be a good leader. It does mean, we believe, that when we wish to develop the traits of good leadership in our own lives we should seek the Lord for wisdom and patience. It means that if we are wise and patient we have some leadership characteristics.

In a review of the best sources we know, among professional books and textbooks, we found several lists of characteristics which are said to be typical of successful leaders. Those which were mentioned in most of the lists are:

1. Empathy
2. Goal achievement
3. Competence
4. Emotional stability
5. Group membership
6. Ability to share leadership
7. Consistency and dependability

As we examine these one by one we shall see that all of them are found, not only in textbooks on leadership, but also in the Bible, as characteristics of good Christians. There is no doubt which scholars believe are needed for successful leadership! However, a list from the Bible would include these in addition:

1. A sense of God's calling, or mission
2. Awareness of being Christ's channel of love to mankind
3. Dependence upon the guidance of the Holy Spirit
4. Exemplary living in accordance with Christian morals and ethics

11 Read these lists again. Then try to write them from memory. Keep them in your heart and check up on yourself in your times of prayer and meditation. This will help you be a good leader.

Now we will consider the seven leadership characteristics which most scholars agree are essential. Our purpose is to answer from a biblical viewpoint this question: What is a leader like? We will encounter most of these characteristics in later lessons as we examine in more detail some attitudes and behaviors associated with successful leadership.

What a Leader Is Like

1. *Empathy*. A leader can see things from the point of view of another person. He tries to understand how others feel. The Bible expresses this in what we call *The Golden Rule*: "Do to others as you would have them do to you" (Luke 6:31). The writer of the book of Hebrews says, "Remember those in prison as if you were their fellow prisoners, and those who are mistreated as if you

yourselves were suffering" (Hebrews 13:3). We are told, also, to be sympathetic (1 Peter 3:8), and to carry one another's burdens (Galatians 6:2). Empathy is essential to Christian service and witnessing, and therefore to Christian leadership.

2. *Goal achievement.* A leader is able to set goals and work toward them until they are achieved. A Christian leader sets goals for himself and his group within the framework of the achievement of God's purposes. The apostle Paul states this plainly: "I press on toward the goal to win the prize for which God has called me heavenward in Christ Jesus" (Philippians 3:14). Throughout his writings the concept of goal achievement is evident. He speaks of his "purpose," his "reason," his "intent," and his "[God's] eternal purpose." (Ephesians 3:1, 10-11 and 2 Timothy 3:10 are examples.)

3. *Competence.* A leader does his work well He has the skills needed for his purposes. He knows facts and where to find information to help others. He works hard and sets high standards for himself and those who follow him. Throughout the Bible there are many references to the need for skill and diligence in the work of the Lord. For examples, see Exodus 35–36; Proverbs 12:27; 22:29; 31:10-31; 2 Timothy 2:15; James 2:14-16; 2 Peter 1:5-10.

4. *Emotional stability.* A leader "keeps his head." He is reasonable, confident, and cheerful. He does not get angry easily, is not willful, and is not easily discouraged. He can react in a peaceful and graceful manner when plans do not work out and difficulties arise. David expresses this concept from the point of view of one who trusts in the Lord. He declares that in all trouble he is still confident and will sing praises. "Be strong and take heart," he says (Psalm 27:14). See also Ephesians 4:31, 2 Timothy 4:5, and 1 Peter 4:7.

5. *Group membership.* A leader has a strong sense of being part of the group. He is aware of a common interest, and enjoys working with others. For the Christian leader, this is the body

relationship explained in 1 Corinthians 12 and Ephesians 4. Absolutely essential to Christian leadership is the understanding that individuals, like parts of a body, find their true life and usefulness when they are "joined and held together by every supporting ligament" (Ephesians 4:16). Every part of the body helps to support every other part. There are various functions as God's people work together, and leadership is one of them. So the leader exists only in relationship to those who follow.

6. *Ability to share leadership.* A leader works well with other leaders. He can accept a place as a middle leader, following others with loyalty and respect. And he can appoint helping leaders, trusting them with control over certain tasks. This characteristic is closely related to that of group membership. The emphasis here is on humility, and trust and respect toward others. A good leader has high regard for other people, and a Christian leader knows that God's method is to work through mankind, His highest creation. Therefore, the gifts and the callings of all are to be respected. We are told to "submit to one another out of reverence for Christ" (Ephesians 5:21). Paul sets the example for leaders in his frequent expressions of appreciation for his co-workers and helpers. Among the many references are Philippians 4:1-3, Colossians 4:7-14, and 1 Thessalonians 1:2-4.

7. *Consistency and dependability.* A leader is consistent and dependable. He communicates in a clear and honest way what he expects from the group and then helps to keep everyone working according to the plans. He does not become enthusiastic about a project and then forget it or change his mind suddenly without informing others. He keeps his word and obeys the same regulations that he sets for others. Jesus made it very clear that consistency and dependability are required in Christian service. "No one who puts his hand to the plow and looks back is fit for service in the kingdom of God" (Luke 9:62). Paul said, "Stand firm. Let nothing move you. Always give yourselves fully to the

work of the Lord" (1 Corinthians 15:58). See also Galatians 5:1 and Ephesians 4:14.

12 Here are seven statements concerning attitudes and behaviors of Joseph. Each of them is associated with one of the leadership characteristics we have listed. Place in front of each statement a number to indicate the appropriate characteristic.

.... **a** He said to Pharaoh, "We will store enough food to last for seven years."

.... **b** He did not get angry at the cupbearer who forgot him.

.... **c** He was aware of his family relationship and felt responsible for the welfare of his people.

.... **d** He continued to trust in God and do his work faithfully, even though he suffered misfortunes.

.... **e** He knew his brothers felt guilty and he tried to comfort them.

.... **f** His master and the warden saw that he did everything well.

.... **g** He was obedient and respectful to his master, to the warden, and to the king.

Let us look back and review what we have accomplished in this lesson. First, we considered Pedro Gonzales, a newly-appointed leader. Then we examined the biblical account of Joseph in order to discover traits, attitudes, and behaviors of a leader in a real situation. Finally, we looked at a list of leadership characteristics as compiled by scholars in textbooks on the subject of leadership. We found that each of these characteristics of good leadership is also a characteristic of good Christians and that Joseph is indeed a good example for us to follow.

Think once more of Pedro. What could we tell him to help him be a better leader? We can see now that he has some problems, can't we? First, he must remember that he is a middle leader, working under the Lord and under the pastor of the church. Then, he needs a more humble attitude. He must be careful not to take pleasure in the thought that he has a position above his brothers and the other young people. He must realize that being a Christian leader is somewhat different from being a boss in a commercial company. A good leader, like Joseph, has respect for those in positions above him and below him. A good leader does much more than give instructions to others. He works with others. He is quick to forgive the mistakes of others, and he continues to love people and expect the best from them, even when they fail him. He will try to guide them into more godly living, as Joseph did his brothers, to accomplish the will of the Lord.

self-test

MULTIPLE CHOICE. Circle the letter in front of the best answer for each question.

1 The "place of leadership in the plan of God" refers to the fact that God
a) has work to do and He accomplishes it in a predictable way.
b) accomplishes His purpose by employing perfect spiritual beings.
c) has a specific way to accomplish His purpose.
d) knows the folly of using people to accomplish His work.

2 An important part of God's plan is that His work will be done by
a) sincere, dedicated people who want to do good.
b) people He chooses, directs, and empowers to accomplish His purpose.
c) obedient angels who have the power and understanding to accomplish His purpose.
d) His people whom He compels to do His work.

3 Our knowledge of God shows that He
a) knows beforehand His purpose and how He will move to achieve it
b) is constantly changing His purpose to accommodate changing times.
c) is the captive of a fixed purpose and method of operation.
d) moves in predictable ways to achieve His purpose as it develops.

4 All of the following except one are evidence that leadership is included in God's plan. Which one is NOT an evidence?
a) Biblical qualifications and responsibilities of leadership are given.
b) Accounts of direct calls and instructions for leadership appear in the Bible.
c) The Bible reveals the concept of leadership in historical accounts and in gifts of leadership.
d) Cultural expectations of able people and societal demands reveal the necessity for leadership.

5 A very basic principle in Christian leadership involves middle management, which means that Christian leaders
a) follow only the Lord.
b) follow other leaders, and all follow the Lord.
c) follow their own inclinations and the Lord.
d) recognize their very limited rights and encourage leadership by consensus under the Lord.

6 Two principles of leadership which Joseph demonstrated when he served in the house of a government official were
a) respect for authority and submission to God's will.
b) his use of force to get his way and fear to secure obedience from those under his authority.
c) the desire to please everybody and the goal of being popular.
d) his sense of self-preservation and his desire to exercise absolute power.

7 In prison Joseph revealed some character traits which are common to all successful leaders: unswerving faith in God, faithfulness in service, and
a) hope that things would turn out well for him.
b) sympathy for the plight of less fortunate people.
c) interest in and concern for other people.
d) the knowledge that people will "let one down."

8 Years of difficulty passed before Joseph saw the part of God's plan that concerned him and his family. Then, with his brothers at his feet, he demonstrated what qualities of leadership?
a) Pride in his part of God's plan, an "I told you so" attitude, and the desire to remind them of their past faults.
b) Competence, efficiency, administrative firmness, and justice.
c) Compassion, understanding of his part in God's plan, forgiveness, and love.
d) Recognition that vengeance is the Lord's, total understanding of God's plan, and acceptance of the inhumanity of people.

9 Diligent service over many years without losing hope coupled with the good counsel he gave Pharaoh indicate which two of Joseph's character traits?
a) Competence and resourcefulness
b) Commitment to God and political ability
c) Longsuffering and administrative ability
d) Patience and wisdom

10 Joseph reveals the kind of attitudes that an effective leader must have. When the ordeal had ended, he did all of the following except one. Which one did he NOT do?
a) He did not boast or try to get revenge.
b) He recognized his own role as God's instrument to benefit others.
c) He reminded his brothers of his earlier dreams and predictions.
d) He put the entire episode into the perspective of God's plan.

11–17 In the following exercise, supply the appropriate leadership characteristic for its definition. The seven leadership characteristics noted in the lesson are listed below.

Empathy

Goal achievement

Competence

Emotional stability

Group membership

Ability to share leadership

Consistency and dependability

11 The ability of a leader to "keep his head" when difficulties arise and things do not work out according to plan is called

....

12 .... is the quality of a leader to work well with other leaders, as well as those above and below him.

13 The ability of a leader to feel with others, to see things from their perspective, is known as ....

14 .... describe the leader who communicates clearly to his group, helps to keep everyone working according to the plan, keeps his word, and obeys the same regulations he sets for others.

15 The characteristic of a leader who sets objectives and works toward them until they are achieved is

....

16 When a leader has a strong sense of being a part of the group, is aware of common interest, and enjoys working with others, we say he has the leadership characteristic of

....

17 .... is the term which describes the leader who works well, has the skills needed for his purposes, knows the facts and where to find information to help others, works hard and sets high standards for himself and those who follow him.

answers to study questions

The answers to your study exercises are not given in the usual order, so that you will not see the answer to your next question ahead of time. Look for the number you need, and try not to look ahead.

7 b) He respected the authority of those over him.
    c) He acted in accordance with God's will.

1 c) accomplish a purpose.

8 b) Joseph went to the prisoners.

2 a 2) The leader has no plan.
  b 3) The leader has a purpose.
  c 1) The leader has a plan.

9 a) He was interested in other people.

3 b) God has a specific way to accomplish His purpose.
    d) God knows in advance what He will do.

10 He told them not to be distressed. He comforted them by reminding them of God's plan.

4 a 3) Direct calls and instructions.
  b 1) Historical account.
  c 4) Qualifications and responsibilities.
  d 2) Gifts of ministry.
  e 3) Direct calls and instructions.
  f 1) Historical account.

11 Check your answer with the lists given under "Leadership Characteristics."

5 a 3) Behavior.
  b 2) Attitude.
  c 1) Trait.
  d 1) Trait.
  e 3) Behavior.

12 a 2) Goal achievement.
  b 4) Emotional stability.
  c 5) Group membership.
  d 7) Consistency and dependability.
  e 1) Empathy.
  f 3) Competence.
  g 6) Ability to share leadership.

6 God chooses leaders in order to accomplish His purposes.

LESSON 2
Leaders Appreciate People

Mr. Loi was late for dinner again. He was tired, and he frowned as his small son pulled at his coat

"I suppose you've been at the church all afternoon," said his wife, in a tone of disapproval.

"Of course," he replied crossly, "you should be glad the church is growing like this. We're starting six more Bible classes. That makes ten new ones since I've been in charge of our Christian education program. I had to see that the literature was ready for all the classes. Then two teachers came asking for help with their lessons. And there was a dispute because no one wants his class in the back room, and I had to go by the carpenter shop to explain about the chairs we ordered, and...."

"Why don't you get someone to help you?" his wife asked.

"People don't have enough interest in the Lord's work. They come late and upset the schedule. Nobody takes any responsibility," he declared, "or else they argue about who is in charge. They stand around wasting time. They make too many mistakes and I have to do it all over. I have to keep everything under very close supervision."

Mr. Loi has an important position in his church. He believes that he is a good leader, and in some ways, he is. He is dedicated to his work, as we can see from his conversation. What else do we learn about him from this same conversation? Do we learn something about the way he feels toward other people? How will this affect his success as a leader?

"Why don't you get someone to help you?"

In this lesson we will study some principles of human relations and discover that how we feel about people is important to good leadership. Our biblical model is Moses, to whom God gave one of the greatest leadership assignments ever known.

lesson outline

Moses—A Leader Relates to People
What Leaders Believe About People
How Leadership Style is Developed

lesson objectives

When you finish this lesson you should be able to:

- Describe leadership principles in the account of Moses and recognize applications of these principles.

- Explain the significance of a leader's beliefs concerning the people with whom he works.

- Evaluate various leadership styles and behaviors in relation to Christian leadership principles.

learning activities

1. Read the opening pages and objectives as you did for Lesson 1. It is important that you do this for each lesson as you continue through the course.

2. Do not neglect the key words. They will help you to understand the material and also to develop useful vocabulary for future studies.

3. Review the accounts of Moses in Exodus 2–7; 11–18; 32; 35–36. The portions actually used in the lesson material are: Exodus 2–3; 4:1-17; 12:31-38; 14:10-31; 15:22-25; 16:1-11; 17:1-15; 18:9-26; 32:1-14; 35:1-35; 36:1-7. Keep your Bible open to the book of Exodus as you study the lesson development section.

4. Study the lesson development and answer the study questions according to the procedure outlined in Lesson 1.

5. Take the self-test at the end of the lesson and check your answers carefully with those supplied at the back of this study guide. Review any items you answer incorrectly.

key words

appropriate	impulsive	relations
assume	manipulate	relationships
assumption	motivated	style
expectations	motivation	theory
frustration	potentialities	
harassing	recognition	

lesson development

MOSES—A LEADER RELATES TO PEOPLE

Objective 1. *Select true statements concerning the call of Moses to leadership and his response to the call*

The story of Moses is a story of leadership. In all literature there is no account so complete and clear in its application to a study of how God relates to leaders and how leaders relate to people.

Moses, like many great servants of the Lord, began early in life to have feelings of *empathy*. That is, he was interested in people. He cared about their condition and wanted to do something to help them. His first effort was impulsive, and undoubtedly he failed to seek the guidance of the Lord. He tried in his own way to fight against injustice. This, of course, led him to kill a man (Exodus 2:11-15). We see, though, when he ran away to hide he still had his sense of justice with him, and his desire to help people was expressed again as he drove away some shepherds who were harassing a group of women (2:16-19).

This act of kindness brought about his association with Jethro, whose daughter he married. One day while he tended the flocks of his father-in-law, he saw the strangely burning bush and went near to examine it. His act was one of a stable man with an inquiring mind, not afraid to approach an unknown situation.

"Moses, Moses!" God called to him from within the bush.

Moses answered, "Here I am." with a quiet confidence, and stood ready to listen. But he hid his face in respectful fear as God announced Himself.

The Lord said, "I have seen the misery of my people. I am concerned about their suffering. So I have come down to rescue them and to bring them up out of that land. So now, go. I am sending you to Pharaoh to bring my people out of Egypt."

We notice the pattern of God's method again. He had a purpose for His people, so He called a leader and gave him a task to do. By this time, however, Moses had become less impulsive and less sure of his own strength. The purpose of God was very great, and the task must have seemed almost impossible for a lone shepherd to accomplish.

"Who am I, to be able to do this?" Moses asked, "What if the people won't listen? How shall I make them understand that the Lord has sent me?"

Moses knew that a leader must act from a position of authority. God gave him that authority in the form of signs and wonders which he could perform in the name of the Lord. God promised to be with Moses and help him in the task. He made no promise of personal honor or reward for Moses, but He promised to help him accomplish the greatest purpose on earth. Still, Moses hesitated.

"I can't speak very well," he declared, "Please send someone else to do this work."

At this point God became angry with Moses. It is good to be humble, but humility must be balanced with faith in God and confidence that He will keep His promises. God told Moses that Aaron would speak for him. The two of them should assemble the elders of Israel and explain the plan of God. In this way everyone in a position of leadership would understand and accept his own responsibility as God gave the directions to Moses. Now Moses committed himself fully to the will of God, and the Bible tells us several times that he "did just as the Lord commanded."

1 Circle the letter in front of each TRUE statement.

a Moses was not concerned about people until he heard God's call.
b God expressed concern for people before He gave Moses a leadership task.
c God promised Moses that people would honor and respect him.
d The experience of Moses teaches us that leadership requires both humility and confidence.
e The leadership of Moses was based on God's authority.
f Moses understood that he was accepting a great responsibility.

"What Am I to Do with These People?"

Objective 2. *Name four ways of working with people which Moses learned from Jethro, and demonstrate a way to apply them.*

Leaders Appreciate People

As he followed the commandments and guidance of the Lord, Moses was able to organize the elders and prepare the people for the moment of their exodus from the slavery of Egypt. God worked in the heart of Pharaoh and sent the plagues upon the land. At last the order went forth, "Leave!... Take your flocks and herds . . . and go" (Exodus 12:32).

Can you imagine 600,000 men plus all the women, children, herds, and flocks beginning in the dark to abandon their houses and rush out into the open country (Exodus 12:37)? If you have ever had the duty of organizing a conference or retreat, or even an evening of evangelism visitation, then you know what a task it was for Moses and his helping leaders to organize that exodus.

In the first enthusiasm of the escape, according to the Bible account, everyone did just what the Lord commanded Moses. It is a principle of human behavior that when an activity is new and exciting people will follow their leader without question. But soon enthusiasm dies and problems are faced. Then people may question and grumble and even turn against the leader and blame him. This is what happened to Moses.

2 Read Exodus 14:10-12; 15:23-25; 16:2-3; 17:1-3. These verses are from the accounts of four events during the travels of the Israelites. What did the people do in each case? Write your answer here ....

....

Finally, when the people complained because there was no water, Moses cried out to the Lord, saying, "What am I to do with these people?"

This time, as before, God answered with a miracle to provide for His people. But in this case the Bible account gives us another indication of God's system of working with people.

3 Read Exodus 17:5. Moses received from God three instructions. He was to walk on ahead of the people. He was to take his staff. What was the third instruction?

....

Moses struck the rock "in the sight of the elders of Israel" and water came out for everyone to drink. The elders were witnesses. They had an opportunity to share closely in the ministry experience of Moses. They must have learned from him and gained new faith and inspiration for their own service among the people. Frequently in the Bible records we find this pattern of leaders sharing their ministry experiences. In the New Testament the Lord Jesus Christ and the apostle Paul are examples.

In the next recorded event we see again an illustration of the relationships among leaders and followers. Moses directed Joshua, and Joshua selected men to fight against enemies who attacked the Israelites. During the battle Moses held up his hands to the Lord. When his hands became tired he lowered them, and the enemy began to win the battle. So two of the men stood (one on each side of Moses as he sat on a rock) and held up his hands. The battle was won, and the Lord said to Moses, "Write this on a scroll as something to be remembered" (Exodus 17:14). It is a good thing for every leader to remember, as well, the importance of the middle leaders who go out to battle and the quiet followers who stand near and hold up his hands.

Like all good leaders, Moses was intensely interested in *goal achievement*. He was dedicated and diligent in his work, and since his success required the cooperation of the people, he was painfully disappointed when they failed to be as dedicated as he was. He loved the people so much that he was willing to give his life for them, but he had to learn that leadership requires another type of love. Leadership love is that which *trusts others, even when they seem weak*, to share the vision and contribute toward the achievement of the goal. Moses learned this truth from his father-in-law, Jethro.

When Jethro came to visit Moses, the two discussed the marvels God had performed and the experiences of the journey. Probably Moses expressed some of his distress because the people grumbled and failed both him and God. Maybe he repeated to Jethro the words he had spoken to the Lord, *"What am I to do with these people?"*

Leaders Appreciate People

Jethro observed Moses in his daily relationships with the people. He saw the dedication, concern, and endless hours of hard work as Moses gave himself completely in the Lord's service. All day the people came to Moses. He acted as judge, counselor, minister, and helper to each of them.

"The work is too heavy for you," declared Jethro, "You cannot handle it alone. Listen now to me and I will give you some advice."

Read again from your Bible the account in Exodus 18:13-26. You will find in the advice of Jethro the following ways of working with people:

1. Teach them the rules and regulations or policies.
2. Show them how to do each task.
3. Give them specific duties to perform.
4. Appoint middle leaders and organize the work with them.

This was Jethro's answer to the question of Moses. Jethro declared that if Moses would do this there would be two results. First, Moses would be able to stand the strain of the work. Second, the people would go home satisfied. Remember these two statements. Later we will find that they represent the ideal results of successful leadership: the goal accomplished, and the needs of the workers met at the same time!

4 Read again Jethro's four ways of working with people, then close your book and try to write them from memory. This is good advice which every Christian leader must follow.

5 Remember these statements which were made by Mr. Loi in our opening story? Place in front of each of them a number from Jethro's four ways of working with people, to indicate what Mr. Loi should do to solve his problem in each case.

.... **a** They stand around wasting time and leave some jobs undone.

.... **b** They come in late and upset the schedule.

.... **c** Nobody takes responsibility, or else everyone argues about who is in charge.

.... **d** They make so many mistakes that I have to do it all over.

You may wish to place more than one number by some of the items. The main point is to recognize that Mr. Loi could be a better leader, feel less strain, and keep the workers more satisfied *if* he would follow the advice of Jethro.

6 Read Exodus 18:22 again. Notice that it contains the same principle of leadership which we found in 17:5. That is, the load of Moses was to be lighter because.

....

The People of God and the People of Moses

Objective 3. *Explain why Moses was willing to work with the people even though they failed him.*

One of Moses' greatest assets as a leader was that he continued to see the potential for good in the people of God. He knew God would work through human beings to bring glory to His name and accomplish His purposes. The actions and words of Moses show that he intended to work with and through the people God had given him to lead. His love for God and his determination to work for God's purpose resulted in love and loyalty toward the people.

Let's look again at Exodus 18:15. When Jethro asked Moses why he spent so much time with the people, what was the reply? *"Because the people come to me to seek God's will."* We see, then, that although the people were rebellious at times, blamed Moses unfairly, and failed to put their trust in the Lord, they still had in their hearts a desire to know God and serve Him. They wanted to learn. They came for advice and help when they were in trouble. They accepted the judgment of the Lord in their disputes. They fought bravely against the enemies of Israel. In spite of the weaknesses he saw in them, Moses recognized all these strengths.

Once, in weakness and fear, when Moses was engaged in a highlight experience of all history—receiving the Word of God on Mt. Sinai—the people fell into the awful sin of idolatry (chapter 32). Our hearts ache with Moses when we read of his return to the camp and his burning frustration as he slammed the precious tablets of stone to the earth.

But in this same chapter (vs. 7-11) we read the most remarkable conversation between God and Moses:

"*Your* people," said God, "whom *you* brought out of Egypt, have become corrupt. . . . Now leave me alone so that my anger may burn against them and that I may destroy them. Then I will make you into a great nation."

But Moses answered, "Why should your anger burn against *your* people, whom *you* brought out of Egypt with great power and a mighty hand? . . . Turn from your fierce anger; relent and do not bring disaster on your people."

"Then the Lord relented."

The people had sinned. They were weak. They needed more teaching and guidance. But they were the people of God, and they were the people of Moses. God made Moses responsible for them, and Moses, in reliance on God, accepted the responsibility. He committed himself to God and to the people, to prepare and develop them as much as he could, with the Lord's help. After the disaster of the golden calf he organized them once again into a productive body. He called forth their best talents and most generous gifts, as we shall see, in the construction of the tabernacle. He taught them the Word of God, assigned them to tasks, and, finally, trusted to them the perpetuation of the work he had to leave unfinished.

7 Circle the letters in front of the best completions for the following sentence: Moses was willing to work with the people even though they failed him because
a) it was an honor to lead such a large group.
b) he knew they had strengths which could be developed.
c) he believed they wanted to do God's will.
d) he wanted God to be glorified through them.
e) he was determined to prove his leadership ability.

WHAT LEADERS BELIEVE ABOUT PEOPLE

Objective 4. *Identify assumptions which Jethro made about the people of God.*

We have considered the good advice which Jethro gave to Moses. We stated this advice in terms of four ways of working with people. We might summarize it by saying simply that Jethro told Moses to *expect more from his followers.*

Some experts in the field of leadership studies say that how we act as leaders is a direct result of what we believe about people. Our beliefs about people are called *assumptions* by some of the writers. What we expect from people and how we treat them, that is, our leadership actions, are based upon these assumptions. For example, we may assume that young people are physically stronger than older people. Therefore, if we were directing a moving project, we would require the younger ones to carry the heavy loads. We would expect them to accept these instructions without complaint.

Think how the words of a preacher could show what he believes about people. Suppose he says to the congregation: "You should be willing to sacrifice some of the time you spend for your own pleasure and use it for winning souls."

What assumptions are made by this preacher? Do you notice these? He assumes that:

1. The people spend time in pleasure.
2. They are selfish with their time.
3. They do not like to do soul winning—it is a sacrifice.
4. They could do soul winning if they were willing.

Leaders Appreciate People

This preacher shows low expectations of the people, since he expects them to love pleasure and dislike soul winning. On the other hand, he expects them to know how to do soul winning. He believes that if they would be willing to make the sacrifice, they could win souls.

But suppose the preacher were to say this: "You will be happy to know we are starting a class in soul winning. Now you can learn more about how to share the Good News with your neighbors." His assumptions are more like this:

1. The people would like to win souls, but they do not know how to go about it. They need training.
2. They are willing to spend time in training and in soul winning.
3. They are concerned about their neighbors.

In this case the preacher shows high expectations of the people, but he believes they are unable to act without some help. He wants to help them develop their potentialities.

8 Remember the advice of Jethro. What assumptions did he make about the people? Circle the letters in front of the best answers.
a) People work well without any organization.
b) Most people can work out all their own problems.
c) Most people will obey rules if they understand them.
d) Many people have leadership ability.
e) Most people can be trusted to make some decisions.

HOW LEADERSHIP STYLE IS DEVELOPED

Objective 5. *Relate examples of leadership behavior to assumptions made about people.*

The most notable study of how assumptions about people affect the development of leadership style is that of Douglas McGreggor. He says that the behaviors of many leaders are based upon what he calls *Theory X Assumptions*. These assumptions are: People do not like work and will avoid it if they can. People wish to avoid responsibility. People have little interest in the achievement of broad goals (such as the goals of an organization or a gospel ministry—often called *institutional goals*).

Mr. McGreggor rejects this set of assumptions and offers another which he calls *Theory Y Assumptions*. These include the following: Work is natural to people; they do not tend to avoid it. People will work willingly toward the achievement of objectives to which they are committed. People not only accept, but seek, responsibility. Most people (not just a few in high positions) can make important contributions to the achievement of institutional goals. Most people have unused potentialities. People will commit themselves to work toward those objectives to which they attach value.

Now we will be able to see how assumptions about people can lead to the development of a style of leadership. *Style* may be defined as a combination of behaviors, or a tendency to act in a certain way. Most books on leadership mention several *styles* which have been observed and described by researchers. Two of these which are mentioned by most writers are the *autocratic style* and the *democratic style*.

A leader who uses the autocratic style is in almost complete control of a group. He makes all significant decisions. He makes rules and enforces them. He gives detailed instructions to those who work under him. He supervises the work closely and personally.

A leader who uses the democratic style works more from within the group. He leads the group in making rules. He allows the group to participate significantly in decision making. He asks for suggestions and contributions from the group. He assigns some important responsibilities to group members.

A leader who accepts the Theory X Assumptions believes that most people are passive and lazy or resistant to work. They need to be "motivated" and given strong control. They must be directed, supervised, pushed, persuaded, and scolded. A leader who believes this may feel that it is necessary to manipulate people, make promises, or threaten them with punishments in order to get them to work toward achievement of the institutional goals. He will tend to develop an autocratic style of leadership.

A leader who accepts the Theory Y Assumptions believes that most people are already somewhat motivated to work toward a goal and that they desire some responsibility. This leader will try to arrange conditions in ways to make possible the best use of talents and abilities. He will give people opportunities to make choices and offer suggestions. He will help them to understand for themselves the value of the goal and make their commitment in a voluntary manner. If such a leader is competent he will develop a democratic style of leadership.

9 Look back again at the story of Mr. Loi. What were his feelings about people? Did he make assumptions more like those of Theory X or like those of Theory Y?

....

....

Of course we know that some people do try to avoid work. Some people need more direction and control than others. There are situations in which the leader must be very firm with his people, give them detailed instructions, and enforce rules that are necessary for the accomplishment of certain purposes. Good leaders learn how to be flexible and use methods which are appropriate with various people in various situations. We will study more about this in later lessons.

The main point to remember right now is that the leadership style you develop, and the degree of success you will have as a leader, depend to a great extent upon the assumptions you make about people. For the Christian leader it is interesting and important to notice that McGreggor's Theory Y Assumptions are descriptive of dedicated and practicing Christians. That is, Christians are already committed to a goal to which they attach great value. Like the people who came to inquire of Moses, most Christians do seek the will of God. They want to share in the work of the body of Christ. They have gifts, talents, and potentialities placed within them by the Lord. They tend to feel honor and pleasure when they are making some contribution to the Lord's work. Therefore, they need, in most cases, a leader who sees in them these qualities and tries to arrange conditions favorable for their development. This is what Moses did when he called the people together and inspired them to build the tabernacle according to God's plan.

10 Read Exodus 35:1-36:7. From the leadership behavior of Moses and the response he received, we can make the following assumptions about the people of God. Match each statement with an appropriate reference. You may use a reference more than once if you wish.

Assumptions

.... **a** People need some definite rules.

.... **b** People need a definite goal.

.... **c** Many people are willing to work.

.... **d** Many people are willing to give.

.... **e** People can be taught skills.

.... **f** People have God-given knowledge and skills.

References

1) 35:10
2) 36:2
3) 35:21
4) 35:35
5) 35:1-3
6) 35:34

Most of the scholars who write about leadership say that people are willing to work best when they feel they are making the most of their capacities. They give more of themselves when they are asked to do something which seems worthwhile. And they like to receive some recognition for what they do.

Certainly the experience of Moses in the building of the tabernacle shows that these principles are true in the Lord's work. You will notice, even, that Moses gave special recognition to individuals. He gave the credit for their abilities to God, but, at the same time, he mentioned in public the names of those, made in God's image, through whom was sent the knowledge and the skill (Exodus 35:30-35).

Do we not believe that the Lord who created the wondrous beauty of the universe could have sent down from heaven a

Leaders Appreciate People

glorious priestly garment for Aaron? But that was not God's method. It pleased Him to tell Moses to enlist and guide the work of those who had the abilities necessary, who were willing, whose own hearts moved them toward a worthy goal.

When we assume that most Christians wish to do God's will and are willing to work, we can see what the basic duty of the leader is. It is to guide people in putting their general commitment to Christ into meaningful action, in order to accomplish God's purposes. As we have seen in this lesson, the leadership principles which will help us do this are those which emphasize trust in people and genuine desire to lead them for the Lord.

Some Practical Applications

11 Suppose you have been appointed to lead a literature campaign to evangelize a community. You meet with a group of Christians who will work with you in the campaign. If you assume they desire to do God's will and are willing to work, which of the following will you do?
a) Preach on the need for dedication to God's work.
b) Explain how the work relates to spiritual goals to which they arc already committed.
c) Explain to them it is very important for Christians to lay aside other duties and interests during the periods of the campaign.
d) Tell them exactly what the goal is and what tasks must be done in order to accomplish i~
e) Give definite assignments and then allow time for them to ask questions.

Now, on separate paper, write some of your reasons for making the choices you did.

When we work as leaders with Christian groups we have the joy of seeing the combined strength, ability, and spiritual power of all the individuals operating together. Leaders who have not learned how to make the most of this marvelous situation create problems for themselves and fail to accomplish Christian goal.

Now that we have reviewed the experiences of Moses, we can go back to look with new insights at the plight of Mr. Loi, and see his greatest flaw as a leader. We can see that his low expectation of the people results in his failure to lead them in a productive way. He sees all their weaknesses, but not their strengths. He fails to claim them as *his* people and *God's* people in the manner we learned from Moses. Therefore he cannot develop their potentialities as individuals nor as a group. The difference between what they do and what they might do is a loss to the work of the Lord. Certainly this calls to our attention the importance of Christian leadership.

There are four principles of human relations in leadership that would help Mr. Loi with his problems.

1. *Let people know how you feel about the situation.* Sometimes leaders complain to others outside the group, but do not tell the group members that there are problems. Mr. Loi might say to his people, "We are so happy for the growth God has given us. It means we all must work harder and get better organized. I really need your help and cooperation. We can do great things together, as God leads us."

2. *Give people opportunities to talk things over and help one another.* Mr. Loi could ask some of the more experienced teachers to help the new ones.

3. *Give people opportunities to make suggestions and be creative.* Mr. Loi could ask the workers for ideas for making the back room more attractive. He could appoint a small group to work on this and give them full responsibility.

4. *Recognize the achievements and abilities of people and express honest appreciation.* Mr. Loi could express his appreciation for teachers who show interest in learning more, for example, and for those interested in the condition of a classroom.

Leaders Appreciate People 57

12 If you were helping Mr. Loi with his leadership problems, what other suggestions would you make? Write a list of your own ideas.

....

....

self-test

MULTIPLE CHOICE. Circle the letter in front of the best answer for each question.

1 God had a purpose for His people, so He called Moses, assigned him a task, gave him authority in the form of signs and wonders, and promised (as He does to all leaders He calls)
a) to bring him immediate as well as eternal reward.
b) protection from the attacks of enemies and criticism of friends.
c) that he would receive recognition and honor from his efforts.
d) to be with him to help him accomplish the greatest purpose on earth.

2 Moses demonstrated *empathy*, an indispensable leadership quality, in all but one of the following. Which one does NOT relate to *empathy*?
a) He was interested in people.
b) He cared about his people's condition and wanted to do something to help them.
c) He refused the Lord's call to help (initially) because of his own humility.
d) He purposed to fight against the injustice that plagued his people.

3 As the exodus from Egypt commenced, we see a principle of human behavior portrayed: When activity is new and exciting people follow their leader unquestioningly, but when problems arise they
a) forget their initial enthusiasm and criticize and blame him.
b) want to give up their ideals and forsake their goals.
c) feel that there must be an immediate change in leadership.
d) want to reexamine their objectives and redefine their purposes.

4 In his dilemma over the lack of water, Moses' experience reveals another principle of leadership: The burden of ministry experiences
a) requires spectacular miracles to inspire people with fresh vision.
b) should be shared with other leaders.
c) can only be lightened by diligent prayer by the leader alone.
d) requires us occasionally to retreat from our goals and be satisfied with our present experience.

5 At the Battle of Rephidim an important leadership principle emerged, which the Lord challenged Moses to record: the great importance of
a) battle tactics and a campaign strategy.
b) middle leaders who go to the battle and the quiet followers who support the leader.
c) morale in the camp of God's people.
d) military preparedness and the will to fight the Lord's battles.

6 Moses had to learn another principle of leadership: Leadership requires a kind of love (leadership love) that is willing to
a) accept incompetent performance from followers.
b) overlook the lack of dedication and commitment in his followers.
c) settle for lower goals and objectives than those originally adopted.
d) trust others to share the vision and help toward the achievement of the goals.

7 Jethro, Moses' father-in-law, gave Moses some wise advice about leadership. Then he said that if Moses would implement these suggestions there would be two results (the ideal results of successful leadership):
a) the people would be loyal and the goals would be achieved.
b) the task would become easy and the people would be happy.
c) Moses would survive and the people's needs would be met.
d) young leaders would be prepared to succeed Moses, and Moses would be regarded as a great leader.

8 One of Moses' greatest assets as a leader was that he continued to see
a) the potential for good in the people of God.
b) visions of how much more could be accomplished than what was originally planned.
c) things realistically; therefore, he never became idealistic.
d) the need to lower his expectations to conform to people's commitment.

9 Concerning Moses' receiving of the Law and the people's concurrent apostasy at Mt. Sinai, God said the people were Moses' and Moses said they were God's. What leadership principle do we see best here?
a) Since the people are God's responsibility, leaders can simply trust the Lord to take care of His people.
b) God makes leaders responsible for His people; they are to rely on God and accept this responsibility.
c) Leaders should not take their ministries too much to heart, for it is really God's work.
d) Actually, spiritual work is a joint partnership: equally God's and man's responsibility.

10 The advice Jethro gave to Moses can be summarized simply as follows:
a) "Lay the law down. Tell the people what you want and make them perform!"
b) "Insist on the complete dedication of your people!"
c) "Be severe in discipline. Make examples of those who fail to produce!"
d) "Expect more from your people. They are an untapped reservoir of potential!"

11 What a leader expects from people and how he treats them, that is, his leadership actions, are based upon
a) the theories of management he has learned.
b) his particular prejudices based upon his past experience.
c) the beliefs commonly held by his society.
d) his beliefs or assumptions about people.

Leaders Appreciate People

12 If a preacher says to his people, "You should be willing to sacrifice some of your funds that you use for your own pleasure and use them to help reach the heathen," he is making all of the following assumptions but one. Which one is he NOT making?
a) People spend their time and money selfishly on themselves.
b) People do not want to win the lost—it is a sacrifice.
c) People are essentially trustworthy and good.
d) People could reach the heathen if they were willing.

13 If a preacher assumes that his people like to share in the Lord's work, that they are willing to learn more about their responsibilities, and that they are concerned about achieving God's purpose in the world, he holds what kinds of expectations (according to the text)?
a) Low expectations
b) High expectations
c) Moderate expectations
d) Reasonable expectations

14-15 Consider each of the following examples to see which leadership style and behavior is employed. Then after each, give your evaluation of the long term effect this style and behavior will have on the leader and his followers.

14 Mr. Land believes that people are basically passive and must be motivated to work. Moreover, he feels that they need close supervision and consistent persuasion. When goals are achieved, he rewards good performers; when they are not achieved, he shows obvious dissatisfaction. Mr. Land establishes all goals and objectives. He gives detailed instructions to all his subordinates, and he watches over all the work closely and personally. Which choices describe best Mr. Land's leadership style and behavior?
a) Uses the democratic style
b) Holds Theory X Assumptions
c) Uses the autocratic style
d) Holds Theory Y Assumptions

....
....

15 Mr. Murphy is a tireless worker. He believes that other people like to work toward the achievement of objectives to which they are committed, just as he does. He sees in his followers an endless source of potential. He leads his people in making rules, and he brings them into the decision-making process. He assigns important responsibilities to some members of his group. He seeks to help nurture the development of talents and abilities that are evident in his followers. He gives his followers the opportunity to make suggestions and contributions. When objectives are achieved, he recognizes publicly the contributions that have been made. Mr. Murphy demonstrates which behavior and which leadership style?
a) Holds Theory Y Assumptions
b) Holds Theory X Assumptions
c) Employs the autocratic style
d) Employs the democratic style

....
....

SHORT ANSWER. Supply the words to fill-in the blank spaces or complete each of the following statements from the following list.

　　Theory X　　　　autocratic style　　recognition
　　Theory Y　　　　democratic style

16 The leader who makes all significant decisions, gives detailed instructions to those under him, and supervises the work closely and personally employs the .... of leadership.

17 The leader who works from within the group, allows the group to participate significantly in decision making, asks for suggestions from the group, and assigns important responsibilities to group members employs the .... of leadership.

Leaders Appreciate People

18 Mr. Cho believes that basically people are lazy and therefore need to be placed under strong leadership and "motivated" to work. He believes that they must be pushed, scolded, threatened, and persuaded to reach goals. He operates under .... Assumptions, and since he believes that it is necessary to manipulate people in order to get them to work he will tend toward an ....of leadership.

19 For the Christian leader it is interesting and important to notice that McGreggor's ....Assumptions are descriptive of dedicated, practicing Christians.

20 According to scholars who write about leadership, most people are willing to work best when they feel they are making the most of their capacities and when they receive some .... for what they do.

answers to study questions

7 b) he knew they had strengths which could be developed.
  c) he believed they wanted to do God's will.
  d) he wanted God to be glorified through them.

1 a False. (Moses was concerned about people before God called him.)
  b True.
  c False. (God promised Moses nothing except that He would be with him.)
  d True.
  e True.
  f True.

8 c) Most people will obey rules if they understand them.
  d) Many people have leadership ability.
  e) Most people can be trusted to make some decisions.

2 They complained, grumbled, and blamed Moses for troubles.

9 He made assumptions more like those of Theory X.

3 He was to take some of the elders with him.

10 a 5) 35:1-3.
  b 1) 35:10.
  c 2) 36:2.
  d 3) 35:21.
  e 6) 5:34.
  f 4) 35:35.

4 Check your answer with that given in the foregoing text

11 The best choices are b), d), and e). Answer a) is not necessary if you assume the people are dedicated and have come to the meeting because they wish to work for the Lord. If you preach in this way, they may feel that you do not understand and appreciate them. Answer b) is the most important, since it makes the present goal a step toward the greatest goal in a Christian's life. This is one of the essentials of Christian leadership. Answer c) is not necessary, since the same purpose can be accomplished in a positive way by answers d) and e). Answers d) and e) show more trust in the people.

5 a 3) Give them specific duties to perform.
  b 1) Teach them the rules and regulations or policies.
  c 4) Appoint middle leaders and organize the work with them.
  d 2) Show them how to do each task.

12 Your answers may differ slightly from mine. Here are some possible suggestions: 1) Appoint a helper and train him. 2) Assign a task to each worker. 3) Make the workers responsible for an early prayer time to help them be on schedule. 4) Put someone in charge of the literature and train him to do the work properly. 5) Make each teacher responsible for his own literature. 6) Call a meeting to discuss ways to improve the program. 7) Show the workers how their efforts have aided in the church growth and soul winning.

6 it would be shared by the people.

LESSON 3
Leaders Grow and Help Others Grow

Pastor Minusan breathed a prayer as he went to answer the knock at his door. He was expecting Hagop to come see him today. He wanted to ask Hagop to be his part-time assistant. He was praying because this was a serious step in his ministry and in the life of young Hagop. He was asking the Lord to help them both to make correct decisions.

The church was growing and Pastor Minusan needed help. The problem on his mind was this: Hagop had been a Christian for less time than many of the other believers. His parents were not believers. He was young and sometimes impulsive in expressing ideas unfamiliar to the group. He did not fully understand all the customs and practices characteristic of this church body.

Pastor Minusan saw in Hagop tremendous potential. Most important, he was convinced, along with the young man himself, that the Lord had called Hagop, and that he could carry out some duties needed in the church at present. He was intelligent, a faithful worker, and an eager student of the Bible.

Still, some people in the church had not accepted him fully. He might be too young. His background might be too different from that of the older believers. "Please, Lord," the pastor prayed as he opened the door, "help us to make the right decision. Help me to do what is best for Your people and Your plan."

"Help us to make the right decision ..."

The situation in which we found Pastor Minusan is complex and extremely significant in our study of leadership. It involves God's plan for the development and perpetuation of His Church. In this lesson we shall examine some biblical examples and principles which will make this clear to us. Also, we will learn more about our own growth and development as Christian leaders.

lesson outline

Paul—A Leader in God's Plan
Leaders Are Called and Developed
Leaders Help to Develop Others

lesson objectives

When you finish this lesson you should be able to:

- Describe leadership principles in the accounts of Barnabas, Paul, and Timothy and recognize and apply these principles.

- Explain what is meant by the statement that leaders are both called and developed.

- Describe and apply some methods of helping others to grow and develop as Christian workers and leaders.

learning activities

1. Read very carefully the books of 1 Timothy and 2 Timothy. Even if you feel you know this material, read it completely. This is essential to your enjoyment and understanding of the material in this lesson. Read also Acts, chapter 19.

2. Study the opening paragraphs, outline, and objectives. Then work through the lesson development according to your usual procedure. After you have completed the lesson, take the self-test and check your answers.

3. Carefully review Unit 1 (Lessons 1–3), then complete the unit student report for Unit 1 and send it to your GTN instructor.

key words

circumcision	dramatic	recruitment
comprehend	Gentiles	reputation
consultant	policy	self-concept
controversy	professional	ultimate
credibility	psychology	unique

lesson development

PAUL—A LEADER IN GOD'S PLAN

Leadership Principles Identified

Objective 1. *Recognize leadership principles in the relationship of Barnabas and Paul.*

"God did extraordinary miracles through Paul" (Acts 19:11). Paul was a special servant of the Lord, specifically chosen and empowered by the Holy Spirit. And, just as marvelous as the incidents in his life, which we all recognize as miracles, was the way he was selected to fill a unique place in history and in God's plan for the perpetuation of the church. In Paul we find an excellent example of the way God works through the instrument of human leadership.

When we first meet Paul in the Scriptures (he was called Saul then), we see immediately that he was a person who could influence others. He had ideas and goals. He was willing to work hard to accomplish his purposes. He took bold action. He organized support for his cause. We recognize in him the qualities and traits which most people admire in good leaders. But sadly, he used all these assets to fight against the work of Jesus (Acts 7:57–8:3 and 9:2). However, we soon discover that the misdirected energies of Saul were useless against the plan of God, as useless as it would be to throw twigs at a battleship.

Let's go back in time and review briefly this unchangeable plan for the perpetuation of the church. While Jesus was on earth He did many wondrous works. His greatest act, of course, was His death on the cross for the salvation of mankind. Next to that, His most important mission was to select and train human leaders who would carry on when He went back to glory. He called out the disciples and taught them. Then He gave them His final instructions, which would be from that moment on the key instructions to Christians in every generation. "Go and preach and teach." The disciples obeyed Jesus, and, filled with the power of the Holy Spirit, these few early leaders influenced hundreds more. The church was set into motion for all time.

There were numerous and varied tasks to be done in the early days of the church. The scriptural record gives us accounts not only of directly spiritual activities (such as preaching and healing), but also of organization, policy discussions, and the constant recruitment and training of new workers. One of the leaders who helped to carry on many of these activities of the church was a faithful and wise Christian named Barnabas. He and the others joined in deciding which specific needs had to be met. There were needs such as teaching Christian doctrine to new converts, providing for the welfare of the poor, and helping new congregations to get organized. For each type of task the elders appointed workers with appropriate God-given abilities.

Among the many needs to be considered by the church, one was frequently neglected. This was ministry to the Gentiles. No one seemed quite equipped to lead this ministry. The disciples understood best the needs and customs of their own people, the

Jews. They did not fully comprehend that God expected them to reach the Gentiles also.

However, God's unchanging purpose included the salvation of people from all races and nationalities. And what does God do when there are purposes to be accomplished? Yes, He calls out people, gives them specific tasks, and guides them in the attainment of His goals.

And Paul was the right person for this unique position in God's plan. Of course all intelligence and all gifts and abilities come from God, and already, before the actual conversion and calling of Paul, God knew that the appropriate knowledge and abilities were there. The dramatic and miraculous conversion was God's way of making His will absolutely clear to Paul and to the church leaders. "This man is my chosen instrument," said the Lord, "to carry my name before the Gentiles and their kings and before the people of Israel" (Acts 9:15).

We notice that God first spoke to Paul (Saul) in a voice from heaven. (*Stop here and read again Acts 9:1-6.*) After that He chose to work mostly through other people to help Paul in his new calling. God allowed Paul to experience the humiliation of being questioned and doubted by the Christians with whom he was called to work. In fact, because of his reputation as an enemy of the Lord Jesus Christ, the disciples at Jerusalem refused to receive him.

Now let's remember Barnabas. (Read Acts 9:26-28.) God had given him leadership gifts, and he had gained the trust and respect of the believers. He did not hesitate to use his position to help others. Showing the stability and the empathy of a true Christian leader, Barnabas became a friend and helper to Paul.

"Isn't he the man who had Christians put into prison?" asked the excited disciples. "How can we trust this man?"

But Barnabas introduced Paul and explained his calling. He supported Paul in every way and helped him to adapt to his new position in the church. This friendship and help were very important to Paul in the early days of his ministry.

Leaders Grow and Help Others Grow

1 What do you think of Barnabas? Name at least four leadership qualities which are indicated by his actions. (You may look at the list in Lesson 1.)

....
....
....
....

2 Circle a letter to show the correct ending: God wanted both Barnabas and Paul in leadership positions because
a) Paul was a better leader and would take the place of Barnabas.
b) different needs in the church require different kinds of leaders.
c) Paul could not do God's work without Barnabas.

We have said already that Barnabas showed *empathy*. That is, he thought of himself in Paul's place and acted as a friend. He showed *stability* in that he was not shaken by the fears of the people. He was firm in his own understanding of God's will. But perhaps his most important leadership trait at this point was his willingness to *share leadership*. He did not hesitate to help another leader. Barnabas knew that Paul had a special place in God's plan. Barnabas had his own place, too. Different needs in the church require different kinds of leadership. (Read Acts 11:22-30.)

Leadership Principles Applied

Objective 2. *Explain how Paul put into practice the lessons he had learned.*

Together Barnabas and Paul made an effective team. They had a glorious ministry in evangelism and church planting. Barnabas continued to have a great interest in the development of other workers, so soon we find another person on the team. His name was John, also called Mark (Acts 12:25).

Evidently John Mark had great potential, but the work of the ministry was difficult. Probably he missed the familiar life in Jerusalem, and became weary with the hardships of travel. So he left the gospel team midway through the first evangelistic mission and went home (Acts 13:13). Later Barnabas wanted to forgive him and take him on another gospel mission, but Paul disagreed (Acts 15:36-39).

At this point it seems that Paul was so eager to get on with the work of the Lord that he was impatient with someone who appeared to be less dedicated. Barnabas, however, knew that God's goals are almost always attained through people. He stood behind John Mark and supported this younger minister, just as he had supported Paul when there had been a need.

Even in the incident of disagreement between Paul and Barnabas we see the plan of God being accomplished Although Paul rejected John Mark at this time, he later changed his mind and accepted him as a co-worker (Colossians 4:10; 2 Timothy 4:11). And, most important, Paul began soon to follow the example of Barnabas. He chose a younger man who had great leadership potential and began to teach and guide him. His name was Timothy.

We find in Paul and Timothy the greatest example of a teacher-pupil relationship since Jesus had taught His disciples. At first Timothy had to be supported and justified before the Jews, much as Paul had been (Acts 16:1-3). Since his father was a Greek, Timothy had not lived according to all the Jewish custom For example, he was not circumcised. There was in the church at this time considerable controversy concerning the need for circumcision. The great apostle Peter had been criticized for accepting uncircumcised persons as friends (Acts 11:1-3).

In this situation Paul could have said, "I have my own ministry to think of." He might have avoided the trouble and responsibility of supporting and counseling another preacher. But he did not. Paul knew that Timothy had been called of God, but because of his youth and his background he might not be able to put his talents into full use. Therefore, he gave Timothy words of instruction something like this:

It is a noble task to be in a position of leadership. Prophecies have been made concerning you, but it is up to you to develop your talents and hold on to your faith (1 Timothy 1:18-19; 3:1).

He encouraged Timothy to respect the law and the customs of the elders, going so far as to see that he was circumcised, in order to avoid controversy. But, at the same time, Paul said, "Don't let anyone look down on you because you are young" (1 Timothy 4:12).

In the midst of a successful ministry, Paul never forgot that he was just one in the leadership line necessary to carry out God's universal gospel plan. He said, "God . . . called us to a holy life—not because of anything we have done but because of His own purpose and grace" (2 Timothy 1:9). This grace, he explained, was given before the beginning of time and was revealed on earth through Jesus Christ "And . . .1," said Paul, "was appointed a herald and an apostle and a teacher" (2 Timothy 1:8-11).

Can you imagine how a great leader like Paul, very sure in his own position, could share so freely and honestly with a young beginning leader? *Now you are a leader, too, in this same stream of God's purpose and grace.* That is the meaning of Paul's words! "Timothy," he continued, "guard what has been entrusted to your care. Don't neglect your gift. Fan it into flame! Be diligent Make progress." (See 1 Timothy 4:14-15; 6:20; 2: Timothy 1:6.)

But he did not stop there, either. He went on to charge the young leader to remember, in his turn, the ultimate goal of helping to develop other leaders to carry on God's work: "And the things you have heard me say . . . entrust to reliable men who will also be qualified to teach others" (2 Timothy 2:2).

3 Here are some statements concerning Barnabas. Write below each a statement to show how Paul followed his example.
a Barnabas was willing to share his leadership with Paul.

....
....

b Barnabas accepted Paul as a person called by God.

....
....

c Barnabas used his own influence to support Paul before others.

....
....

d Barnabas helped Paul get started in his ministry.

....
....

LEADERS ARE CALLED AND DEVELOPED

The Leader's Call and Development Explained

Objective 3. *Identify examples of* **calling** *and* **development**.

Paul spoke often and boldly of his calling. He knew he had been chosen by God for a certain kind of ministry. Probably you have studied in other courses the *ministry gifts*. God has given to the church several kinds of leadership persons to minister in various ways. These include prophets, pastors, and teachers. Remember that Barnabas accepted Paul first on the basis that he had been called of God. It was this that he explained to the others when he supported Paul. Barnabas was not simply introducing a talented new leader. He was giving assurance that he recognized the call of God upon Paul's life. The call was thus recognized as God's claim upon his life, the ground or basis for his ministry.

Leaders Grow and Help Others Grow

We found that Paul recognized God's calling upon the life of Timothy. However, the newly "found" leader was like a tender, young plant which needs to grow, develop, and mature. Timothy needed to develop the skills of leadership, acquire spiritual knowledge and knowledge of people, and mature in judgment. Paul thus gave Timothy many practical instructions concerning the development of his leadership capacities, but he began with the declaration that Timothy had received his leadership gift through a divine message (1 Timothy 4:14). The divine call was thus the basis for Paul's recognition of Timothy's leadership potential.

Of course Paul and Timothy were ministers and preachers. We think of them as very special people. But what about those Christian leaders who are not preachers nor full-time workers in the church? Are they *called*, too?

Certainly there are unique callings in the plan of God. There are indeed separate classifications of workers. Local church bodies need ministers who are called of God and officially recognized as the spiritual leaders—the pastors of the flock. In most cases these persons should have specialized education and should be devoted fully and, whenever possible, exclusively to the gospel ministry. They are to be respected by all members and must be consulted concerning all activities related to local church bodies.

In addition to the full-time ministry, there is a sense in which any true Christian may be called to serve in specific ways. We have seen in the words of Paul to Timothy that even a gifted and called worker needs teaching and development This leads us to the conclusion that all Christian leaders are both called and developed. If we are to use our full potential in the work of the Lord we must assume two major responsibilities:

1. To recognize the importance of God's calling upon our own lives and the lives of others.
2. To develop our own gifts and help others to develop theirs.

People, Tasks, and Goals

4 Following are quotations from the words of Paul to Timothy. Write **1** in front of those which refer to development and **2** in front of those which refer to both calling and development.

.... **a** "Train yourself to be godly" (1 Timothy 4:7).

.... **b** "Do not neglect your gift" (1 Timothy 4:14).

.... **c** "Watch your life and doctrine closely" (1 Timothy 4:16).

.... **d** "Do nothing out of favoritism" (1 Timothy 5:21).

.... **e** "Guard what has been entrusted to your care" (1 Timothy 6:20).

1) Development
2) Calling and development

5 Circle the letter in front of each TRUE statement.

a The term call to leadership refers to the call which is extended to all people to become God's people and become involved in His service.

b The call to leadership is the Christian leader's basic claim to a valid ministry of leadership.

c Having been called by God and perhaps possessing certain observable native talents, the new leader has all that is necessary and all he will ever need to be an effective leader.

d The leader who is set apart by God's call and who truly desires to be used of God begins a lifetime of development as he endeavors to fulfill God's purpose for his life.

6 Read each of the following Scriptures and answer the question(s) associated with each.

a Ephesians 4:11-16. Why did the Lord give the ministry gifts to His people?..

....

b I Corinthians 12:4-11. Gifts are given to whom?.....................

Why are gifts given? ....

....

Leaders Grow and Help Others Grow

c Romans 8:29. Believers have been predestined to what?

....

d Ephesians 1:4-5, 11-12. God has predestined believers to what? ....

e 2 Peter 3:18. Believers are commanded to do what?

....

....

The Leader's Development Examined

Objective 4. *Recognize true statements concerning leadership development.*

In order to understand the importance of leadership development we must know exactly what is included in the concept *leader*. We know that persons are called by God to meet various needs. Some of these who are called and used by God are not true leaders. They are outstanding individuals. Sometimes they are called "up-front persons." Among these are the prophets. Isaiah and John the Baptist are biblical examples of prophets. They influence many people and bring glory to the Lord. Their main ministry is communication of God's Word, rather than working with others.

Some of the "up-front" persons are more like performers, or "stars." They are greatly admired by others. Often their influence is great and they are effective in the work of the Lord. Usually, however, their popularity fades and they leave little behind them because they have called too much attention to themselves. They seldom train anyone to carry on after them, so even if they build a work much of it is lost eventually.

Other "up-front" persons are "bosses," or supervisors. They think in terms of getting a task accomplished. They expect others to obey them because they are in control. Often they accomplish specific purposes. They get jobs done. But the people who work under their orders are unhappy, take little interest in the work, and develop no talents to help them accomplish other and greater purposes.

If you desire to be a true leader, your best gift probably is that you really love and respect people and want to work with them in the Lord's service. You notice in Paul's letters he speaks to Timothy on two levels. In one sentence he gives instructions concerning Timothy's own life and conduct. In the next he tells Timothy what to teach others. Thus Paul demonstrates to Timothy, and to all of us who read these letters, that a leader is constantly aware of the task and the people. A leader is constantly learning and growing and helping others to learn and grow.

Some Examples from Paul's Letters

For Timothy to learn:	Train yourself to be godly.
For Timothy to teach:	Godliness has value for the present and for the life to come.
For Timothy to learn:	Set an example for the believers in speech, in life, in love, in faith, and in purity.
For Timothy to teach:	The overseer must be above reproach. If anyone does not know how to manage his own family, how can he take care of God's church?
For Timothy to learn:	Turn away from godless chatter.
For Timothy to teach:	People are not to have an unhealthy interest in controversies, arguments, and constant friction. They are not to gossip.
For Timothy to learn:	Do not rebuke an older man harshly, but exhort him as if he were your father. Treat younger men as brothers, older women as mothers.
For Timothy to teach:	People should put their religion into practice by caring for their own families.

Leaders Grow and Help Others Grow

These examples demonstrate to us the significant truth that a good leader is never very far from those he leads. The best way to develop our own abilities is to begin at once to help others to develop theirs. Timothy was not instructed to become fully trained and at some point he would be a leader who could take charge of others. He was guided into the beautiful truth that good leaders remain teachable and involved in the lives of their people.

7 Circle the letter in front of each TRUE statement. Then correct each false statement in the space provided below each statement.

a Popularity means about the same thing as leadership.

....

b Good leaders respect the abilities of others.

....

c A leader must have his own gifts completely developed before he can help others.

....

d The leadership style of Paul was similar to that of a "boss."

....

e Some great and influential persons are not true leaders.

....

LEADERS HELP TO DEVELOP OTHERS

Objective 5. *Identify examples of methods used by leaders to help others develop their gifts and abilities.*

Turn back to the first page of this lesson and review the situation of Pastor Minusan and Hagop. This illustration is given to remind us that what we learn from Barnabas, Paul, and Timothy is important for leaders of today. God still works through people, and they are still called and developed in the scriptural way. Leaders like Pastor Minusan see the need for helpers as the work grows. Dedicated believers such as Hagop feel the touch of God upon their lives and wish to accept leadership responsibilities.

As the work of the Lord progresses needs arise and leaders are sought to fill appropriate positions. The more mature and experienced leaders must understand how to recruit and develop younger leaders. Younger Christians, and those who are just beginning in leadership roles, must accept guidance and direction. Whatever your position is at present you need to understand both the position of Pastor Minusan and that of Hagop.

Probably the most important goal you will ever attain as a leader is to help develop the leadership potential of others. For example, if you are a youth leader you will need to help young people assume responsibility for leading family members and schoolmates into the church. If you lead men, you help train them to be leaders in their homes and work places. Every Christian needs some form of leadership training.

8 Scripture teaches that Christian leaders must
a) be older than the persons they lead.
b) be called to pastoral ministry.
c) respect and help one another.
d) not desire leadership roles.

9 Effective leaders recognize the need to develop younger leaders. Dedicated leaders often recruit other potential leaders and
a) send them to leadership training schools.
b) evaluate and observe them carefully for a few years.
c) personally give them "on the job" training.
d) load them down with many responsibilities.

How to Help Others Develop

Objective 6. *Recognize effective principles of leadership.*

The first modern books on leadership were written by people who were interested in commercial goals and industrial production. These books gave instructions for getting people to do the will of a leader or "boss." Christian leaders read some of these books and began to use many of the same methods. In most of the earlier studies of leadership the emphasis was upon methods of persuasion. Christian leaders, anxious to do the work of the Lord in efficient and effective ways, wanted to know how to establish control and

Leaders Grow and Help Others Grow

authority. They wanted to motivate people—keep them working to attain the goals which the leader felt were important.

Recently commercial and industrial leaders, and leaders in government and education, have agreed that their methods did not work very well. They have announced the discovery of new and better methods of leadership. It should not come as a surprise to Christians that these "new" methods are very similar to those used by God's greatest leaders and described for us in the Bible.

Since beginning this study guide your writer attended a two-hour seminar conducted by a famous consultant on leadership. He used all the latest expressions of psychology and management He described dozens of leadership situations and problems. We waited expectantly for him to tell us the great new discovery. But suddenly his fountain of fine words was dry.

"Well," he said, "after extensive research we have reached the conclusion that only one type of method is really basic and consistently effective. That is a method based upon caring for people." Caring for people! We did not have to pay a fee and listen two hours to a wordy professor to know that! We learned it in our Bible classes, didn't we? Why is it so often difficult for us Christians to accept the fact that all real truth is God's truth? There is no wisdom, and no effective positive method of working with people, for which we cannot find a foundation in the Scriptures.

10 Circle the letter of each TRUE statement
a Earlier modern books on leadership stressed the importance of getting people motivated to do the will of the boss.
b People who are persuaded to attain the goals which their leaders feel are important are generally high achievers.
c More recent studies in the field of leadership indicate that only one method of leadership is basic and consistently effective: caring for people.
d When leaders care enough about the task to be accomplished and about the needs of their people, they will share their burden with leaders from among the people; consequently, they will find that their task is lighter, their objectives are achieved, and the needs of the people are met (as Moses learned).

Let's examine some of the principles given in the best professional writings on leadership. We will find that all of them are compatible with the teaching and behaviors of Barnabas and Paul.

Be aware of talent and ability in the people you wish to lead. In the case of Christian leadership, this includes recognition of God's calling on the life of another person and divine gifts.

Accept differences in people. Do not believe that every difference is a problem to be eliminated. Remember the different backgrounds of Paul and Timothy were accepted and became assets in the work of the Lord.

Help people adapt their different qualities to the situation. Support them among other workers and leaders so that they feel accepted. Help them to recognize needs which they can fill. Remember the words of Paul indicate that he was pleased to be able to fill a unique place as an apostle to the Gentiles.

Help people understand exactly what is expected and required of them. Explain and interpret the attitudes and behaviors which are appropriate in each situation, so that each person has a chance to adapt. Let people know the reasons behind your requirements and actions. Help new people get acquainted with the background, history, and special customs of a group. Remember how Paul accomplished this in his letters to Timothy, reminding him of the past and preparing him for the future. Paul gave Timothy specific instructions and training.

Let people know that you care about them as people, not just as workers. "Caring" is not superficial. It is genuine. It is expressed in actions and attitudes as well as in words.

Express appreciation for good work. There is an important warning with this. Appreciation in this case should not be personal. Do not say, "I like you. You are nice." This may make a person feel good for a moment, but it seldom helps him to develop his talents and gifts. You must accurately evaluate the person's abilities and contributions. People need to be appreciated and recognized for real achievements. The most effective word of appreciation is something like this: "The program you planned was excellent. It met a real need."

Recognize the fact that development of others enlarges your own effectiveness. There is no place for competition in God's work. When a leader is afraid to help develop another he weakens his own position. Leaders do not develop credibility with others nor confidence in themselves and the Lord by being self-assertive and authoritarian. Our own feelings of self-worth or self-concept are important, as long as we recognize that we are servants of our sovereign Lord. And, according to the experts, self-concept is the result of how others respond to us. The best way to have a good and Christian self-concept is to help someone else develop his concept of himself as a person important in the Lord's work. A leader increases his own influence and effectiveness when he helps others and surrounds himself with competent workers. If a leader is insecure in his own position and fails to recognize the contributions of others, then he becomes weaker.

Share goals and decision-making as much as possible. Instead of trying to get others to work toward your goal, let them know that the goal is theirs, too. You don't just announce this, of course. You make it plain that this is not a case of someone helping you in your ministry. It is rather that they have their own ministry with goals identical to yours. You can reach your goals only if your workers reach their They can reach their goals only if you reach yours. This is the basic principle of working as a body. Christian leaders who expect to make all the decisions and get others to help them in their ministry are almost certain to fail. More success comes to those leaders who invite others to help in decision-making. Such leaders do not say, "Work for me." They say, "Let's work together for the Lord."

Help people to develop order and discipline. Most people work better if they have clear directions and work according to plans which they understand. Making strict rules will not bring success, but providing appropriate structure will. A good leader knows how to plan; set deadlines and standards, organize, and coordinate his workers and materials. In our next lesson we will learn more about how to plan, coordinate, and organize.

Questions for meditation and self-analysis. What gifts and abilities do you feel you have received from the Lord? Do you think of this course in leadership as one step in the development of these gifts and abilities? What have you learned from the biblical examples that will help you to grow as a person and as a leader? Can you think of specific ways you might use your knowledge to help someone else?

11 Circle the letter of each TRUE statement
a To be truly effective, a leader must recognize the wealth of talent and ability within a group he leads.
b Part of the challenge of leadership lies in the need to adapt people's qualities to different situations so that tasks are accomplished and their needs are met.
c If you tell your people repeatedly of your love for them, you need not communicate your methods nor goals to them; they will understand.
d In expressing appreciation or extending recognition for a person's contributions, you must make the message intensely personal—not job-related nor "official."

12 As leaders develop the leadership abilities of others they must be most keenly aware of which one of the following?
a) As leaders develop the talents of others, their own influence will naturally diminish.
b) Leaders maintain long term control better if they ignore the contributions and suggestions of others.
c) Leaders develop credibility with others by being self-assertive and authoritarian.
d) A leader develops a healthy self-concept in the process of helping another person develop his own self-concept.

13 All of the following but one represent effective leadership principles. Which one is NOT an effective leadership principle?
a) A good leader develops a plan, sets standards and deadlines, organizes, and allocates wisely the resources at his disposal.
b) The efficient leader gives clear-cut directions, communicates instructions effectively, and follows the plan.
c) The leader who elects to make all the decisions, assume all responsibility alone, and run a "tightly disciplined ship" will inspire others by his selfless dedication.
d) The wise leader invites others to share in decision-making, making the goal not *his*, but *ours*.

self-test

1 As an accepted and respected leader Barnabas demonstrated an important leadership principle: He used the influence of his position to
a) secure apostolic approval for policies that he favored.
b) help develop the capabilities of others.
c) obtain places of prominence for his family members.
d) ensure that he would never lose his status of prestige and power.

2 The fact that Paul and Barnabas were very different illustrates another principle of leadership:
a) any leader's effectiveness is of necessity limited.
b) younger leaders who have the benefit of greater training are naturally better leaders.
c) different needs in the church require different kinds of leadership.
d) many leaders need to be trained in order to obtain a few good ones.

3 In the incident involving John Mark's rejection, we see that early in his career Paul was primarily interested in the task. Barnabas, however, recognized that the key to long term effectiveness in the ministry lay in the development of
a) a less demanding personnel policy.
b) trained leaders who could multiply the teacher's effectiveness.
c) missionary teams made up of men like himself who believed that the requirements for Christian service should be less rigid.
d) personalities who did not feel threatened by younger leaders.

4 The style of leadership development demonstrated by Jesus, as well as by Barnabas and Paul, can be described best by which of the following statements?
a) Personally instructs and advises, gives opportunity to observe the master teacher, gives opportunity to apply lessons, reviews results, and assigns task
b) Gives opportunity to learn by observation, by on-the-job-training
c) Instructs repeatedly in areas of doctrine and leadership, lectures on morals, commissions to service, and commits performance to God
d) Chooses those with background in spiritual matters and formal education, keeps close to self for short time, assigns to ministry, reviews performance occasionally if convenient

5 Of Paul's method of leadership we can say most accurately that he
a) encouraged people to leadership positions; starting was their concern.
b) was alert to leadership potential and helped called persons get started.
c) left the initiative of responding to the call to the individual.
d) was not particularly interested in developing leaders until much later.

6 We can most accurately interpret the statement "leaders are called and developed" to mean that
a) a leader's call is more important than his development.
b) training is not more important than a divine call.
c) leadership is equally the responsibility of God and people.
d) from the "call" a leader gains his right to lead; whereas, from his development he gains the skills for effective leadership.

7 Recognizing the fact that Christian leaders are called to their positions by a sovereign act of God, other leaders and the body of Christ should respond by
a) encouraging the called ones to move out and fulfill the terms of their call.
b) providing such potential leaders with classes in leadership and management training.
c) providing both the place and the environment where leadership skills can be developed and applied under the direction of seasoned leaders.
d) sending them to schools where they can learn the arts of leadership.

8 The matter of *calling and development* leads us to the conclusion that if we are to use our full potential in the work of the Lord, we must recognize the importance of God's calling upon our lives and
a) thus develop our own gifts.
b) the lives of others and help them develop their own gifts.
c) thus fulfill it by serving others and helping to develop their gifts.
d) the lives of others and develop our own gifts and help others develop theirs.

9 Which one of the following sentences describes most accurately the differences between "up-front" persons who are not true leaders and those who are true leaders?
a) Performers are self-centered and rarely plan for the continuation of their work.
b) Bosses are task-oriented and care little about the feelings and needs of the people.
c) True leaders are both task and people oriented; they seek to grow and they work to help others grow.
d) Answers a) and c) above accurately explain all the differences.
e) All of the above—a), b), and c)—accurately explain these differences.

10 Earlier modern books on leadership stressed the importance of persuading people to do the will of the boss and attain his goals. Recently experts in the field have acknowledged that these methods
a) were highly effective and produced favorable results.
b) did not work very well.
c) were totally ineffective.
d) would probably have been effective in an earlier period.

11 Current studies indicate that the only type of leadership method which is really basic and consistently effective is one which
a) limits leadership to the will of the majority.
b) stresses the cooperative nature of management.
c) rests upon authoritarian premises.
d) is based on caring for people.

12 All of the following but one are principles of leadership taken from the best professional writings on leadership. Which one is NOT?
a) "Be aware of talent and ability in the people you lead."
b) "Accept differences in people."
c) "Help people to understand exactly what is expected and required of them."
d) "Help people to adapt their different qualities to the situation."
e) "Keep the strain of decision-making as well as problems from your people."

13 Jose is terribly afraid to develop leaders because as he has trained new leadership the focus of attention has shifted from him to them. Which principle below does Jose need to embrace and internalize so that he can approach his job more positively?
a) Let people know that you care about them as people.
b) Recognize the fact that the development of others enlarges your own effectiveness.
c) Share the goals and decision-making as much as possible.
d) Help people to adapt their different qualities to the situation.

Leaders Grow and Help Others Grow 89

14 A leader increases his own effectiveness and influence when he
a) helps others and surrounds himself with competent workers.
b) gets jobs done on schedule by tough management and close supervision.
c) does most of the leadership work himself and delegates only unimportant tasks to his subordinates.
d) mixes well with his people but retains full control of decision-making processes.

15 In the matter of goals and decision-making, the best policy is to
a) try to get others to work toward your goal.
b) conceal your goal by declaring that it is a "ministry."
c) sell yourself as one who cares; then plead, "Come work for me."
d) share goals and decision-making so that you can say truly, "This is our work."

Before you continue your study with Lesson 4, be sure to complete your unit student report for Unit 1 and return the answer sheet to your GTN instructor.

answers to study questions

7 a False. (Popular persons are not always good leaders.)
 b True.
 c False. (A good leader is constantly learning and developing.)
 d False. the style of Paul was that of a teacher.)
 e True.

1 You may have indicated the following: empathy, emotional stability, ability to share leadership, and group membership. Or you may have used any of the other traits listed in Lesson 1.

8 c) respect and help one another.

2 b) different needs in the church require different kinds of leaders.

9 c) personally give them "on the job" training.

3 a Paul took the time to groom Timothy for his role as a leader, recognizing God's call on the younger man's life.
 b Paul referred to Timothy's call in his letter (1 Timothy 4:14).
 c To the Romans Paul represented Timothy as his fellow worker (Romans 16:21). Paul asserted to the Corinthians that Timothy was carrying on the Lord's work just as he (Paul) was (1 Corinthians 16:10).
 d Paul recognized leadership potential in Timothy; therefore, he made the young man a part of his evangelistic team and began developing his potential (Acts 16:1-3).

10 a True.
 b False.
 c True.
 d True.

4 a 1) Development.
 b 2) Calling and development
 c 1) Development.
 d 1) Development
 e 2) Calling and development

Leaders Grow and Help Others Grow

11 a True.
 b True.
 c False.
 d False.

5 a False.
 b True.
 c False.
 d True.

12 d) A leader develops a healthy self-concept in the process of helping another person develop his own self-concept.

6 a To prepare them for works of service and to help them become spiritually mature.
 b To each believer. For the common good.
 c To be conformed to the likeness of Christ—to mature spiritually.
 d To be His holy and blameless children and to bring glory to his name.
 e To grow in grace and knowledge of the Lord—in a word, to become spiritually mature. It is evident that the Lord's purpose for His children is that they be productive and mature. The process of maturity takes place under the influence of wise leadership and within the framework of body ministries. Second Peter 3:18 and John 15:1-8 and other verses of Scripture indicate that growth and development are expected as a normal outgrowth of spiritual life.

13 c) The leader who elects to make all the decisions, assume all responsibility alone, and run a "tightly disciplined ship" will inspire others by his selfless dedication.

Unit 2
TASKS
WHAT LEADERS DO AND HOW THEY GUIDE OTHERS IN THE WORK

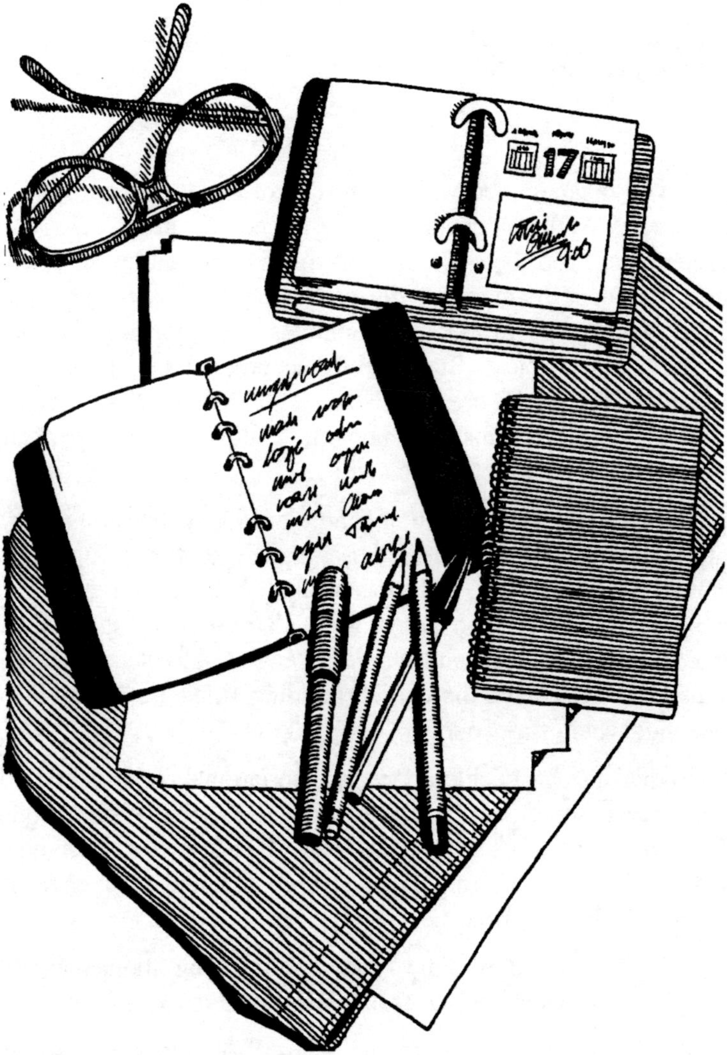

LESSON 4
Leaders Plan and Organize

"I was disappointed with the results of our visitation project last week," William declared as he faced the group. He was disappointed, too, because only six of his committee members were present. This morning, during Sunday school time, he had asked them to remain for a few minutes after morning worship to discuss the project. But several had other plans, or for one reason or another did not stay. He could understand. "All people have personal problems," he thought, "I must be aware of their needs, too, and not be too demanding."

"Since the pastor put me in charge of this visitation ministry I feel a great responsibility," he explained to the group. "We should all get behind our pastor and help him reach this community with the gospel. I want all of you to show your dedication to the Lord and work harder throughout the coming week. We must have the church building filled for the revival meetings which start soon."

"What did we decide about transportation?" John asked. "I believe you mentioned that we might find some way to help those who live too far away to walk. I visited a mother with several children who might come to church, but they have no means of transportation."

"Yes," admitted William," we were thinking about that. I'll see what I can work out. Does anyone else have a question?

"There are two young people in my Bible class who would like to go with me on visitation," said Mary, "Do you think it's all right for me to take both of them?"

"... I feel a great responsibility"

"Yes," answered William, "it will be good experience for them."

"That's what I thought," Mary replied, "but I asked the pastor, and he said it was better to take just one at a time."

"W-e-l-l I, don't know, maybe in that case . . .

lesson outline

David—A Competent Leader
Leaders Plan and Coordinate
Leaders Organize

lesson objectives

When you finish this lesson you should be able to:

- Describe leadership principles in the accounts of David and recognize and apply these principles.

- Outline plans for a specific project and prepare appropriate worksheets.

- Explain the concept *organization* and describe some types and principles of organization.

learning activities

1. Review Bible accounts of the life and work of David. Think in terms of this course and look for examples of leadership traits and behaviors. Important Scripture portions are: 1 Samuel 16:1-22; 17:21-58, chapters 22–26; chapter 30; 2 Samuel 5:1-7; 7:1-25; 1 Chronicles chapters 17–19 and 22–29. This is a long reading assignment. You may be familiar with much of the material. Your objective now is to read it for the purpose of seeing David as a leader called out by God to accomplish His purposes. You will learn much concerning leadership if you follow carefully the example of David.

2. Study the lesson development and answer the study questions in the usual manner.

3. Look over the key words. If they are unfamiliar to you check their meaning in the glossary.

4. Take the self-test at the end of the lesson and check your answers carefully with those given at the back of this study guide. Review any items you answer incorrectly.

key words

accountability	conceited	servitude
allocated	handicapped	strategy
casually	magnificent	techniques
climactic	relevant	

lesson development

DAVID—A COMPETENT LEADER

Objective 1. *Recognize from scriptural accounts the importance of competence in the acts of David.*

Before we discuss the place of David in God's plan for leading His people, let's go back to our story of William. We left him in a most embarrassing position, didn't we? He had been trapped into a place where he must either disagree with his pastor or reconsider his own opinion in the presence of those he wanted to lead and inspire. What would you do? William allowed the subject to be forgotten as another question was asked.

"What about the literature? I need some more. I asked the Sunday school secretary if she had ordered extra copies for our visitation project, and she said that wasn't her responsibility."

"Another thing," Jim interrupted, "there were three of us in the same neighborhood last week, and I doubt if anyone visited in the Northtown area. I've heard there are several new families up there who should be invited to attend our church."

"That's a good suggestion," William smiled his approval and spoke enthusiastically, "Now let's get out there and cover the territory! Let's all work hard! We can have this church filled next Sunday!"

"Amen! Amen!" said the members of the committee.

This brief description of a committee meeting brings to our attention several important leadership principles. How many of them can you name? What good leadership qualities do you recognize in William? Do you think he represents a sincere Christian in his attitude? Is he willing to accept a leadership position and yet be subject to the leadership of another? Does he seem enthusiastic? Does he have a goal, or purpose in mind which he is working to accomplish? Is he considerate in his attitude toward the other workers?

Why are these good qualities not sufficient to make him an effective leader? What is needed to bring success to the committee in this illustration? We will find in the account of David's life and work answers to these and other questions.

Up to this point in our course the emphasis has been upon people—people who lead and people who follow. Now, in Unit 2 we will turn our attention more fully to the TASKS—the "jobs" and techniques involved in leadership. Our biblical example, David, did not lack any of the qualities usually associated with leadership. But most remarkable was the efficient and consistent way in which he put together his assets and resources to bring about extraordinary results.

The Bible acquaints us with David as a total man: shepherd, soldier, poet, lover, father, and king. Brave, guilty, repentant, forgiven, and triumphant he reveals to us the variety and complexity of human experience. This indicates the marvelous depth of God's planning. David was provided with the background and elements necessary for the tasks ahead. Physical development, courage, and self-reliance came as he cared for the sheep and protected them from danger. As he walked alone with the flocks he learned to think for himself, use initiative and imagination, and express his feelings and ideas in powerful, inspiring words.

We know that he began life in a lowly position. His call to leadership came as the prophet Samuel selected him, at God's direction, and let him know, in a simple, almost secret way, that he was to be the king (1 Samuel 16:1-22). And "the Spirit of the Lord came upon David in power." Then he went back to the sheep, with the marvel locked in his heart. Later, in the household of King Saul, his position was one of humility and servitude.

It seems a contrast to this humility to hear David say boldly that he would go and fight the giant Goliath, when everyone else was afraid. It did not sound humble to state firmly, "I can accomplish that task." His elder brother scorned David, saying, "You are conceited!" (1 Samuel 17:28-32).

David soon proved something that all good leaders know: humility and courage to act are not opposites. Often they go together, as they did on that day when David slew the giant.

Of course David knew he was not acting in his own strength. The Spirit of the Lord had come upon him in power, and therefore he could speak boldly and confidently. Nevertheless, David did not rely upon enthusiastic words. He referred to actual accomplishments and skills which the Lord had allowed him to acquire. "I killed the lion and the bear," he declared (1 Samuel 17:34-37).

Leaders Plan and Organize

We know that God could have stricken Goliath dead without a stone. God could have sent a stone flying by miracle power, without David or a sling. But when there is need for action to accomplish His purposes, we find that usually God works through persons in whom the appropriate abilities have been developed. David had already developed skills. He used confident words to convince others. He used strategy. He used strength and ability. Although he knew the power was from God, he did not act in a careless, unstructured manner. He went about the task as he had learned to do. Notice that he did not casually grab up any little rock. He selected five smooth stones from the stream, and put them into his shepherd's bag. There was system and order in his behavior.

Questions for meditation and self-analysis. Read Psalm 144:1. Do you recognize in this passage the fact that David felt competent, and yet took no personal glory? How did he become competent? What skills and abilities do you have? Has the Lord taught your hands? Has he given skills to your fingers? Do you feel that the abilities you have developed can be used in some special tasks for the Lord's work?

He Became Their Leader

After his dramatic victory, David had an opportunity to accept honor and praise. He could have been in control of thousands of people immediately. His humility and good sense are shown by the fact that he did not take advantage of personal popularity. He willingly took orders from King Saul. He fit himself into the organizational structure. He obeyed as a soldier and moved up in the ranks according to his skill and conquests. He accepted tasks that were necessary in the movement of the nation toward its common goals.

Many pages of the Old Testament are devoted to accounts of David's activities. These are historical writings, but they give numerous details of David's leadership methods. Three of the most important principles related to his success are:

1. He consistently sought God's will.
2. He was loyal and considerate in dealing with both superiors and followers.

3. He recognized the need for excellence and competence, for which he gave the glory to the Lord.

We know that eventually David received the crown which had been promised to him. As king of Judah, and all Israel, he was able to subdue the surrounding enemies. This kept him occupied in many battles, which he led with courage and skill.

After he was firmly established in his kingdom, David's great desire was to build a house for the ark of the covenant—a temple of the Lord. But the Lord revealed that it would not be his privilege to be present during the actual construction of this temple. His part was to supply the plans and the provisions (1 Chronicles 22:1-4). The record of these activities is a unique model for organizational processes and structures.

David Made Extensive Preparations

At this point in the historical record we see that David believed his lighting exploits had a second major focus, that of providing opportunities to amass materials for the temple (1 Chronicles 22:14). As we read the books of Chronicles we are conscious of a thrilling episode in God's dealing with mankind. The theme is not celebration of formal worship nor miracles, but it is planning, organization, job descriptions, and fund raising!

David engaged stonecutters and other workmen. He provided stone, iron, bronze, and logs for them to work. He appointed specific supervisors, officials, judges, gatekeepers, and musicians. The assignments were clear. The plans were detailed and were the result of much preliminary work and prayer. David said to his son, Solomon:

> "May the Lord give you discretion and understanding . . ."
> "I have taken great pains to provide for the temple of the Lord..."
> "You have many workmen" (1 Chronicles 22:12-15).

He gave Solomon plans for the temple, its buildings, storerooms, inner rooms and courts. He gave instructions for all the work of serving in the temple, and the articles to be used in the service, as "the Spirit had put in his mind" (1 Chronicles 28:11-12).

"All this is in writing," said David, "because the hand of the Lord was upon me, and He gave me understanding in all the details of the plan" (1 Chronicles 28:19).

Through years of varied experiences and circumstances David maintained his firm purpose. He planned with an aim as unerring as that which buried the stone in Goliath's giant brow. He admitted his failures and repented of his sins. He gave the Lord credit for his skill and recognized that God gave skill to many others. Without resentment he accepted his role as one leader in the sequence of God's order.

Then came that climactic time when David had decided to challenge the workers and officially commit the responsibility to Solomon. We can imagine the scene as he called that great assembly in Jerusalem. There he summarized, openly, before the officials and helpers of all ranks, his previous activities and his plans for the future. Nothing was forgotten. Nothing was uncertain. When that meeting was over the people whom David addressed as "brothers" knew their duties. They knew their relationships to one another. They knew what resources were available and something of the costs and sacrifices involved.

Without boasting, but in terms of information sharing, David explained his feelings and actions. Then he made a concrete commitment, saying, "In my devotion to the temple of my God I now give my personal treasures of gold and silver" (1 Chronicles 29:3).

From this position of personal involvement, he could challenge the others to follow him in consecration of themselves to the work of the Lord, in service and in giving. Of course the people responded to his magnificent leadership. They gave themselves and their possessions freely to the Lord.

David prayed and led the people in worship. "Praise the Lord your God," he encouraged them enthusiastically. And they all praised the Lord (I Chronicles 29:10-20).

Turn back to the beginning of this lesson and review the example of William and his committee.

1 List at least three ways in which William followed the example of David.

....
....
....

2 List at least three ways in which William failed to follow the example of David.

....
....
....

3 David's bold announcement that he would fight the giant indicates that he
a) was conceited.
b) wanted to excel before his brothers.
c) was a born leader.
d) had confidence that the Lord would use him.

4 David told his experiences with the lion and the bear to
a) demonstrate his position with facts.
b) show greater faith than his brothers.
c) prove that he was chosen to be king.
d) demonstrate his physical strength.

5 David carefully chose five stones. This behavior seems to indicate
a) lack of confidence.
b) training and competence.
c) public demonstration of his skills.
d) rejection of Saul's armor.

LEADERS PLAN AND COORDINATE

Planning is Thinking and Writing

Objective 2. *Identify the purpose behind a plan.*

Almost every task which is done well is done twice. First it is done mentally, in the minds of those who have leadership roles. This process of thinking through what is to be done is what we call *planning*.

Everyone plans in more or less unconscious ways. It is one of the essential human qualities to be able to imagine and picture how something is to be before actually doing it. We try to predetermine, or work out in advance, a course of action, thinking what we would do under various circumstances. Leaders develop the ability to do this more formally and more efficiently than others.

In most studies of leadership functions, the word *planning* is at the top of the list. Leaders must plan, and the better they are at planning the more likely they are to be successful. So let's find out just what the process of planning includes.

1. *Analysis and forecasting.* Leaders observe carefully what present conditions are and then predict or estimate how matters will proceed in the future.

2. *Establishment of purposes and goals.* Leaders have clear ideas of the reasons behind their actions. They know what the purpose of each task is and what result or outcome is desired. The desired outcomes are what we call objectives. Every good plan includes stated objectives. We will study this in more detail later.

3. *Outline of a specific course of action.* In terms of leadership functions, this is called *programming*. It includes making a list of steps which will be taken in order to effect the desired outcomes, or achieve the objectives.

4. *Scheduling.* Making a calendar or time line is an essential part of both goal-setting and programming. Without specific time lines, goals and programs become impotent.

5. *Statement of proposed methods and procedures.* The plan must be practical and workable. Therefore, leaders must be able to state in advance what methods are appropriate and available for use in each step of the programs they outline.

6. *Financial considerations.* In studies of leadership functions this is called *budgeting.* Most plans require that some degree of attention be given to the expense involved, how money is to be raised, allocated, and accounted for. Even leaders who are not responsible for formal budgeting must consider these matters in order to make practical and realistic plans.

7. *Personnel considerations.* Leaders decide in advance how many persons are needed to carry out a program or project, and what qualities or skills the persons should have. Selecting the right people for particular tasks is an extremely important part of planning.

8. *Compliance with policies and standards.* Every plan is made within a framework of *policy.* That is, there are established values and standards which guide every action within an organization. Christian leaders, of course, are guided by scriptural principles and also by the policies of the higher leadership in the church or institution.

Many leaders find it helpful to express the planning process in the form of questions. The answers to these questions reveal the essentials of the plan:

1. Why should this work be done? This leads to thoughtful analysis of the present situation.
2. What is to be accomplished? This leads to the establishment of objectives.
3. How will the work be done? This leads to outlining procedures.
4. When will the work be done? This leads to the time schedule.
5. What is the best way available to do the work? This leads to consideration of specific methods.

6. What will the work be done with? This leads to budgeting and consideration of facilities and materials required.
7. Who will do the work? This leads to personnel selection and making of specific assignments according to the skills and gifts of the persons available.
8. What standards and guidelines must be observed or set for the workers? This leads to consideration of existing policies and also to setting standards of quality.

Kinds of Plan:

Most leaders use three kinds of plans. These are:

1. General plans for a period of time, such as a calendar of activities for the year and an organizational chart.
2. Plans for specific activities which are repeated periodically, such as procedures for committee meetings, and workers' training programs.
3. Plans for individual projects, such as a particular conference or special day program.

We have said that planning is both thinking and writing. The *planning* which is a process usually requires a *plan* which is a written document Competent leaders use a few basic tools for making both long-range and daily specific plans.

Planning Tool.

1. *The "To Do" list*. Every leader must keep a list of plans and duties for each day. This may be no more than a sheet of paper or a notepad, or special forms may be purchased or made. Items to be listed on a daily basis include:

Appointments	Phone calls to be made
Tasks to be done	Phone calls received
Assignments to be made	Materials needed
Letters to write	Financial or expense data

You will find a suggested form for a daily reminder sheet in the appendix.

2. *The calendar.* Every leader needs two calendars. One is a large pad with space to write for each date. This is for long-range planning. Such a calendar can be made from any writing tablet if prepared ones are not available. The other calendar is a small one to be carried at all times. Important dates from the large planning calendar should be marked on the small one for quick reference.

3. *A small notebook.* The small calendar may be a page of a pad or notebook which can be carried at all times. The good leader is always prepared to make notes concerning the events of the day and to write ideas as they come to mind. The pad is used also for writing names to remember, phone numbers, and addresses.

4. *Work planning sheets.* Plans for all major projects should be written out in detail. Most leaders design worksheets or forms which are appropriate for their own purposes. Such forms should include space for:

Date
Name of leader
Names of other persons or committee making the plans
Name of project with description and objectives
List of specific tasks to be done
Assignments of persons to do each of the tasks
Materials and equipment needed for each task
Date for completion of each task

6 Read again the section on planning tools which you have just completed. Study the suggested forms which are conveniently located in the appendix. Think of a real or imaginary situation in which you might be responsible for making plans. Design a suitable worksheet, or copy one which is suggested, and fill it in appropriately. This is a practice exercise for your own benefit. It is not a test.

Coordination

Coordination is working the plan. After the plan is finished, your next task is to get all the components together in the most

Leaders Plan and Organize

productive way. Coordination is the process of seeing that the right people are in the right place, at the right time, with the right materials and that they understand how they are to work together to accomplish a task.

Look back at the questions we asked to help you in the planning process. What components or elements are suggested by these questions?

7 Write the planning component (right) which is suggested by each question (left).

.... **a** Who will do the work?

.... **b** What will the work be done with?

.... **c** What is to be accomplished?

.... **d** When will the work be done?

.... **e** How will the work be done?

.... **f** Where will the work be done?

1) Time
2) Place
3) People
4) Methods
5) Materials
6) Objectives

Questions for mediation. Think back over the biblical accounts of David's leadership role. Was he a good coordinator? Did he consider all the planning components? In regard to his plans for the temple, could you answer each of the questions we suggested?

8 Which one of the following statements identifies best the purpose behind planning?
a) Basically planning is the activity by which we determine our objectives.
b) Planning is done in an attempt to justify our course of action.
c) Planning is the attempt to predetermine a course of action and how to respond to various circumstances that might occur as we endeavor to reach our objective.
d) Essentially, planning is the attempt to determine how each one fits into the structure and what are his responsibilities.

Problems and Obstacles

Objective 3. *Name three obstacles to planning in Christian work.*

Sometimes you hear leaders say, "What's the use? I had everything planned, and then..."

"My workers didn't follow the instructions."
"My supervisor changed his mind."
"My helper was ill."
"The whole situation was different from what I expected."

Probably you have had or will have this type of frustrating experience. You make careful plans and see them pushed aside. Then you may see someone who seems to have no plan at all enjoy great success in a project. Do not be discouraged or allow this to cause you to depreciate the value of planning. Just be aware that planning in itself does not bring certain success. That is one of the reasons some people give for not planning.

There are two other obstacles which we should consider. One is that in Christian work someone may accuse a leader of leaning upon his own programs rather than upon the guidance of the Holy Spirit, Certainly our Bible studies have shown us that the Spirit guides at the planning stage just as surely as at the action stage. Therefore, we must not be greatly affected by people who criticize planning and programs in the church.

Probably the greatest obstacle to good planning is that it takes so much time and hard work. Thinking and writing are two of the most difficult human activities Try it by testing how much easier it is to stand up and give a testimony than ft is to write it in advance. We know that the Lord is able to guide us in writing as surely as in speaking; therefore, it is not logical to say that we are speaking in the power of the Holy Spirit if we do it suddenly in church but are not working by His power if we are writing out plans in advance! This misunderstanding must be overcome before a leader can be most effective. Time and hard work are necessary, along with the guidance of the Spirit.

9 Name three obstacles to planning in Christian work.

....

....

....

Following are some suggestions to help you avoid the obstacles and do effective planning:

1. *Submit your plans to the guidance of the Spirit.* Make them a matter of sincere prayer.

2. *Maintain an attitude that all plans are flexible.* This is one of the greatest challenges to leadership—to keep plans both specific and flexible.

3. *Do not expect all plans to work out.* A wise leader knows that the act of planning makes him more capable of reaching his goals, even if the original plan must be abandoned. In most cases, a person who has a plan feels more competent and is able to gain respect and cooperation when a situation changes. Whenever possible, anticipate problems. Think ahead and try to imagine what changes are possible in the situation and what you might do.

4. *Plan numerous minor objectives which will help you reach the major objective or goal.* For example, if your major objective is to provide meals for a regional conference, minor objectives may be to provide storage space and to collect food items. Plans for reaching a particular minor objective can be kept flexible, and changes can be made without affecting seriously the total plan. We will discuss major and minor objectives in another lesson.

5. *Be sure that the plans are understood and accepted by everyone who is responsible for making them work.* Remember how David explained his plans and gave the people opportunities to express their personal commitment. Explain to your workers the purpose and importance of every part of your plans. Assure them of your appreciation for their contributions. As David did, have them join you m prayer and praise, submitting the plans to the guidance of the Spirit.

LEADERS ORGANIZE

Objective 4.   *Recognize descriptions of organizational types, and draw an organizational chart.*

We have learned that the concept *plan* includes both a process of planning and a written document or outline to guide activity. The concept *organization* also includes two major ideas. One is the process of getting people into relationships for efficient work on a task. The other is the structure, or formal plan, which shows people how they are expected to relate to one another.

Types of Organization

Several types of formal organization are possible. Probably the one with which you are most familiar is the one called *direct line organization*.

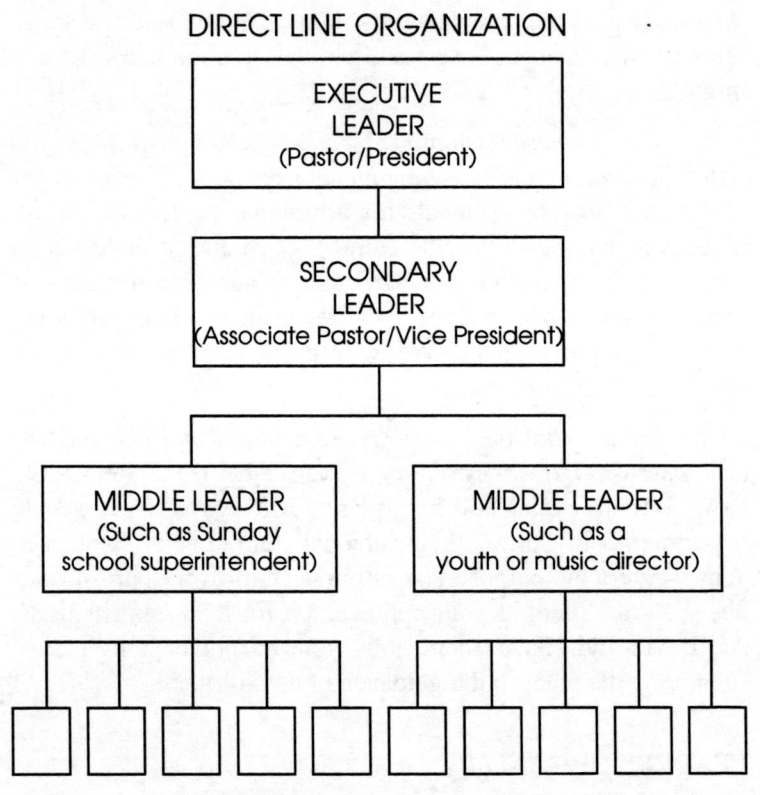

DIRECT LINE ORGANIZATION

```
              EXECUTIVE
               LEADER
          (Pastor/President)
                  |
              SECONDARY
               LEADER
    (Associate Pastor/Vice President)
                  |
        ┌─────────┴─────────┐
   MIDDLE LEADER        MIDDLE LEADER
  (Such as Sunday        (Such as a
school superintendent)  youth or music director)
```

Small churches may not have a secondary leader, and the middle leaders are directly under the pastor.

Leaders Plan and Organize

Military organization is the most extreme example of this type. Its basic characteristics are that the executive leader has the controlling authority and work is done through a line of secondary and middle leaders. Each person is supervised directly by the person above him. The workers are supposed to communicate only through the supervisors and not go directly to the executive leader.

Another type of organization is called line-staff. This type is used in most large modern organizations. It has a chief executive who is advised by a staff of persons who have special knowledge and abilities. They give advice and direction to the executive, and then he supervises middle leaders, as in the direct line organization.

LINE-STAFF ORGANIZATION

```
YOUTH PASTOR    PASTOR    MUSIC DIRECTOR

LAYLEADER    LAYLEADER    LAYLEADER

WORKERS         WORKERS
```

A third type of organization is called *functional*. In a business or company this means that an employee may work with several different supervisors, according to the type of work (or function) involved. The leaders are concerned mainly with the tasks rather than the people.

In most Christian work there is a combination of these types. The pastor is the executive leader. He may have secondary leaders, such as assistant pastors. There are middle leaders, such as Sunday school superintendents and music directors. In a direct line organization, a worker, such as a member of the choir, would be under the choir director. The choir director would be under the music director; the music director under the assistant pastor. This kind of true line organization is seldom used in churches. Usually all leaders have direct relationships with the pastor, so the pattern is more like a line-staff organization. Then, because church work includes a variety of tasks, the leaders may find themselves relating to the other leaders and workers in functional ways.

The relationships of a pastor in the church organization are indeed complex because of this variety of tasks and functions. The pastor is the spiritual head of the congregation. He is the executive leader in the organizational structure and therefore the supervisor in his relationships to other leaders. Also, he is counselor and teacher to individual members of the flock. In order to maintain an effective organizational operation, the various roles of the pastor must be understood.

THE RELATIONSHIPS OF THE PASTOR

EXECUTIVE LEADER- ADMINISTRATOR

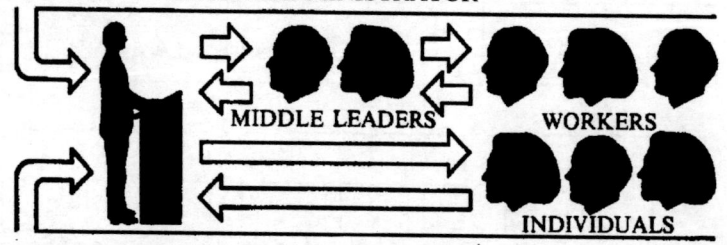

SPIRITUAL HEAD TEACHER COUNSELOR

As spiritual head, teacher, and counselor, the pastor relates directly to every individual in the congregation. But as the executive leader, or administrator in the organization, he must do much of his work with people through other leaders, to whom he delegates responsibilities and authority.

This combination of relationships can result in very effective church work. On the other hand, it can bring about some problems, especially for middle leaders who feel insecure or are

Leaders Plan and Organize 113

not competent in their positions. Remember what happened to William in our illustration? One of his workers asked his opinion. After he had spoken she announced that a different answer had been given to her by the pastor. Not only is a situation such as this a personal embarrassment for the middle leader, but it causes him to lose the respect he needs in order to get his tasks accomplished.

William did the right thing when he refused to make an issue of the matter. But he could have avoided the situation if he had had a clear understanding with the pastor concerning his duties and relationships. The pastor and the middle leaders should meet frequently to pray together and talk over the work. They should agree to maintain responsibilities for specific parts of the work. Then, if a worker goes to the pastor with a question concerning matters which have been delegated to another leader, the pastor should either advise the worker to go to the leader or invite the leader into the discussion. A leader should never try to handle alone a matter which is the responsibility of the pastor or another leader.

This is wise and efficient organization, and it makes the task easier for all parties. The pastor can trust his helpers to carry out their part of the work. The middle leader can maintain his effectiveness with the group. The workers feel secure knowing how they fit into the structure and how they should proceed when they have questions.

YOU AND ORGANIZATION

Objective 5. *Select a statement which explains the leader's relationship to organization.*

Most leaders relate to organization in two ways. First, they must understand how they fit into an existing organization. Second, they must know how to establish and maintain organization in their own areas of responsibility. As we have seen, successful leadership depends upon the qualities of the leader and the structure in which he works. A good leader may be handicapped by a poor organizational structure. A good organization may be handicapped by poor leadership. It takes both to accomplish the tasks and reach the goals in Christian work.

Therefore, when you assume a position of leadership you will want to be sure you understand the structure. If there is an organizational chart, study it Ask your superiors to explain the details of your position. Be sure you know what is expected of you. You may get a written job description (which is a list of your basic minimum duties), but the important part is the feeling that you and everyone involved have clear understandings. If you are to supervise others, there should be a meeting where your position is explained to the group.

How to Organize

If you are to start a new organization, or begin with one which needs renewal, you have a great responsibility. Here are some suggestions to guide you:

1. Make a task analysis—a fist of all the jobs or work items which have been delegated to you or must be done to reach the objectives.

2. Decide how many persons or positions will be needed to accomplish the tasks. List the specific tasks for each person or position.

3. Make a chart to show how the positions will relate to each other and to you and other leaders.

4. Appoint people to fill the positions or be responsible for the tasks. (Do not fill positions which may be more or less permanent until you have qualified persons. It is better to leave positions open and plan to recruit or train new people.)

5. Provide immediate information to all those who will work with you, and plan to see that they have help and training as needed. Try to give everyone the same information at the same time and allow people to ask questions.

Leaders Plan and Organize 115

6. Have a definite plan for accountability. That is, each person must know what is expected and what the conditions and limitations are. Use the planning questions: When? Where? How? Specify how workers are to record and report the results of their work. Set time limits. Explain relevant policies of the organization which may affect the work. Include in the original plan a way to evaluate or measure results so that you and the others will have an opportunity to learn from experience and make improvements in the future.

10 Draw an organizational chart which you believe represents an organizational structure with which you are familiar.

11 Match the type of organization (right) with its correct description (left).

.... **a** The executive leader is advised by a specialized advisory group. He supervises middle leaders, who interact with individuals who are under them.

.... **b** The executive leader has controlling authority. Each person is supervised directly by person above him. Workers communicate only through supervisors.

.... **c** The executive leader is head of organization. He is supervisor in relationships with other leaders. He is also responsible directly to every individual in his organization.

1) Direct line
2) Line-staff
3) Pastoral

12 In his relationship to organization, the leader must understand
a) how he fits into the organization.
b) what is expected of him.
c) how he fits into the structure and how to establish control and maintain organization in his area.
d) what are the limits of his authority and what is the process by which he establishes control.

self-test

TRUE-FALSE. Place a **T** in the blank space in front of each TRUE statement. Place an **F** in front of each FALSE statement.

.... 1 In the experiences of David we see that the call of God usually comes after a potential leader has demonstrated his natural skills and abilities.

.... 2 Humility and courage are complimentary qualities. Courage comes because an unfailing God is the source of one's strength; humility comes because all the glory belongs to Him.

.... 3 David's great victory over Goliath established him as a leader. Thereafter he was free to pursue his own goals.

.... 4 Three principles which emerge from David's leadership methods are: 1) He consistently sought God's will; 2) He was loyal and considerate in dealing with subordinates and superiors; and 3) He strove for excellence and competence, giving glory to God.

.... 5 While David was not permitted to build the temple, he was challenged to prepare for its construction. This division of responsibility demonstrates David's incompetence as a builder.

.... 6 Preliminary planning and organization are part of the "thinking" stage of leadership. The truly important part, however, is the carrying out of the plans which is the "doing" stage.

.... 7 In David's example of preparation we learn that each leader is just one in the sequence of leaders: one prepares, one builds; but God alone makes possible the achievement of the task.

.... 8 In his preparations for the building of the temple, David demonstrates some principles of good leadership: consistent planning, adequate instructions for those involved, and appropriate provision of materials for the completion of the task.

.... **9** Only those tasks which are characterized by "poor planning" are done twice.

.... **10** Planning is a comprehensive process that involves time, energy, and expense; therefore, it is essential only in major jobs which require larger sums of money and greater numbers of people.

.... **11** Planning is essentially a thinking or mental process.

.... **12** The exercise of planning is a guarantee of certain success.

.... **13** In Christian work "planning" is viewed as an obstacle because some accuse the leader of leaning on his programs instead of the Holy Spirit.

.... **14** Scripture shows that the Holy Spirit anoints at the planning stage just as He does at the action stage of a task.

.... **15** Plans that are flexible, backed by prayer and contingency plans, and understood and accepted by everyone are certain to be successful.

.... **16** *Organization* includes getting people into relationships for efficient work on a task and *structure* or a plan shows how they are expected to relate to one another.

.... **17** Lines of authority must be respected in an organization if the needs of the people are to be met and the position of leaders is to be respected.

.... **18** Frequent communication is necessary to eliminate potential conflict between members of the leadership group and the leader in their relationships with people.

.... **19** If an individual who is under a middle leader goes directly to the top leader, the leader should handle the matter himself without consulting the middle leader involved.

.... **20** Both good organization and good leadership are required to accomplish the tasks and reach the goals in Christian service.

answers to study questions

7
  a 3) People.
  b 5) Materials.
  c 6) Objectives.
  d 1) Time.
  e 4) Methods.
  f 2) Place.

1 Suggested answers: He wanted to do a project for the Lord's work; he asked the people to be dedicated; he asked the people to work; and he spoke enthusiastically of the work.

8 c) Planning is the attempt to predetermine a course of action.

2 You should have noted that: He did not plan ahead, he did not give clear instructions, and he did not provide materials.

9 Three obstacles to planning in Christian work are: 1) plans do not always work; 2) people criticize Christians for planning; and 3) planning takes time and hard work.

3 d) had confidence that the Lord would use him.

10 Your answer.

4 a) demonstrate his position with facts.

11
  a 2) Line-staff.
  b 1) Direct line.
  c 3) Pastoral.

5 b) training and competence.

12 c) how he fits into the structure and how to establish control and maintain organization in his area

6 Your answer.

for your notes

LESSON 5

Leaders Communicate

Afke was leader of the men's ministries group in his church. He had plans for a new project and was enthusiastic.

"This is our opportunity to do something very good for the church," he told his wife. "The men m my group are all good Christians and eager to serve the Lord. They are capable men, too. Even though they are busy they are willing to give time for a project like this. I'll make it as easy for them as I can."

Later, in the men's meeting he announced his plans. "You will find your assignment quite easy," he assured the men with a confident smile, "because I have worked out all the details."

Mr. Andberg had joined the group recently. Before moving here he had been an active worker in another church. He was looking forward to having a place of service. He felt his experience was valuable, and he wanted to work for the Lord During the discussion time in the meeting he spoke out boldly. "This is a project I understand," he declared. "You don't have to work out every detail. I will do my part."

"Well, this is my responsibility," Afke answered, "I'll give you an assignment as soon as I have completed the plans."

That evening Mr. Andberg complained to his wife. "That Afke thinks he knows everything. He is interested in his own power and thinks none of us is capable. Says he'll make everything easy for us. Thinks he's the only one who wants to work for the Lord."

That evening Afke complained to his wife. "That Mr. Andberg thinks he knows everything. He wants to show off his ability. Doesn't want to cooperate with the group."

"... Thinks he knows everything"　　*"Doesn't want to cooperate ..."*

Afke and Mr. Andberg illustrate for us what may be the greatest problem in Christian leadership. It is the failure of leaders to communicate their real meaning to those with whom they work. In this lesson we will learn to understand and solve such problems.

lesson outline

Joshua—Leader With a Clear Message
The Communication Process
Leaders Overcome Barriers

lesson objectives

When you finish this lesson you should be able to:

- Describe leadership principles in the accounts of Joshua and recognize and apply these principles. define and illustrate the concept communication.

- Explain communications principles which are important in leadership situations.

- Listen as an effective leader, and provide feedback.

learning activities

1. Read Joshua chapter 1; 3:1-13; 4:1-8; 6:6-17; 18:1-8; 21:43-45; and chapter 22.

2. Work through the lesson development and answer study questions in the usual manner.

3. Take the self-test at the end of the lesson and check your answers carefully with those supplied at the back of this study guide.

key words

assertive type	evaluative words	prejudice
courageous	figurative meanings	responsive type
descriptive words	intuitive	spontaneously
equality	perceptions	vaguely

lesson development

JOSHUA—LEADER WITH A CLEAR MESSAGE

Objective 1. *Identify examples of communication in the book of Joshua and name the seven types mentioned.*

In the life and work of Joshua we can find an illustration of almost every characteristic and behavior associated with leadership. He learned from Moses first to follow and then to lead and inspire others. He had problems with people and made some mistakes when he failed to seek the guidance of the Lord. He laid out careful plans. He set the example in courageous action. He worked through others, such as the spies and Rahab, in order to reach his objectives. There is no doubt that Joshua was a typical leader and a model in many ways. For this lesson, however, we will limit our study to one outstanding characteristic of Joshua: He understood and utilized with unique success the basic principles of communication. He was a leader who knew how to communicate with God and man.

We began this lesson with a situation which illustrates the failure of a leader to communicate properly. Afke believed the men were capable, but busy. He was sincere in his desire to help

Leaders Communicate

them. Mr. Andberg was sincere in his desire to work for the Lord. Yet each man misunderstood the meaning which the other tried to express.

The fact that it is possible for God's people to misunderstand one another is made plain to us in one of the incidents in the book of Joshua. Remember that the tribe of Reuben, the tribe of Gad, and the half-tribe of Manasseh received their share of land on the east side of the Jordan. They went with the other Israelites to possess the land west of the Jordan. When the battles were won, they were given a blessing by Joshua and sent back to their inheritance (Joshua 22).

"When they came to Geliloth near the Jordan in the land of Canaan, the Reubenites, the Gadites and the half-tribe of Manasseh built an imposing altar there by the Jordan" (Joshua 22:10). This made the other tribes so angry that they wanted to fight a civil war. It had been agreed that no altar for sacrifice was to be erected except at Shiloh. The purpose of this was to keep the worship of the true God completely separate from any heathen altars which might be placed anywhere. So the Israelites accused their brothers of rebellion—breaking faith with the agreement and disobedience against God.

The people of Reuben, Gad, and the half-tribe of Manasseh were horrified. "No!" they cried, "We had no plans to make sacrifices in this place. You do not understand our meaning. We simply want everyone to know that we are a part of the same people who worship the true God at Shiloh! We want to honor the Lord, not disobey Him. We want the future generations to know that we are a part of His people!"

Do you see how these who had so recently fought side by side were now ready to fight each other? But as soon as the other tribes understood the true meaning of the altar they were pleased. Everyone rejoiced. Communication made the difference.

1-3 If you have not reviewed Joshua chapter 22, do so now. Give special attention to verses 11-24. Then circle the letter in front of the best completion for each sentence.

1 When the Israelites heard that an altar had been built at Geliloth they
a) knew why it was built.
b) asked why it was built
c) imagined why it was built

2 The Israelites were angry and decided to fight because
a) the other tribes had sinned.
b) they thought the other tribes had sinned.
c) they were always ready to attach wrong motives to others' actions.

3 The representatives from Israel went to the other tribes and
a) asked them why they built the altar.
b) asked them to take the altar down.
c) accused them of rebellion against God.

4 What could the Israelites have done in order to avoid the misunderstanding?

....

....

5 What could the people of Reuben, Gad, and the half-tribe of Manasseh have done to avoid the misunderstanding?

....

....

This account is significant because it helps us to see why the people needed a leader like Joshua. The Lord knew that the great need at this time was for clear instructions and careful guidance every step of the way. Here at the beginning of a new life in unknown circumstances there must be a strong leader who would listen to the Lord and bring understanding to the people.

Joshua was trained by Moses to be a brilliant general. Even more important, he was taught to know and follow the Word of God. His call to leadership came with God's command and God's promise: "Lead these people to inherit the land ... Be strong and very courageous ... The Lord your God will be with you ... (Joshua 1:6-9).

Evidently Joshua had a humble attitude toward himself as a person, for God told him several times not to be afraid. Yet, when he was sure of his calling, he began to demonstrate at once his courage and confidence. His first act of leadership was to give clear directions and precise instructions to the officers: "Go through the camp and tell the people, 'Get your supplies ready. Three days from now you will cross the Jordan here to go in and take possession of the land the Lord your God is giving you for your own'" (Joshua 1:10-11).

From this point on Joshua shows great ability to communicate with his people and deep understanding of the importance of various kinds of communications skills. We find in the book of Joshua seven distinct types of communication. Keep your Bible open so you can refer to the examples as we discuss each one briefly. You may wish to mark them in the Bible for future reference.

Words of Instruction
Joshua 2:1; 3:2-4, 9; 8:3-8

Officers went throughout the camp explaining to the people exactly what they should do. Joshua made certain that everyone heard and understood when plans were being made for the various activities in the march and the conquest. Special directions were repeated for the various tribes. Individuals and groups were called out for special assignments. Each action was explained for all of those who shared in the responsibilities. "Come here and listen," said Joshua (Joshua 3:9). No detail was overlooked. Every person received the information needed in order to do his part.

The results of this careful instruction are evident in the mission of the spies to Rahab, the crossing of the Jordan, the fall of Jericho, and all the successful campaigns. The people, with very few exceptions, "did as Joshua commanded them" (Joshua 4:8). Because they knew what was expected of them, they were able to act with confidence and in cooperation with one another.

Words of Encouragement
Joshua 3:5; 10:24-25; 23:5

Joshua said to his men, "Come here and put your feet on the necks of these kings . . . Do not be afraid; do not be discouraged . . . This is what the Lord will do . . ." (Joshua 10:24-25). Joshua shared moments of victory and encouragement with his followers. He helped them to see that each triumph was more than a task completed. It was a promise for the future, too. It was evidence of the Lord's blessing which could be expected to continue. In this way the people were strengthened in their faith and their devotion to their mission.

Commands and Orders
Joshua 6:16

Joshua as a military leader found it necessary to give many direct commands and orders. We see from our example in the fall of Jericho that there are times when a leader must require complete obedience. Joshua sets for us the example of a leader who treats his followers with care and respect. The people soon began to trust and respect him, too. Then when the need for obedience arose they were willing to respond. This is a lesson which all leaders, especially those who work with very young people, need to learn.

Information (Teaching)
Joshua 24:1-13

Joshua reminded the people of their history and purpose. As a wise leader, he knew it was his duty to keep them informed and aware of important facts affecting the work as a whole. Basic truths and scriptural teachings must be made constantly fresh to people who work for the Lord. Joshua did not say, "Everyone should know this by now." He repeated God's words patiently again and again. Communication is never a completed project. It is a process for which every leader is continually responsible.

Persuasion (Exhortation)
Joshua 23:6-16; 24:14-24

Much of the communication in Christian work takes the form of exhortation, or preaching. Some leaders seem to think that all communication is of this type. They seem always to be urging the people to act, trying to persuade them to do the will of the leader. When persuasion is used too much in this way it ceases to be effective. Joshua gives us examples of good use of persuasion. The Lord led him to speak to the people concerning their commitment for the future. Notice four main elements in the words of Joshua All effective persuasive communication follows this pattern:

1. *Appeals to the mind.* "You know what has happened before, so it is logical for you to believe that God will continue to work in the same way" (See Joshua 23:14-16).
2. *Warns.* "If you violate the covenant of the Lord . . . the Lord's anger will burn against you" (Joshua 23:16).
3. *Challenges.* "Be very strong" (Joshua 23:6).
4. *Gives opportunity to respond.* "Choose for yourselves this day whom you will serve" (Joshua 24:15).

Records and Reports
Joshua, chapters 12–20

Communication may be in written form, as well as in spoken language. Joshua performed one of the essential duties of leadership by maintaining good records and writing reports of the activities. In this way the results of his efforts were communicated accurately. They may not enjoy filling in forms and keeping records, but all good leaders agree that such work is necessary. How much less we would understand about God and His people if His chosen leaders had not kept records!

Symbolic Communication
Joshua 4:1-9

"What do these stones mean?" Communication is the process of getting *meaning* from one person to another. This is accomplished not only by spoken and written language but also by various kinds of symbols. Joshua used a pile of stones to communicate a most important message. Symbolic communication used in our churches today includes the arrangement of furniture, such as the altar, and the type of clothing worn by ministers. Kneeling, clapping, and waving are symbolic communications. A good leader learns that the people find meaning in his bodily movements and facial expressions, whether or not he intends for them to do so. Therefore, it is important to understand how to communicate effectively through symbols as well as words.

6 Try to repeat from memory the seven types of communication for which examples are found in the book of Joshua. Then match each type of communication (right) with the example which illustrates it (left).

.... **a** "Choose for yourselves this day whom you will serve ... As for me and my household, we will serve the Lord" (24:15).

.... **b** "Joshua copied on stones the law of Moses" (8:32).

.... **c** "Come here and listen to the words of the Lord your God" (3:9).

.... **d** "Each of you is to take up a stone on his shoulder ... to serve as a sign" (4:5-6).

.... **e** "Do not be afraid; do not be discouraged ... Be strong and courageous" (10:25).

.... **f** "This is what the Lord, the God of Israel, says" (24:2).

.... **g** "But keep away from the devoted things, so that you will not bring about your own destruction" (6:18).

1) Instruction
2) Encouragement
3) Commands
4) Information
5) Persuasion
6) Records
7) Symbols

THE COMMUNICATION PROCESS

Leaders Recognize Barriers

Objective 2. *Describe the communication process and some barriers to communication.*

Now that we have examined several examples of communication we are ready to analyze the process. Let's begin with a list of the parts or components which we have observed.

First there is the *source* of the material which is to be communicated, or the person who wishes to communicate. The source person has an intent, or a *meaning*. This may be an idea, a feeling, or some information. There is a *receiver* to whom the meaning is directed. The receiver is not an empty vessel but is a person with *perceptions* which probably will have some effect upon the meaning which is received. The source person must select a *method* or methods, such as language and other symbols, by which to express the meaning. The purpose of the communication process is to have the receiver understand the meaning exactly as it is intended by the source person.

Most of us never realize how difficult it is to accomplish this purpose. Between the meaning which is intended and the meaning which is received are numerous barriers. One way to understand the communication process is to consider some of these barriers. Then we will see how good leaders communicate effectively by overcoming the barriers. Following is a brief description of seven barriers which are most likely to cause problems.

1. Language. Some words have more than one meaning. Some words have distinct meanings in certain geographical areas. Many biblical terms have special or figurative meanings. Remember the problem Nicodemus had with the term born again? (See John 3:1-12.) Communication is not satisfactory unless the speaker (or source person) and the receiver understand words in the same way.

2. *Symbols*. Much of what we communicate is not spoken at all. One pastor relates that he was first induced to join a Bible class by the way the teacher held her Bible. "I knew she loved that book," he said, "and I wanted to find out why it was so special to her. She held it tenderly and turned the pages in a loving way." This was symbolic communication of a positive kind. Barriers to communication are created when symbols (gestures, movements, facial expressions, voice tone) do not agree with the spoken message. For example, suppose a person said, "I love the Bible," and then threw it down carelessly and forgot it. What would be communicated—love or disrespect?

3. *Customs*. Every group of people develops certain ways of behavior which are called customs. Sometimes these ways are

accepted so completely that people believe they are the only right ways. For example, in some groups women are expected to shake hands when they meet and in other groups they are expected to touch their cheeks together. When such customs are not observed properly, communication breaks down, sometimes to the point of painful misunderstanding.

4. *Prejudice.* We cannot communicate effectively with people we do not accept as our equals in the sight of God. In the Bible we have several references to prejudice which interfered with communication. Because the Israelites generally considered Samaritans and all Gentiles inferior to themselves, even the gospel of Jesus could not be communicated adequately. For this reason the Lord spoke to Peter in a vision and guided him in overcoming the barrier of prejudice (Acts 10).

5. *Status.* Most people find it difficult to communicate with those in positions which the society considers lower or higher than their own. Usually it is easier for two farmers to communicate with each other than for a farmer and a hired field worker. There are wealthy Christians who never witness to their servants. There are Christian servants who never witness to their employers. Dedication to the Lord and love for souls are made ineffective because of communication barriers in these cases. An essential skill which must be learned for successful leadership is how to communicate with individuals on various social levels and in various organizational positions. The first step is to be aware of the status barrier and sincerely desire to overcome it.

SOURCE PERSON	METHOD	RECEIVER PERSON
INTENT OR MEANING	LANGUAGE, SYMBOL	PERCEPTIONS

6. *Age and sex.* Closely related to status are the age and sex of those who attempt communication. Older leaders may find it particularly difficult to reach young people. Their values and interests may be very different. For example, a leader announced that the young people who cooperated with a certain project would be rewarded by a dinner at the pastor's home. The young people were not impressed. They preferred a picnic by the lake. The leader felt embarrassed and angry. The project was not a success.

Relations between males and females all over the world have been strained by the modern conception of equality for women. Sensitive Christian leaders will not ignore this issue. They will think about it, pray, and try to understand the values and the needs of both sexes and all the age groups. This is a difficult task, but Christian leaders have the advantage of knowing that everyone has a place in God's great circle of love.

7. *Personality.* Every group situation is composed of unique individuals. A major leadership task is to bring understanding and cooperation so that group goals will be accepted and accomplished. In order to do this the leader must communicate with the individuals. He must not make the mistake of believing that the message he sends will be received in the same way by every person in the group. He must realize that the end result of the communication process is not the meaning intended by the sender, but rather the meaning perceived by each receiver.

7 Based on what you have learned in this lesson, write in your own words a definition of *communication*.

....
....

8 Based on what you have learned in this lesson, write in your own words a definition for the term *barrier to communication*.

....
....

9 Think of a situation in your own experience where there has been misunderstanding because of some barrier to communication.

The Significance of Perception

Objective 3. *Explain the significance of perception In the process of communication.*

We have said that the perception of the receiver determines the meaning of a message. In other words, the message actually means whatever the receiver thinks it means. Therefore, we must know something of how he perceives in order to communicate with him.

The way a person perceives is partly the result of factors we listed previously such as age, sex, status, and customs. Two other significant factors are personality traits and field of experience. Experts in the study of communications use the personality type classifications of Carl Jung to explain how different interpretations (or perceptions) result from the same message. According to this classification there are four personality types, as follows:

1. Thinking people, who want a leader to explain everything with careful attention to facts and logic.
2. Feeling people, who need emotional inspiration and challenge.
3. Sensing people, who need demonstrations and examples.
4. Intuitive people, who are quick to jump to conclusions and look for hidden meanings.

Leaders who understand that these four personality types may be represented in their groups will be able to present balanced messages. They will understand why some in the group respond more at one time than another. They will be able to approach individuals in the most appropriate manner and make assignments suitable to the needs and interests of the workers. They will be able to offer training and guidance in the most effective ways. Because they understand that these types of behavior are typical, they will not feel personally offended or angry when someone fails to understand a message.

Another way to classify personality types is by the degree of dependence or independence expressed. The dependent person (sometimes called *responsive type*) needs to receive detailed instructions from a leader. The independent person (sometimes called *assertive type*) needs opportunities to express his own ideas. He wants the leader to give more general suggestions and allow him freedom for creativity. Obviously it is greatly to the leader's advantage to know how these types interpret a message.

All perception is dependent upon the *field of experience*, and all communication is dependent upon a shared field of experience. That is, messages can be sent and received only if the sender and the receiver share basic fields of experience, such as language. In addition to the basic shared experiences of a group, each person has a particular set of experiences which causes him to think and feel in certain ways. This includes dramatic experiences, such as fighting in a war and living through a storm, and the personal life situations, such as occupation and marriage. Meanings attached to certain items, places, people, ideas can be changed tremendously because of an experience. Therefore, when there is a greater amount of shared experience, there is a better foundation for communication. All communication must begin in the area of shared experience, and all messages from a source person must pass through the field of experience of the receiver. This can be illustrated in a drawing.

THE COMMUNICATION PROCESS

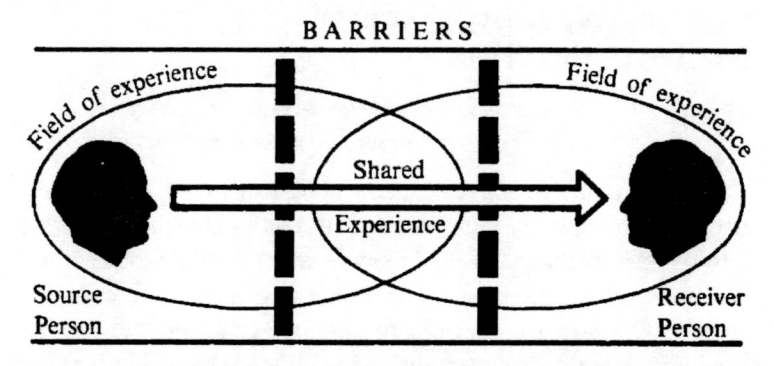

Communication is effective when there is shared experience and when barriers are overcome

10 The director of Christian education is leading a staff meeting. He says, "We need a special room for the very young children. There is one room in the church which we could use if we provide the necessary equipment."

"Yes," said Miss X, who was a nurse, "we need safe cribs and plenty of sheets so we can keep it clean."

"Yes," said Mrs. Y, who had five children, "but first we should get a rocking chair for mothers and some toys."

Which of the following statements is illustrated by this conversation?
a) The leader is not sending a clear message.
b) The nurse is the assertive type of personality.
c) Field of experience affects perception.
d) The mother is a thinking person.

11 Review the illustration with which we began this lesson. If you were to classify Mr. Andberg according to Jung's personality types, you would call him

....

If you were to classify him as a dependent or an independent type, you would call him

....

LEADERS OVERCOME BARRIERS TO COMMUNICATION

Objective 4. *Explain how leaders can achieve satisfactory communication between themselves and the people they lead.*

At this point we have leaned enough to avoid the greatest error leaders make in their attempts to communicate. That error is to believe that whatever they say is understood by the hearers. We are now aware that good communication is a complex process. Our next step is to learn what we can do to be sure the receiver perceives our messages as we intend them. We learn to overcome the barriers to communication by turning them into gateways. Following are some practical suggestions:

1. *Know what you wish to communicate.* Find out how well you can communicate with yourself. Write out or express aloud in meditation exactly what you have in mind before you make a formal presentation or an important announcement. Have a clear, precise objective rather than a hazy idea as to the subject of your communication. Get into the habit of making notes and outlines.

2. *Know as much as possible about the people with whom you wish to communicate.* We see from our previous discussion that a leader will never be able to send messages which every receiver will understand in exactly the same way. Nevertheless, very good results are achieved by leaders who understand the principles of perception, personality types, and the field of experience. The more you know about your people, the more you share their field of experience, and the more likely you are to communicate with them in a satisfactory manner.

3. *Show genuine respect equally for people* (their gifts, talents, and interests). Give them reasons to believe that what you say is important to them as well as to you.

4. *Choose correct and precise language.* Speak in an honest, open manner, not vaguely as though you were keeping to yourself some important information you cannot share with them. Use exact words wherever possible. That is, do not use terms such as these: a lot; only a little; a short time; your fair share. If there is a problem, speak it out clearly to the involved parties. Never leave a vague impression that some unnamed person is at fault. Someone is sure to misunderstand and feel hurt or angry.

5. *Encourage response.* One way to find out whether or not your messages are being understood is to ask for questions and comments. If you are in charge of a particular group, establish regular information channels. Make certain persons responsible for reports and announcements. Indicate by your manner and words that ail contributions are welcome.

12 Remember Afke? Which of these rules of good communication did he fail to observe?
a) Know what you wish to communicate.
b) Choose correct and precise language.
c) Know as much as possible about the people with whom you wish to communicate.

Listening is a Part of Communication

Successful leaders know how to listen as well as to send messages. There are four stages in the listening process. First is *hearing*. This is the physical reception of sound waves. The next stage is *attention*. We hear many sounds to which we pay no attention, so most of them are meaningless. When we select a sound from among those we hear, this is attention. When we give attention to a sound we can begin to *understand* it as a message. The last stage of the listening process is *remembering*. When we have understood a message and put it into the mind's storage, we can say we have completed an act of listening.

Effective listening begins with putting your attention on what is being said by another person. This requires effort. For example, adults may hear children speaking and not really listen. What they say is not considered important enough to make that special kind of effort required to listen. If you feel superior to a person you may find yourself not really listening to what he says. If you are in a hurry or have your mind on another matter, you may hear words and even answer without really listening.

You can develop listening skills if you are motivated to do so. You can say to yourself, "I want to understand this person's idea (or problem) exactly as he intends me to understand it." You must believe that the person is important and that his message has some significance. Remember and practice the following rules for effective listening.

1. Concentrate your physical and mental energies on listening.
2. Demonstrate interest and alertness with your body and eyes.
3. Avoid interrupting the speaker.

4. Do not show strong disagreement until the speaker has completed a message. Look for opportunities to indicate agreement with body movement such as leaning forward or nodding your head.
5. Search for meanings and avoid getting hung up on specific words.
6. Be patient. Do not act as though you are in a hurry.
7. Ask questions when you don't understand, but keep your questions quiet and objective.
8. Do not respond emotionally, but answer in an objective manner after the message is completed.
9. Try to separate facts from opinions in what you hear, so that you will have a basis for evaluating the message and giving a reply.
10. Try to discern what type of response the person expects—information, help, or simply assurance and caring.

13 A group member said, "The devil has interfered with our plans, and six of our workers are absent. What shall we do?" The leader answered, 'Don't blame the devil for everything." Which rule for effective listening did the leader fail to observe?

....

Feedback is a Part of Communication

Successful leaders know how to reply as well as to send messages and listen. A communication cycle includes transmission of a message from sender to receiver and then a return message, which is called *feedback*. The return message may be verbal or nonverbal. We have mentioned this in our discussion of listening, as good listening is a type of feedback.

When people try to communicate with a leader and do not receive adequate feedback they tend either to feel rejected or to reject the leader. Have you spoken into a recording device or in an empty room? It is not the same as talking to people, is it? The difference is that there is no feedback. This is similar to the uncomfortable feeling people have with a leader who does not give good feedback.

An important effect of feedback on the communication process is to help both the speaker and the hearer understand correctly. Sometimes you can tell by facial expressions (nonverbal feedback) whether or not people are understanding your message.

Another effect of feedback is the development of self-concept. In a leadership situation the leader uses feedback to encourage people and help them to believe they are capable of accomplishing the tasks and reaching the goals. Too much negative feedback (pointing out faults and mistakes, scolding) can cause people to become discouraged and feel incapable of achievement.

Feedback affects performance very definitely. Studies show that workers who do not receive feedback from their leaders lose interest in their tasks. Good performance results partly from good self-concept Also there is satisfaction in knowing that the leader is interested and aware of what each worker is doing. Much feedback comes spontaneously, but good leaders can learn how to provide feedback in conscious and effective ways. As you lead people in Christian service, the feedback you give often will be in the form of helping with tasks and evaluating what has been done. For example, you may be leading a group of teachers, and you want to help them improve their performance. In group discussions, or individually, you will find opportunities to let them know what the desired outcomes are and how you feel about their work. Here are some suggestions to guide you in providing this type of feedback.

1. Emphasize performance, not personality. You will say to a worker, "This work needs to be improved," without giving the impression that you think he is careless or not dedicated to God.

2. Use descriptive words rather than evaluative words. It would be better to say a teacher needs to study more than to say he is lazy.

3. The timing of feedback is important. When a worker asks for help or advice it should be given immediately if possible. People should not be corrected when they are discouraged or when time is too limited for discussion.

4. Amount of feedback is important. Usually it is better to give a small amount of feedback at a time. On the other hand, the leader must not leave a person feeling uncertain.

14 Write a brief description of the communications process.

....

....

15 What are the main responsibilities of the leader in the communications process?

....

....

self-test

1 Joshua demonstrated valuable leadership principles in his tenure as Israel's leader. Which one of the following is NOT one of these principles?
a) He explained every action to all who shared responsibility for that action: instruction.
b) He issued specific imperatives that required implicit obedience: commands.
c) He stressed obedience and appealed to the memory of the generation which failed: threat.
d) He strengthened the people's faith and devotion by words of comfort and challenge: encouragement.

2 Israel needed to know God's statutes and ordinances—they needed *information*. And lest they forget, Joshua spoke convincingly to them about their spiritual obligations (*persuasion*). Available information over the long-term requires
a) a strong oral tradition and good communication.
b) an organized priesthood which interprets tradition and administers its sacraments.
c) a culture which is sensitive to the values of the past.
d) records which communicate the responsibilities and privileges of spiritual life.

3 Jasper entered a church which was filled with people. The reverent worship, the dignity of the anthems of praise, the ministry of the Word, and even the strong, wooden benches and the massive pulpit created a feeling of confidence and strength. His impressions were the result of
a) symbolic communication.
b) his strong religious superstition.
c) his extreme sensitivity to religious experience.
d) his cultural conditioning to spiritual phenomena.

4 The purpose of the communication process is to have the receiver
a) hear clearly the message that is sent by the source person.
b) understand the meaning of the message exactly as it was intended by the source person.
c) perceive the message of the source person as he believes it should be understood.
d) and the source person operate from identical frames of reference.

5 Communication is not satisfactory unless the source person and the receiver
a) perceive reality in the same way.
b) share the same attitudes and outlook on life, as well as the same prejudices.
c) understand words in the same way.
d) have the same comprehension of figurative language.

6 In Fred's country friends greet one another with three light kisses on the cheek. When he returns from abroad, Fred ignores this custom, causing people to react strongly to his foreign ways. Since custom has not been followed and misunderstanding has occurred, we can say best that
a) Fred's people are extremely prejudice.
b) Fred has sinned grievously.
c) both Fred and his friends need to reconsider the issue of customs.
d) communication has broken down.

7 The end result of the communication process is the meaning
a) intended by the sender.
b) that any impartial witness would attach to the message.
c) perceived by the receiver.
d) obviously indicated by the plain meaning of the words.

8 The greatest error leaders make in their attempts to communicate is to believe that
a) it is possible to be understood by people.
b) whatever they say is understood by their hearers.
c) the gap between leaders and followers can be bridged by any medium of communication.
d) they will receive a sympathetic hearing from the majority of their people.

9 Listening is an important part of communication. We have completed an act of listening when we have
a) physically heard a message.
b) heard a message and given our full attention to it.
c) heard, given our attention to, and understood a message.
d) understood a message and put it in our mind's storage system.

10 Feedback, the return message from the receiver to the source person, completes the communication cycle. Feedback is vitally important for all the following reasons but one. Which one is NOT one of these?
a) Feedback helps both speaker and hearer to understand correctly.
b) Feedback is an important means of developing people's self-concept.
c) Feedback enables the leader to judge the people's reaction to established policies.
d) Feedback has a significant effect on the performance of workers.

11 Match each specific barrier to communication (right) with its correct description (left).

.... **a** The unique quality of a person that sets him off from all others

.... **b** Characteristics that 1) differentiate one generation from another and 2) that state appropriate behavior for men and women

.... **c** Composed of words which convey meaning

.... **d** The attitude which refuses to accept others as equals in the sight of God

.... **e** Accepted standard of behavior for any group of people

.... **f** The attitude which makes it difficult for one to communicate with those on higher or lower social level than his own

.... **g** Nonverbal communication devices (for example, gestures, facial expressions, tone of voice, movements)

1) Language
2) Symbols
3) Customs
4) Prejudice
5) Status
6) Age and sex
7) Personality

12 Match each practical communication suggestion (left) with its appropriate descriptive title (right).

.... **a** Determine to know in advance the people's perceptions, personality types, and field of experience.

.... **b** Avoid the use of vague terms. Use exact words as you speak openly and honestly.

.... **c** Ask for questions and comments. Encourage contributions.

.... **d** Demonstrate appreciation equally for people and for their talents, gifts, and interests.

.... **e** Rehearse your presentation to see that you have your message clearly in mind. Use notes and outlines.

1) Know your material
2) Know your audience
3) Respect your audience
4) Use precise language
5) Encourage response

TRUE-FALSE. Write **T** in front of the TRUE statements, and **F** in front of those which are FALSE.

.... **13** Understanding the various personality types helps the leader present balanced messages and relate better to his people.

.... **14** The dependent person requires considerable attention and detailed instruction from his supervisor.

.... **15** The independent person generally reacts strongly to heavy supervision and the giving of detailed instructions.

.... **16** When the source person and the receiver share basic fields of experience, they have the basic ingredients necessary to communicate.

.... **17** People within a given society share the same particular set of experiences which make them think and feel in the same predictable ways.

answers to study questions

8 Your answer. I have suggested the following: A barrier to communication is anything which keeps the meaning intended by the source person from getting to the receiver.

1 c) imagined why it was built.

9 Your answer.

2 b) they thought the other tribes had sinned.

10 c) Field of experience affects perception.

3 c) accused them of rebellion against God.

11 Intuitive. That is, he is ready to jump to conclusions and see hidden meanings. Independent.

4 They could have asked the other tribes why they built the altar before making accusations and preparing to fight.

12 c) Know as much as possible about the people with whom you wish to communicate.

5 They could have sent a message to the Israelites to explain what they were doing.

13 He failed to observe rule 5: Search for meanings and avoid getting hung up on specific words.

6 a 5) Persuasion.
 b 6) Records.
 c 1) Instruction.
 d 7) Symbols.
 e 2) Encouragement
 f 4) Information.
 g 3) Commands.

14 Your answer should be similar to mine. I've noted that "a source person sends a message which is received and understood by the receiver. The receiver then returns a message, which is called feedback."

7 Your answer. I have suggested the following answer as a possible definition: Communication is getting meaning from one person to another.

15 The leader must endeavor 1) to make the message clear, 2) to be sure the message is understood, and 3) to give adequate feedback. The essential responsibility of a leader is to be sure his messages are understood and to provide opportunities for response.

LESSON 6
Leaders Solve Problems and Make Decisions

"Things sure didn't go very well last Sunday," Saven remarked "We need to pray for our Sunday school."

"That's right," agreed Bella She was leading the monthly meeting of the Sunday school committee. After a time of prayer she continued the discussion.

"You say you didn't feel good about last Sunday. What is the problem?"

"The adult classes are too close to those noisy boys," said Leif "Is there any way we could move the classes around?"

"Moving the classes is no answer," Marta declared. "It's a matter of discipline. We should make those boys be quiet."

"The problem is the parents," Leif proposed. "Maybe we should put out a notice asking the parents to cooperate."

"I hate to say this," Saven spoke slowly, "but maybe it's the teacher. He just doesn't hold their attention, and that's why they're so noisy. Could we find someone else to teach that class?"

"Or we could give him a helper," Marta suggested. "Two working together might be effective."

Bella spoke very little, but she was performing one of the most important tasks of leadership. She was guiding her people to analyze problems and seek solutions for them. In this lesson

"... What is the problem?"

we will examine the methods of the great leader, Nehemiah. We will learn from him and from modern scholars how to solve problems and make decisions.

lesson outline

Nehemiah—A Wise and Decisive Leader
Leadership Involves Problem-Solving
Leadership Involves Decision-Making
Group Dynamics

lesson objectives

When you finish this lesson you should be able to:

- Describe leadership principles in the account of Nehemiah and recognize examples and applications of these principles.

- Describe a formal problem-solving procedure.

- List decision-making styles and evaluate them.

- Give a brief explanation of the term group dynamics and discuss the two dimensions in group work.

learning activities

1. It will be beneficial, and we believe interesting, for you to review the entire book of Nehemiah. Of special importance for this lesson are chapters 1–5; 6:15-7:3; 8.

2. Work through the lesson development and answer the study questions in the usual manner. When you have finished, take the self-test and check your answers.

3. Carefully review Unit 2 (Lessons 4–6), then complete the unit student report for Unit 2 and send it to your instructor.

key words

authoritarian	downtrodden	ridicule
confidant	faction	routine
consequences	harmonize	symptom
dimensions	imminent	

lesson development

NEHEMIAH—A WISE AND DECISIVE LEADER

Objective 1. *distinguish leadership characteristics and leadership functions from the account of Nehemiah.*

During the period after Cyrus had decreed that the Jews could return to Jerusalem, Nehemiah was cupbearer in the Persian court His position and popularity had resulted in good personal fortune for him. He had wealth and privileges. Nevertheless, his heart was with his own people and he was concerned for his beloved homeland. When he heard that the walls of Jerusalem were in ruins, he wept and prayed. He felt that God was calling him to a great task (see Nehemiah chapters 1 and 2).

"Why do you look so sad?" the king asked.

"Because our city is a wasteland, with the gates burned. It is a sorrow and a disgrace."

"What would you like to do about it?" the king inquired.

Leaders Solve Problems and Make Decisions

At this point begins one of the most complete illustrations of leadership that has ever been written. Nehemiah was motivated by a love for Jerusalem, the city of his God and his people. The value he placed upon Jerusalem was far greater than any personal gain or ease he had as a popular confidant of the king. Nehemiah had vision. He was able to comprehend the total situation and recognize the need for action. He could see a clear goal and a possible means of reaching it. He did not hesitate to tell the king exactly what he had in mind. With suitable respect, but with boldness he spoke: "I want you to send me to Judah, to rebuild the city of my fathers."

We see that the Lord guided Nehemiah to go through the proper channels and present plans in a reasonable way. "How long will it take?" the king asked, and Nehemiah tells us, "I set a time." He was in no way vague nor hesitant. "I need letters of safe-conduct, too," he continued, "and permission to use timber from the king's forests."

Next we find that Nehemiah carefully studied the situation in detail. Riding around the walls, he inspected the damage and no doubt planned in his mind how the work should proceed. When he felt he was in possession of all essential information, and was sure of God's leading, he called together all the priests, nobles, officials, and other workers to place the matter before them (chapter 2).

He communicated to them, clearly and honestly, the plan he had in mind and the goal to be attained. He lead them to face reality, giving them an accurate description of the situation. He motivated them by letting them see that his goal was theirs, also, saying, "Come, let us rebuild the wall of Jerusalem, and we will no longer be in disgrace." He gave assignments which included repair of the walls *near their own houses*. He kept records so that it could be reported what had been done by each group of workers (chapter 3).

Nehemiah, like most leaders, had problems both from within his own people and from the outside. Enemies tried to stop the project by fighting and to discourage the workers with ridicule and insults. Nehemiah organized his people for work and for self-protection. Most important, he worked among them personally and gave them words of encouragement. "Don't be afraid," he counseled them. "Remember the Lord, who is great and awesome" (4:14).

While they were working day and night with all their strength and living under the threat of imminent attack, it was a sadness to Nehemiah to realize that some of his people were taking advantage of others. Some had managed to keep much property during the days of captivity, and others were destitute, without enough to eat. Nehemiah saw that the poor were being cheated. He did not make excuses for the wealthy and powerful in order to maintain his own high status. He said plainly, "What you are doing is not right. Stop cheating the poor." As a godly leader, he knew that no goal can have meaning unless those who work toward it are doing God's will and are living in peace with one another. The people are important, as well as the task and goal.

Nehemiah's official position was that of governor of Judah. Yet he refused to accept any of the special privileges that might have been his. Instead of having special meals for himself, he prepared large meals for those who were in need. He had enough money for his personal needs, so he took no salary for his services to his people. He devoted himself completely to the work and did not acquire any land or money for himself (5:14-18).

There was no doubt of the success of Nehemiah's leadership, for the main objective was reached—the wall of Jerusalem completed—in 52 days.

Leaders Solve Problems and Make Decisions 151

1 Each of the sentences illustrates a leadership characteristic or a leadership function. Place before each a number to indicate which of the following is most appropriate.

Leadership characteristics

1) Empathy
2) Competence
3) A sense of calling

Leadership functions

4) Planning
5) Organizing
6) Motivating others

.... **a** Nehemiah said, "Come, let us build the wall so we will not be a disgrace."

.... **b** He examined the wall carefully and provided the correct materials.

.... **c** He told them the hand of God was upon him.

.... **d** Although he was rich, he supported the position of the poor.

.... **e** He thought about what he would say to the king.

.... **f** He assigned each group to a definite part of the work.

LEADERSHIP INVOLVES PROBLEM-SOLVING

Objective 2. *Identify and explain elements of the problem-solving process.*

Our brief review of the experiences of Nehemiah has shown us that he had the characteristics and carried out the functions of leadership. A closer examination of this material will reveal to us what is perhaps the greatest strength of Nehemiah's leadership: With confidence in God, he accepted the responsibility of *solving problems* and *making decisions*.

Students of leadership functions have devised several models of the problem-solving process. Usually they suggest three main stages. Each stage has several steps.

> ## STAGES IN PROBLEM-SOLVING
>
> *First Stage*: Defining or formulating the problem and deciding to act
>
> 1. Analyze and describe the situation (or general condition).
> 2. State the problem in specific terms.
> 3. Decide if action is needed.
>
> Second Stage: Selecting a solution and taking action
>
> 1. Consider alternative solutions (and advantages and disadvantages of each).
> 2. Select a course of action and outline specific procedures.
> 3. Implement action and monitor each procedure.
>
> *Third Stage*: Evaluating the outcome of the action. If the outcome is satisfactory, the problem is solved. If not, it is necessary to ask these questions:
>
> 1. Was the problem defined correctly?
> 2. Was the correct solution chosen?
> 3. Was the action carried out properly?

These three stages of problem-solving are evident in the experiences of Nehemiah. What we call a "problem" is something we identify from a situation which makes us feel uneasy or distressed in some way. We feel that "something is wrong." We feel tension or frustration. Nehemiah said he was "sad" about the condition of which he was aware. The condition was that the survivors of Judah were in great trouble and disgrace. Next note that Nehemiah questioned the messengers. He was making an analysis of the situation before deciding to ask help from the king. Later he examined the walls in person, so that he could describe the situation in detail. This illustrates the first step in problem-solving. Know exactly what the situation is. Ask: What kind of trouble or unrest is involved?

Leaders Solve Problems and Make Decisions

Out of the general condition of unrest, we must identify a definite problem which can be attacked. In this case the general state was the trouble and disgrace of the people. The specific problem was that the walls of Jerusalem were broken down and burned. Nehemiah understood the connection between the condition and the problem. The trouble and disgrace were the result of broken walls. He stated this clearly. This is the second step. You must know what the specific problem is and be able to state it clearly.

Nehemiah decided that action should be taken. Then he proceeded through the second stage of problem-solving, working out the steps of the action and seeing that they were made effectively. Not only in the case of the first major problem, but several times, as other problems arose, we find that Nehemiah used strategies such as we have described.

2-3 In the following examples, a general condition or situation will be given. You are to select the specific problem and the appropriate solution from among those listed. Circle the letter which indicates your choice in each case.

2 In Nehemiah 4, the general condition was that the Jews were being insulted and attacked.

The specific problem was
a) the Samaritans and the Ammonites were plotting together.
b) work on the wall was being hindered.
c) the Jews were complaining too much.

Nehemiah's solution was to
d) attack the enemy armies.
e) equip the builders with defensive weapons.
f) preach to the complaining Jews.

3 In Nehemiah 5, the general condition was that people were complaining and bringing accusations against their Jewish brothers.

The specific problem was
a) the poor had to borrow money.
b) sons and daughters were sold into slavery.
c) unlawful usury was being charged.

Nehemiah's solution was to
d) require that the Law of God be observed.
e) ask people to be more loving to each other.
f) start a welfare system to help the poor.

We can see from these examples that it is necessary to separate the specific problem from the general condition in order to look for solutions. Let's turn back to our illustration of the teachers' meeting and see how this may work in a church in our own time. In this situation the problem is to be solved, not by one person, but by the group. In most of our present leadership situations it happens in a similar manner. Let's see how a group works through the stages of problem-solving.

The First Stage

What is the general condition according to Saven in our brief story? "Things didn't go very well last Sunday." Many of the problems you will face as a Christian leader will be introduced to you much like that. Someone feels dissatisfied. There is tension and unrest. Your first responsibility in problem-solving is to be sensitive and aware of these first indications of trouble. Then you must allow the situation to progress so that the real problem comes out in a way that will lead to its solution. It is easy to make mistakes at this point.

Suppose Bella had said, "Yes, it was pretty bad. Nobody did a very good job. Everybody's been letting down lately. We have to be willing to work harder for the Lord."

This would have cut off consideration of the real problem. Feelings might have been hurt. The others would have been afraid to express their concerns because it might make them seem unwilling to do God's work just because of some small problem.

On the other hand, suppose Bella had said, "Oh, everything was pretty good. We have to look on the bright side. We Christians shouldn't get discouraged."

Probably that, too, would have kept the others from continuing with the real issue. They would have felt ashamed to complain.

Leaders Solve Problems and Make Decisions 155

But Bella did in this case what a good leader should do. She did not show approval nor disapproval. She allowed group members to express their feelings and ideas. Let's notice how they proceeded.

From a vague feeling of tension and dissatisfaction, someone identified a specific factor: noise. Noise was causing the feelings. There is a tendency for people to do as Leif did and try to define the problem without analyzing it. He said, "The adult classes are too close to the boys." But that was not the problem, was it? What was the problem? Was it noise? No, noise was a *symptom* of the problem, not the problem itself. Many times people confuse symptoms with problems, and the leader must guide them to analyze all the events and factors more carefully. In this case, the group began to look for the cause of the noise. Was it inadequate discipline? Was it careless parents? Was it inadequate teaching? The group was trying to define the problem.

Typical Sequence for Defining a Problem

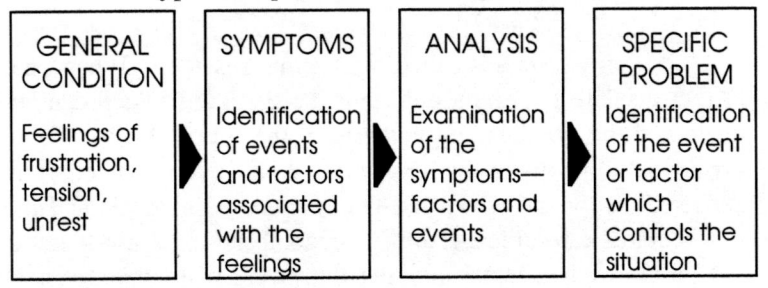

GENERAL CONDITION	SYMPTOMS	ANALYSIS	SPECIFIC PROBLEM
Feelings of frustration, tension, unrest	Identification of events and factors associated with the feelings	Examination of the symptoms—factors and events	Identification of the event or factor which controls the situation

4 In the illustration of the teachers' meeting:

a The general condition was

....

b The symptom, or factor associated with the feeling, was

....

c Analysis of the situation brought out possible causes for the noise such as

....

When the group members have completed this analysis they should be able to agree upon a statement of the problem. How would you state or define the problem if you were Bella? It could be something like this: *Classroom activities are not holding the attention of the boys.*

It is now obvious that no solution could be found until the problem was defined. This is always the first stage in problem-solving.

The Second Stage

The group members have defined a problem and decided that some kind of action needs to be taken. In our illustration they did this informally. As you understand these processes more thoroughly you will be able to guide a group through the steps with or without a formal structure.

The members begin to propose solutions such as sending notes to the parents, changing teachers, and getting a helper for the teacher. What other ideas could you suggest? Perhaps more suitable chairs, better teaching materials, or a teachers' training class for all the teachers.

These proposals are called *alternative solutions*. When one of them is selected, the group must discuss steps which can be taken and the possible consequence of the action. Who will be involved? Will there be expense? What exact outcome is expected? How and when will the outcome be evaluated? This step requires careful leadership. The members of the group must not be allowed to leave thinking the problem is solved. They must be aware of the specific action steps and how they are to be carried out. The leader must then implement the action, and continually monitor it, as Nehemiah did, working among his people along the wall.

The Third Stage

After a specific period of time the members should be given an opportunity to express their feelings concerning the outcome of the solution. In some cases a formal progress report may be required. In a case such as that of the noisy classroom this may be an informal discussion. Is the plan working? Is the general condition more pleasant? Should some other actions be taken? If the outcome is mostly positive the leader should express appreciation. If it tends to be negative the leader should offer understanding and encourage further efforts.

5 Write from memory the three stages in problem-solving and the steps included in each stage.

LEADERSHIP INVOLVES DECISION-MAKING

Objective 3. *Select true statements concerning decision-making.*

Decision-making is related closely to problem-solving. The mental processes and procedural steps are very similar. The main difference is that decisions are required in many routine situations just to keep the work moving ahead. In each case there is a condition of need—something needs to be done or a particular course of action must be selected from alternative possibilities.

There are times when a leader must decide personally what action to take (or not to take). At other times he participates in decision making with his superiors. Often he leads a group in decision-making activities. You need to learn how to be effective in each of these situations.

Nehemiah Made Decisions

Think back over the book of Nehemiah. How many decisions did Nehemiah have to make? For example, when he heard of the condition of Jerusalem, he had to decide to commit himself. He decided to ask for a leave of absence from the court. This could have brought him trouble, or even death, for the will of kings was absolute in those days. He decided to ask the king not only for time off but also for materials and letters of safe conduct. Then he examined the wall and made a decision to put the matter before a committee. He took the risk of sharing his burden with others. He asked them to make a decision, too. Later, he made decisions concerning how to deal with the enemies. Should he fight them or just defend the work on the wall? He made the decision to risk his position by rebuking the wealthy Jews for charging usury and cheating the poor. He required them to make a decision to give back what they had taken and stop charging usury. In every case Nehemiah acquired the necessary information, so the issue or problem was clear to him. Then he had the courage and wisdom to make a definite decision. In this way he provides the example for all good Christian leadership: Have adequate information. Understand the risks and be willing to take the consequences. Make the situation clear to those who work with you. Make definite decisions, and give others opportunities to express definite decisions.

Steps in Decision-Making

1. *Be confident in the Lord.* Faith has a place in decision-making. Throughout the book of Nehemiah we are made well aware that Nehemiah's trust was not in himself but in God. But he did not call upon the Lord to build the walls by divine intervention. God could have done it as easily as He pulled down the walls at Jericho; however, He chose to work through the mind and will of Nehemiah and those Nehemiah would lead. In most cases God works through means that men call "natural." Some person such as Nehemiah must make the decisions which place all natural means at the disposal of God's divine plan.

2. *Collect information.* Identify and describe the situation. Good decisions are based upon facts and knowledge. Be sure that what you have been told by others is correct. Examine the details for yourself or see that a competent helper examines them and reports to you. Try never to jump to conclusions or be pushed by emotional people into making decisions too quickly.

3. *List alternative courses of action.* In some cases you may decide to take no action, or to delay action to see if the situation changes. Usually there is more than one possible solution. Most good leaders never say, "I have no choice."

4. *Think of advantages and disadvantages.* List possible risks, consequences, and obstacles. Consider the expense and effort required for various alternatives. Be willing to make some adjustments. For example, if a worker is very skilled at a task

but constantly arrives late, you may have to decide to allow for the lateness in order to take advantage of the skill.

5. *Think of the persons involved in your decisions.* How will your decisions affect others? Who else should be advised before you take action? Whose opinions and ideas should be considered?

6. *Seek help and suggestions from qualified persons.* Never be afraid to "lose face," nor to admit you need help. It is strength, not weakness, to share decision-making with others.

7. *Test your decisions.* Look back, not in regret or indecision, but in honest appraisal of your action. Learn from your mistakes.

Obstacles to Decision-Making

1. *Failure to form clear objectives.* If we are not sure what end we are working for, then we find it difficult to decide what action to take. For example, a leader is told that a well-known evangelist is visiting in the area. It is suggested that he be invited to speak, sing, and play his guitar at the teachers' meeting. The leader had planned a discussion concerning biblical doctrine. How will he decide what to do? If he sets the objective of the meeting to have the teachers leave feeling happy and inspired, then he will choose the evangelist. If he sets the objective to have the teachers leave the meeting with a better understanding of a doctrinal issue, he will decide to have the discussion. This is not to say that one decision is "better" than another. It is to say that the decision is based upon the desired outcome, or the objective, which the leader has in mind. When you find yourself in the position of not knowing how to decide an issue, ask yourself honestly, "What is the objective?"

2. *Feelings of insecurity.* A leader may be afraid to act. This may be a result of his own personality, or it may be because he does not have a clear understanding of his position and his relationship with other leaders. As we have seen, most leaders in Christian work are middle leaders. A youth leader and a Sunday school superintendent, for example, must be sure they understand

their responsibilities and their relationship with the pastor. They must be sure that their decisions will be supported. If they feel insecure they may refuse to make decisions, and they may be too embarrassed to ask for the help they need from the pastor.

3. *Fear of change*. It is always more comfortable to keep on doing things in the customary way. Almost everyone resists change to some extent. A leader may hesitate to make a decision because he fears the response of the people to change. A good leader accepts the need for change and tries to move in a way which will prepare his followers to accept needed changes.

4. *Failure to face facts honestly*. There is a tendency in Christian work to fear making evaluations because this may seem to be a lack of faith. Leaders make decisions with inadequate information because they are afraid to ask questions and find out how people really feel. Unless you are willing to evaluate a situation and understand the real needs of people you cannot make good decisions.

Styles of Decision-Making

In most situations Christian leaders guide a group m decision-making. The degree to which the group is involved changes according to the circumstances. For example, if the group members have very little experience, the leader may have greater responsibility for making the decisions. If the members are competent, experienced Christians, then they should be encouraged to take more responsibility. Decision-making styles range from extremely authoritarian, in which the leader makes all the decisions, to the extremely democratic, in which the group members act with relative independence. These styles may be described as follows:

1. The leader makes the decision and announces it to the group.
2. The leader makes the decision and then "sells" it to the group. That is, he urges the group to accept his decision, giving the members no real choice.

3. The leader presents a decision and invites the group to ask questions. Discussion may be encouraged, but the decision is not really changed by the group.
4. The leader presents a tentative decision and invites the group to discuss it. He may then make some changes on the basis of suggestions from the group.
5. The leader presents a problem which he has defined and asks the group to suggest alternative solutions. Then he makes the decision.
6. The leader describes a situation and sets some limits or guidelines, and then asks the group to make the decision.
7. The leader allows the group to analyze a situation, define a problem, and make the decision, according to the process which we have discussed. In this style the leader guides the group to act within limits of higher authorities, such as church policies, and he provides information. This is true group decision-making. We will discuss it further in the section on group dynamics.

6 We learn from the example of Nehemiah that
a) good Christians do not have to go through the decision-making process.
b) faith in the Lord is required when natural means fail.
c) decisions must be made by natural means only.
d) the Lord guides people in the decision-making process.

7 The most effective style of decision-making
a) depends upon the specific situation.
b) is neither authoritarian nor extremely democratic.
c) usually is authoritarian if the leader is strong.
d) is the democratic style because more people are involved.

8 Circle the letter in front of each **TRUE** statement.
a The most competent leaders make their decisions very quickly.
b There is only one truly effective way to solve most problems.
c It is not a lack of faith to consider the risks and the expense involved before making a decision.

Questions for meditation and self-analysis: Look back at the *Styles of Decision-Making* and try to think of a situation where each one might be appropriate. Is there one style which you feel is best for you most of the time? Why?

GROUP DYNAMICS

Group Dynamics Explained

Objective 4. *Identify examples of the two dimensions In group work.*

Since most decisions involve groups in one way or another, it is necessary for the leader to understand the concepts *group* and *group dynamics*. The first basic truth is that human beings are essentially social—that is they need each other and work best when they work together. The second basic truth is that a true group is not just any collection of people. It is a collection of people who act together and influence one another. A group decision is not just one person's decision which is accepted by everyone else. It is a decision to which the group members have given thought and personal interest.

One of the amazing truths about groups is that regardless of how different people are as individuals they can form some kind of common ground in order to work together toward some end which they think is worthwhile. This should be especially true of Christian groups, since the common ground of faith and belief is the basis of Christian fellowship. *Group dynamics* is a term used to describe the special kind of power and action that comes from people working together. An illustration of this is a family or a clan in which the members feel that they are a part of one another. They act as a unit. The strength and satisfaction felt in contributing to the decisions and activities of the group are different from any which come from working alone.

The advantage of working in groups is not only in the satisfaction experienced by the members but also in the quality of work which can be accomplished. Obviously some members of a group will have more knowledge and skill than others. But a good leader will see that everyone has an opportunity to contribute. Special status should not be given to individuals, but rather there should be a recognition of different types of contributions. For example, a person with little skill might have a gift of faith or a happy spirit which encourages the other members when problems arise. There is an old saying that a hundred ditchdiggers could build a bridge. It might be crude, but it would serve its purpose. In contrast, only one very accomplished architect would have much more difficulty building a bridge. Probably a bridge he tried to build alone would be even more crude than that built by the unskilled laborers. On the other hand, the architect and the laborers working together could build a very fine bridge.

Dimensions of the Group

When we speak of *group dynamics* we have two ideas in mind—the people and the task. These are sometimes called the *dimensions* of the group. One is the *social dimension*—how the members of the group relate to one another, how they feel about one another, and how they feel about their own place and contributions in the group. The other is the *task dimension*—how the members contribute in various ways to the accomplishing of the work. It is the responsibility of the leader to guide in the development of the two dimensions. Following are some suggestions for group leadership.

The Social Dimension

1. *Encourage the members.* Help them to be warm and responsive to one another. Give recognition to all members.

2. *Express group feelings.* Emphasize team spirit. Help individuals to overcome personal feelings and prejudices. Do not use competitive techniques. Strictly avoid favoritism. Share yourself as a team member.

3. *Harmonize differences.* Help the members to accept various opinions without conflict. Suggest compromises. Point out the similarities and agreements among members and their ideas.

4. *Keep the communication channels open.* Try to make everyone feel free to express ideas and opinions.

5. *Set standards.* Make some rules if necessary. For example, set time limits so some will not use all the time. Do not allow ridicule or criticism of individuals. Discuss the ideas, not the personalities. Do not waste time on minor issues. Maintain a truly Christian atmosphere.

The Task Dimension

1. *Initiate or propose objectives and tasks.* Guide the group in definition of problems. Suggest ideas and procedures. Assign specific tasks. Set time limits for tasks to be completed or progress reported.

2. *Provide information and help.* Guide the group in seeking information which you do not have.

3. *Interpret, clarify, and offer explanations.* Clear up confusions, give examples, make applications of ideas.

4. *Summarize, or pull together, related ideas.* Restate ideas to help the group members see how they relate. Help them recognize their points of agreement and make definite decisions.

5. *Provide reward and recognition.* When progress is made or a task is completed, never allow the fact to go unnoticed. Emphasize the quality of the work rather than the personal qualities of the workers.

6. *Provide structure for evaluation.* Help the group members to evaluate their accomplishments in a realistic way without becoming either too discouraged or over-confident. Guide them to give the Lord glory for success, and yet be aware of their own contributions. Help them to develop new and better skills as a result of their experience, whether it is positive or negative.

9 Mark the following examples 1 for social dimension, or 2 for task dimension.

.... **a** Before the meeting, the leader arranged the chairs in the small circle.
.... **b** Two members were appointed to find materials for the nursery class.
.... **c** The leader explained the duties of altar workers during the evangelistic campaign.
.... **d** The leader asked a new member to lead in a chorus to open the meeting.
.... **e** The leader suggested that each person take two minutes to express his opinion on an issue.
.... **f** The leader proposed that the group work on a series of weekly objectives for the coming year.

1) Social dimension
2) Task dimension

How Decisions Are Made In Groups

Objective 5. *Recognize and evaluate decision-making styles.*

Decision by Voting or Majority Rule

In many societies the most common procedure for decision-making in a group is by formal voting. This may be done in a carefully structured meeting, using the form called *parliamentary law* or *parliamentary procedure.* In case you are not familiar with this process, or have not been involved in its use recently, we will explain it briefly here. For your further information and reference, a brief outline of parliamentary procedure is given in the appendix at the end of the course.

When a meeting is conducted according to parliamentary procedure, the leader is known as the presiding officer, or the chairperson. The duty of this leader is to organize the meeting by giving permission for the members to speak, one at a time, and then calling for a vote to decide what action should be taken. This system assures that only one item can be considered at a time, that everyone who wishes may give an opinion, and that the action taken will represent the desires of the majority.

The presiding officer is not supposed to give his opinion or try to influence the vote. He may present a subject for discussion. For example, the group may be planning a youth retreat. The leader may suggest that the group make some decisions concerning the details. One member may indicate by standing or raising his hand that he wishes to speak. The leader gives permission.

"I move that we invite Reverend X to be the main speaker," says the member. This is called a *motion*. That is, one member is proposing that the subject of inviting Reverend X be discussed and voted upon.

In formal parliamentary procedure it is necessary to have two people agree on a motion before it can be discussed by the group. This agreement is called a *second*. Another member of the group says, "I second the motion."

Then the leader says, "It has been moved and seconded that Reverend X be invited as the main speaker. Is there any discussion?"

One by one the members may rise and give their opinions. Some may suggest different speakers. Some may prefer to have a panel of young people instead of a speaker, or a music program. When it seems that everyone who wishes to speak has had an opportunity, the leader asks, "Are you ready to vote?"

If there is no objection, he continues, "Everyone who is in favor of inviting Reverend X to be the main speaker, please raise your hand." Voting may be done by standing, by voice, or by writing the vote on slips of paper.) Everyone who is not in favor indicates his vote in the same way. In most cases the motion is said to *carry* or win if a majority of the members vote in favor of it.

Making decisions by majority rule seems fair and logical to many people. However, there are problems to be considered. Some members may feel very strongly against a decision which the group has voted to accept. They may feel that the voting is a kind of contest and they are the losers. Instead of truly cooperating with the majority, they may make a minority faction within the group. They may look for opportunities to compete and try to win some other point. This could keep the group divided instead of working in harmony.

10 In the foregoing discussion of voting and decision by majority rule, we see all the following as positive values except one. Which one is NOT a positive value?
a) It encourages discussion of the issues and full participation.
b) It provides a framework for orderly discussion, since rules of procedure are employed and only one issue is considered at a time.
c) It provides the leader with a mandate to act boldly, since what the majority decides is undoubtedly right.
d) It produces a decision that represents what the majority feels is the best decision.

Decision by Consensus

The weakness of majority rule is that when the meeting ends, someone is on the losing side. This situation can be avoided if the leader can guide the members to make decisions by consensus. Consensus does not mean that everyone agrees completely, but the feelings and attitudes of people are different when the meeting can end in a spirit of consensus, rather than competition.

Consensus means that each member expresses a willingness to go along with the decision, even though he may not be completely convinced that it is the best one possible. In order to bring about this condition, the leader must be patient and understanding with all members. He must be sure that all have had real opportunities to explain how they feel and give their reasons. If they leave the meeting feeling understood, they are much more likely to cooperate and join in carrying out the group decision. Sometimes people even get a certain satisfaction out of giving in if they are not made to feel downtrodden. They feel they did get their points across and have made some contribution to the group processes.

11 Suppose you are involved in a meeting in which a consensus is being sought. Discussion has proceeded until all the alternatives have been explored. A consensus is reached at last. How would such an ending differ from one in which the majority had won a vote? Write your answer in your notebook.

Decision by Unanimous Consent

In Christian work something is possible which can seldom be attained in other types of organizations. It is possible because the goals of Christians are ultimately shared and because we can rely upon the guidance of the Holy Spirit to have perfect agreement and unity. We know from Scripture and from practical experience that unity does not always exist. Actually, perfect unity is not necessary in every case, and we must be careful not to blame ourselves unduly if we do not achieve this happy state in all our group work. But we can be very tender and sensitive to the moving of the Holy Spirit. We can be constantly aware that His desire for us is that we

> Make every effort to keep the unity of the Spirit through the bond of peace . . . prepare God's people for works of service, so that the body of Christ may be built up until we all reach unity in the faith and in the knowledge of the Son of God and become mature, attaining to the whole measure of the fullness of Christ (Ephesians 4:3, 12-13).

Leaders Solve Problems and Make Decisions 169

12 Match the type of decision-making (right) with its appropriate example (left) based upon a leader's words.

.... **a** "It would seem that we have arrived at agreement on a course of action. While not exactly perfect, this course seems to be best given the facts. I appreciate the willingness of all of you to support this course—even though it may not have seemed best"

.... **b** "Having reached a point at which all agree as to the rightness of the proposed course, we may proceed"

.... **c** "The vote has decided the issue: 16 for and 8 against. We shall proceed on the basis of this decision."

1) Majority rule
2) Consensus
3) Unanimous consent

13 Turn to the appendix and read "Pointers on Parliamentary Procedure" and then answer the following questions.

a List the five "Essential Principles of Parliamentary Law."

....

....

b How many "Essential Rules Discussion" are given?...............

c How many methods of voting are given? .... How many types of votes are listed? .... The most votes cast regardless of the majority is called a ....

d When conducting a meeting, the chairperson never says, "You are out of order." Instead, he should say,

....

e The presiding officer (or chairperson) prepares an .... for each meeting.

f The value of a set procedure in conducting business is that

....

....

g The rules for "Processing a Main Motion" ensure that

....

....

> This is the final lesson in Unit 2. After you have taken the self-test, review Lessons 4 through 6 and answer the questions in Unit Student Report 2. Follow the directions given in the unit student report booklet.

Leaders Solve Problems and Make Decisions 171

self-test

TRUE-FALSE. Place a **T** in the blank space in front of each TRUE statement and an **F** in front of each FALSE statement.

.... 1 Nehemiah's love for Jerusalem, coupled with his vision for its restoration, as well as his boldness in initiating action as the hand of God was upon him, give evidence of a divine call.

.... 2 We are permitted to see Nehemiah's competence after he arrived in Jerusalem, for he sent a delegation to evaluate the damaged walls and recommend repair procedures.

.... 3 Although he was wealthy, the fact that Nehemiah was deeply moved by the plight of the poor is an indication of his empathy.

.... 4 The aspect of leadership we see in Nehemiah's thinking through in advance his course of action before he went to see the king is *planning*.

.... 5 Having evaluated the needs, developed a course of action, and shared his vision, Nehemiah permitted the available manpower resources to find an appropriate place of work.

.... 6 Nehemiah gave an accurate analysis of the situation: what was and what was needed. Then he ignited his people's spirits, motivating them with words which demonstrated that they shared common goals.

.... 7 The first stage in the problem-solving process is to define the problem, which includes analyzing the general condition, stating the specific problem, and deciding if action is needed.

.... 8 Having defined the problem, one moves to the second stage—selecting a solution—which includes considering alternatives, choosing a course of action, and implementing the action.

.... 9 The third stage of problem-solving concerns evaluating the outcome of the action. If these three stages of problem solving have been followed, the outcome will be satisfactory.

.... 10 Once an alternative solution is selected, action steps and possible consequences discussed, as well as related matters, members may leave convinced that the problem is solved.

.... 11 At a specified time, members should be given an opportunity to express their feelings regarding the outcome of the solution. If the outcome is generally good, appreciation should be expressed; if it tends to be negative, the leader should offer understanding and encourage further efforts.

.... 12 In general we can say that problem-solving relates to major needs, whereas decision-making concerns solutions to minor problems.

.... 13 Nehemiah made decisions based upon adequate information, a clear understanding of the risks involved, clear communication with his co-workers regarding the issues, making a definite decision, and giving others an opportunity to express definite decisions.

.... 14 Christian leaders find certain obstacles to decision-making, among which are failure to form clear objectives, feelings of insecurity, fear of change, and fear that if they make evaluations they will appear to lack faith.

.... 15 Generally, a Christian leader guides his group in decision-making, rarely involving the group in the process of making decisions.

.... 16 While decision-making styles run the entire spectrum from the extremely authoritarian to the extremely democratic, most decisive leaders employ the authoritarian style.

.... **17** Even though members may be competent, experienced Christians, they should not assume more responsibility for decision-making, for this would be an indication of carnality and pride.

.... **18** *Group dynamics* rests upon the assumption that people are social and need each other, work best when they work together, and that as they act together they influence one another.

.... **19** While people, being social, do like working together better than working alone, they do not normally produce the same high quality work that they do when working by themselves.

.... **20** How the members of the group relate to one another, how they feel about one another, and how they feel about their place and contributions in the group concerns the *task dimension* of group dynamics.

.... **21** Providing reward and recognition, as well as structure for evaluation, is part of the *task dimension* of group dynamics.

.... **22** Decisions that are reached based on majority rule are generally arbitrary and leave the minority feeling beaten and resentful.

.... **23** Consensus gives the impression that all of the people are in agreement and that there is no dissent.

.... **24** The process of arriving at a decision by majority vote does have some negative aspects, but generally it has much to commend it.

.... **25** A decision by unanimous consent is a measure of the truly spiritual church. It is evidence of spiritual maturity and perfect unity.

answers to study questions

7 a) depends upon the specific situation.

1 a 6) Motivating others.
b 2) Competence.
c 3) A sense of calling.
d 1) Empathy.
e 4) Planning.
f 5) Organizing.

8 a False.
b False.
c True.

2 b) work on the wall was being hindered.
e) equip the builders with defensive weapons.

9 a 1) Social dimension.
b 2) Task dimension.
c 2) Task dimension.
d 1) Social dimension.
e 1) Social dimension.
f 2) Task dimension.

3 c) unlawful usury was being charged.
d) require that the Law of God be observed.

10 c) It provides the leader with a mandate to act boldly, since what the majority decides is undoubtedly right.

4 a things didn't go well. Teachers felt dissatisfied.
b noise.
c inadequate discipline, careless parents, inadequate teaching.

11 Your answer. The difference may be subtle. In both cases the issue would be aired fully. It would seem that the difference lies in the fact that consensus comes less dramatically and leaves no losers, whereas the vote divides a group into two parts: winners and losers. Handled appropriately, the majority rule decision-making process can be an effective method; without sensitivity and Christian charity it can be divisive.

5 Refer to the three stages and the steps included in this section.

12 a 2) Consensus.
   b 3) Unanimous consent.
   c 1) Majority rule.

6 d) the Lord guides people in the decision-making process.

13 a 1) Courtesy and justice to all, 2) consider one item at a time, 3) the minority must be heard, 4) the majority must prevail, and 5) the purpose of rules is to facilitate action, not obstruct it.
   b five.
   c eight; four; plurality.
   d "The motion is not in order."
   e agenda.
   f it helps to expedite business, ensures continuity with the past, links current decisions with future meetings, and ensures that decisions are reached in an appropriate way—not arbitrarily.
   g only one item of business is before the group at a time, that it is handled fully and fairly before another is introduced.

Unit 3
Goals
HOW LEADERS ESTABLISH OBJECTIVES AND WORK WITH PEOPLE TO ACHIEVE THE GOALS OF THE CHURCH

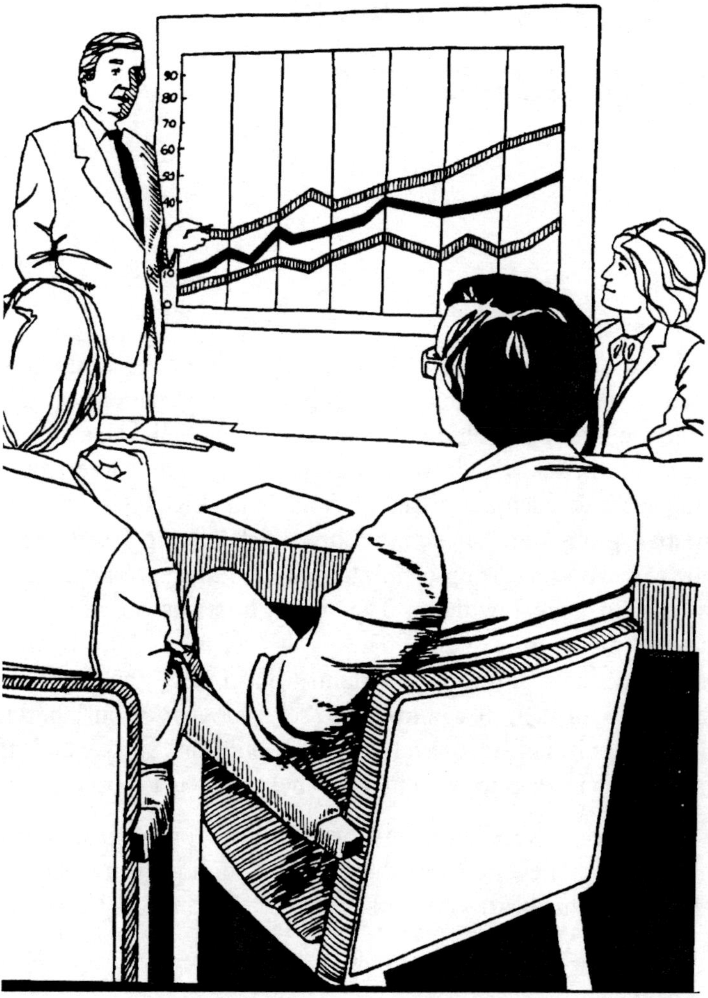
90
80
70
60

Lesson 7
Leaders Accept Responsibility

"We are facing a great challenge! All over the world there is tremendous social change and population movement. Rural people are moving to cities. People are leaving their countries in search of better conditions. Many who come here have languages and customs different from ours. People from non-Christian groups are accepting Christ and looking for a place among us. A large group of immigrants in a distant part of this city has no gospel witness. The new Christians among them have no place to worship. They can't come to our church because of transportation problems, but I feel that we are responsible for them. I would like to set aside part of our church income to help build a church there. I would like for several of you to act as leaders in that church to help them get started."

These words were actually spoken by a pastor. He had called a meeting of believers to ask their support for a project the Lord had placed in his heart. Some of the people began to object.

"But we hardly have enough money to pay our own expenses."

"How could we give up the blessings and fellowship in our church to mingle with those folk? Anyway, we don't have enough workers in our own church. And isn't that neighborhood dangerous?"

". . . I will help in the new project"

Then a young man stood and spoke out clearly. "My brothers and sisters," he said, "I feel we must examine our attitudes concerning the purpose of the church. We can't be satisfied to be a happy, comfortable community of God's people. There is a more important goal. While we are having our own needs met in the church, we should be working toward the goal of reaching others and sharing our love. I will help in the new project."

This true situation of our time illustrates some of the most serious issues related to Christian leadership: understanding the importance and the nature of objectives and goals, and willingness to accept responsibility for attaining them. The Bible account which will guide us in an examination of these principles is the story of Esther.

lesson outline

Esther–A Willing Leader
Leaders Understand the Nature of Goals
Leaders Accept Responsibility

lesson objectives

When you finish this lesson you should be able to:

- Describe leadership principles in the accounts of Esther and recognize and apply these principles.

- Recognize kinds of goals and objectives and explain their importance and effects.

- Demonstrate understanding of the concepts *responsibility* and *reality*.

learning activities

1. Read the book of Esther. Even if you are familiar with it, read it again for the specific purpose of finding principles of leadership. You may wish to make some notes as you read.

2. Look over the key words. If they are unfamiliar to you, check their meanings in the glossary.

3. Work through the lesson development and answer the study questions in the usual manner. When you have finished, take the self-test and check your answers.

key words

abolished	exiles	rationally
competencies	exotic	scepter
defiance	institutional goal	status
dire	operational goal	
enchanted	privation	

lesson development

From the beginning of this course we have emphasized three main ideas in the concept of leadership. These are: The people who lead and follow, the tasks they do, and their *goals*. In Unit 1 the focus was upon *people*. We gave our attention mostly to the characteristics of leaders and their relationships with people. In Unit 2 the focus was upon *tasks*. We considered the functions of leaders and the techniques of leadership. In Unit 3 the focus is upon *goals*.

In this lesson we will study the nature and importance of goals and objectives. Lesson 8 will teach us how to use objectives in planning and working. In Lesson 9 we will consider how to motivate people and help them to achieve objectives and goals.

Of course, in life situations it is not possible to separate the ideas of people, tasks, and goals. We will see in the story of Esther, for example, how the three are related and combined.

ESTHER—A WILLING LEADER

Objective 1. *Recognize examples of leadership characteristics, tasks, and goals.*

Individuals find themselves in positions of leadership in several ways. Often a leader seems to emerge as a consequence of the needs of a group. The leader is followed because he appears to be the one through whom the group can have its needs met. There must be a *goal* (perhaps a problem to be solved) for a leader to be necessary. The kind of goal or problem will then determine or greatly influence the kind of leader needed. This is one reason why no set of leadership characteristics can be outlined. Most leaders seem to have some characteristics in common, but others can be very different, as we have seen from our biblical examples.

The story of Esther is a precise example of leadership emerging to meet a need. The book begins with a description of the problem situation. Can you picture the events described in this unusual chapter of history?

At a time when King Xerxes was celebrating his wealth and power, his wife, Queen Vashti, refused to obey him. In order to prove his power and authority he made a public decree to divorce her and have her removed from the palace.

In that land an official notice from the king was a law forever and could not be changed even by the king himself. The king began to miss his wife, but he was bound by his official decree so that he could not take her back. He was advised to fill the queen's place with a virgin selected from the most beautiful girls in the kingdom. He would have a kind of beauty contest and choose a new queen.

Among the king's subjects were the Jewish exiles. Many of them had adapted to their life in captivity, and, because of their character and ability, had attained positions of leadership. One of these was Mordecai. His cousin, Esther, was like a daughter to him, since her mother and father were dead. She was lovely and graceful. In the search for beautiful virgins Esther was one of those selected to go before the king. Mordecai told her not to mention that she was of the Jews. The king did not inquire concerning her background. His interest was in her beauty and fine manners. He liked her better than any of the others, and chose her to be his queen. She was given the queen's palace, royal robes, a crown, maids to serve her—all the privilege and luxury of her status.

On the king's staff of high officials was Haman, a proud and selfishly ambitious man who hated the Jews. He became extremely angry because Mordecai would not bow to him. "Not only does he offend me," Haman complained bitterly, "but he is one of those Jews. I'll find a way to punish him and all his people with him!"

Haman made the king believe that the Jews were a danger and a source of trouble. He implied that they were disrespectful of the crown and should be abolished He persuaded the king to sign a decree, and plans were started to kill all the Jews on a certain day.

When Mordecai heard this news he realized that there was one possible chance for the Jews to be saved. Perhaps if the king knew the death order included his queen he would do something to save her and her people. She was the only person in a position to meet the need of this hour. So Mordecai asked Esther to go before the king and request mercy for all the Jews.

How could she do that? Surely Mordecai knew she could not walk up to the king without an invitation. There was a strict law that any person who did that would be seized by the king's aides and put to death. That law could not be changed. The decree to kill the Jews could not be changed. What could she do? Of course, if the king wished he could extend his golden scepter to a person who approached him, but it would be a fearful risk.

Leaders Accept Responsibility

"You know the law," Esther told Mordecai, "and the king has not called me for thirty days."

Then Mordecai reminded Esther that she was a Jew. "Just because you are the queen you cannot expect to escape," he said. "If you help the people now you will be helping yourself, too. Perhaps you have been allowed to have your royal position for such a time as this."

It is interesting to note that the name Esther means *star*. She was in a high position because God had given her the qualities and the opportunities to be a kind of star. But for Esther, as for all others who are called by God, the position was not for her personal power and enjoyment. She could not be a star alone. Her position was for the benefit of her people. At this point Esther chose to be a true leader. "All right," she agreed, "I will go even though it is dangerous. If I perish, I perish. I will take the consequences of my decision."

Esther not only had some leadership characteristics but also began immediately to behave as a leader. Already a plan was forming in her mind, and she realized that all the people should be involved. She needed their complete support. She asked them to fast for three days, promising that she and her household would fast also. She stated these details clearly.

During those three days Esther did much more than fast. She was busily planning and making preparations. She designed a set of procedures. She would ask the king and Haman to eat with her so that she could select the proper time and manner to make her request. She would show respect for the law as much as possible and give the king a chance to think of a solution. She put her helpers to work making ready for the banquets.

Then, on the third day, she put on the royal robes and went to the throne room. She acted boldly but with quiet dignity. She put herself into a position where she could be killed for defiance of the king's rules. She was willing to do this because of the importance of her goal. Yet she was careful not to offend anyone needlessly. She wore the correct garments for the occasion and spoke in the accepted manner. The king was pleased. She reached out, humble in her victory, to touch the golden scepter.

Esther followed her plan rationally. She did not cry out immediately her concern for her people, but asked the king to dine with her so that the matter could be approached in the best possible way. Little by little she led him to understand the situation and to be persuaded on behalf of the Jews.

1 Each of the following sentences expresses either leadership characteristics, tasks, or goals related to the person and work of Esther. Write the number of the appropriate designation in the blank space in front of each sentence.

.... **a** She wanted her people to be saved.

.... **b** She was bold and courageous.

.... **c** The king had to be persuaded.

.... **d** The meeting was planned in advance.

.... **e** She gave instructions clearly.

.... **f** She was courteous and gracious.

.... **g** She accepted responsibility.

.... **h** She was rational and systematic.

1) Leadership characteristic
2) Task
3) Goal

LEADERS UNDERSTAND THE NATURE OF GOALS

Objective 2. *Distinguish between institutional goals and operational goals or objectives.*

Look back at Exercise 1 which you have just completed. You see that **a** (She wanted her people to be saved) and **c** (The king had to be persuaded) are both called *goals*. How are they alike? What do they have in common which makes us call them *goals*? You note that they both express desired outcomes, or some kind of end result toward which we can work. How are the two goals different from each other? When we remember the story of Esther we can see the difference. *She wanted her people to be saved* is the final goal for everything Esther did. In order to reach this final goal she had to persuade the king to release them

Leaders Accept Responsibility 185

from the decree of certain death. The final goal is reached by means of making and reaching other goals. In Christian work our final goal is spiritual and very broad. We call it our *institutional goal*. The greatest of all is to win the world for Christ. Within each local Christian body or project there are institutional goals. In order to reach them we set *operational goals*, which we might also call *objectives*.

Notice again how Esther moved from one objective to another. She had to gain the approval of the king. She had to be sure that he understood the entire situation so that he could act appropriately. Since he could not overrule a previous decree, a way had to be found to save the Jews and still keep the law. When it was decided that the Jews could defend themselves, this condition of the king's honor was preserved. Because she had a clear and important final goal she was able to set for herself and her helpers a series of definite objectives. As each objective was achieved she moved closer to the final or institutional goal.

2 Think of the modern example at the beginning of this lesson. What is the situation which seems to require leadership?

....

3 How is the pastor similar to Mordecai?

....

4 Suppose the people begin to work on the project suggested by the pastor. Can you write an institutional goal for them?

....
....

5 Suppose you are the young man who accepts a position of leadership to get this project started. Write two objectives you will have to achieve as you work toward the goal.

....
....

Why Objectives Are Important

Objective 3. *Identify some effects of goals and objectives.*

Since the final or institutional goals of Christian work seem obvious, many leaders are not aware of the importance of stating clear objectives. They tend to feel that "doing the Lord's will" and "winning souls" are clear enough. Some may be reluctant to state specific objectives because they wish to remain open to the leading of the Spirit. However, as we have learned in the lesson on planning, we must seek spiritual guidance in the planning stages in order to be at our best as leaders. People work better and are happier in their work when they have clear objectives. Much unrest and waste in church work is the result of failure of the leadership in this regard, and stating objectives can have powerful effects in your efforts as a leader.

1. *Objectives help us save time, energy, and resources*. By stating clear objectives we can direct the use of our resources toward specific ends without waste and confusion. Without objectives, some tasks may be forgotten while others are duplicated. Money may be spent for something that is not essential, while a real need is unmet. One person may be doing too much and others too little.

2. *Objectives inspire cooperation*. People see the need to work together when there is a clear reason for their cooperation. They sometimes fail to respond to a leader who says, "Now let's all work together on this." Just "working together" seems aimless if the desired result of their effort is not clear.

3. *Objectives provide a basis for evaluation*. The best performance of any activity can be assured only when there is some way to measure it. If results are not evaluated people can be satisfied with a very low standard of performance. They are just busy and don't know what they accomplish. If we state the objectives in advance we can measure results. In this way we can help workers to see the need for improvement, or, on the other hand, we can give them the satisfaction of knowing exactly how well they have done. We can discover weak places in organization and direct our efforts intelligently.

4. *Objectives help us discover gifts and talents*. When a desired result is stated people realize more clearly what gifts and talents are needed in order to accomplish the purpose. We begin to see in ourselves and others specific competencies related to the proposed task. Probably Esther never thought of herself as capable of what she accomplished until she understood the need which had to be met. When we are thinking of specific objectives, we can assign workers whose qualities are best suited. Workers are more likely to volunteer, and new leaders emerge as a result.

6 Stephen is a carpenter. He hears the pastor asking for volunteers for a church work day. To which of the following announcements do you think he would be more likely to respond? Circle the letter in front of the statement you choose.
a) We want as many as possible to come help us fix up the church.
b) One of our objectives is to repair six window frames.

7 Circle letters to indicate which effects the following objective statement may be expected to have: Our objective for the visitation work this week is to have three teams of two persons make five calls each.
a) Inspire cooperation
b) Save money
c) Provide a basis for measurement

8 Circle the letter in front of the statement which most clearly expresses the main idea in our discussion of the effects of objectives.
a) The major effect of stating objectives is to get more work done in less time.
b) The true purpose of goal-setting is to make the leader's work easier.
c) Good objectives help get the work done and also affect the attitudes of the people.

LEADERS ACCEPT RESPONSIBILITY

Objective 4. *Select illustrations which explain how commitment to a goal brings freedom.*

Answer b) in the exercise you have just completed certainly is not true. Setting clear goals and objectives for yourself and your workers is one of the most difficult tasks of leadership. It is difficult because it requires absolute honesty and the willingness to accept responsibility at any cost.

Remember our example of the city church. The pastor said he felt responsible. He was willing to make some sacrifices by using part of the church funds and some of the workers to start a new church. He was willing to risk criticism from his people by asking them to make sacrifices, too. It was a similar situation with Esther. As Mordecai challenged her she began to feel responsible for her people. When people think in terms of the true purposes of the church, and the objectives are made plain to them, they become willing to make commitments and assume responsibility.

The young man who volunteered to serve did so because he had begun to understand the true purpose of the church. He was willing to face reality and take responsibility.

Some understanding of how to face reality and accept responsibility has come to us from a psychiatrist, William Glasser. As he worked with unhappy people who could not adjust to the demands of their society, he found that much of their failure came from their refusal to face reality. They were continually making excuses for themselves. They blamed their problems on other people and on circumstances. If Esther had had such an attitude she would have said, "If only I were not a woman. If only the king were not so stubborn." But she was willing to admit the facts and work with what she had.

This, according to Glasser, is the only way to have a successful and productive life. Certainly it is the only way to be a successful leader. Glasser suggests that satisfaction in life comes from willingness to endure privation, if need be, in order to reach goals. He says that commitment brings freedom. If we consider the consequences honestly and then decide to take appropriate action we gain self-confidence and become more effective as leaders. Christian leaders have the extra advantage of knowing that self-confidence comes only as a reflection of confidence in the Lord.

Leaders Accept Responsibility 189

9 Write the words of Esther which show she understood the consequences of her commitment and was willing to accept responsibility.

....

How did this commitment bring her freedom? Don't you think she was now free from much of her fear? She had freed herself from excuses. She had proved to herself that she was capable of making a difficult decision. She was free to move forward in faith.

10 Circle the letter in front of each illustration which explains correctly, according to the foregoing discussion, how commitment to a goal brings freedom.
a) John has evaluated the consequences of his decision to enter Bible school as a result of his response to the call of God to enter the ministry, has resolved to see it through, and now moves to implement his plan. He is calm and confident and no longer worries about whether he will make it. Having chosen a course of action, he is no longer torn by indecision. Now he can focus all his attention on his one goal.
b) Rebecca makes a quick decision to quit her job and travel to a foreign field to help with the Lord's work. She justifies herself because she loves the possibility of working in a foreign, exciting land. Stubbornly, she decides no one will change her mind. She hopes that things will go her way. She believes she has expressed true freedom of action in what she has done.
c) For some time God has been dealing with Thomas about full-time Christian service. Now after much heart searching and prayer, he commits himself to start a church in a new area where there is a great need. He makes the decisive break which he has always feared, leaving his job, home, and friends. Furthermore, he initiates a plan of action and begins services in the new city, sensing, in spite of many uncertainties about the future, God's approval on his actions. Strangely, he isn't even concerned about future needs—funds for food and other necessities. He has confidence that God will see him through.

d) Peter thinks about his call to the ministry and what his response should be. To relieve his conscience and be free from the compulsion he feels, he reasons: "I'm not qualified, people frighten me, I'm not well-educated, and the work is too hard—even for a highly qualified person. No, I could never be successful in the Lord's work. Up to this point I've always been successful. There's no point in reversing this trend." Having resolved the matter in this fashion, he attempts to forget it.

11 Perhaps it would be helpful for you to see what your attitude is toward the following qualities of leadership required of successful leaders. Mark an X in the appropriate column to indicate your response.

	A Usually	B Sometime	C Seldom
Are you willing to accept responsibility at any cost?			
Are you willing to be absolutely honest in your relationships with those whom you lead?			
Are you willing to sacrifice for the good of the people you lead?			
Are you willing to risk criticism by asking your followers to sacrifice so that goals may be reached?			
Are you willing to challenge people to accept the true purpose of the church—even though this may represent a departure from the church's previous institutional goals?			
Are you willing to face reality, admit the facts, and work with what you have?			
Are you willing to set realistic goals and standards, give specific instructions to your followers, and make sure they understand how to proceed?			

Leaders Accept Responsibility

	A Usually	B Sometime	C Seldom
Are you willing to face privation, if need be, to reach your goals?			
Do you understand that when you consider the consequences honestly before you take action, you gain self-confidence and become more effective as a leader?			
Are you willing to test the reality of a goal by being willing to measure it and report the results to your followers?			
Are you unwilling to accept excuses by setting standards of performance and helping followers to live up to the required standards?			
Are you willing to give full credit for the success your followers achieve and recognize their good qualities and improvements?			

Now that you have finished with your evaluation, give yourself three points for each response in Column A, two points for those in Column B, and one point for those in Column C.

Leaders Help the Workers to Face Reality

Objective 5. *Select true statements concerning reality thinking.*

Objectives must be realistic. There may be a temptation to claim great results "in faith." Certainly faith and confidence in God should be expressed. But if people become emotionally involved and have unrealistic expectations they will be easily discouraged and less likely to cooperate in the future. The leader is responsible to be absolutely certain of his position of faith before he makes claims and involves the emotions of others. You can test the reality of a goal by asking yourself if you are willing to measure and report the results to those who work with you. Do you believe it can be attained with reasonable effort?

The obstacles must be explained. A leader, guiding his people toward real goals, does not try to make the task look easy or gloss it over in any way. Most workers appreciate a leader who admits difficulties and requests their prayers and suggestions. When a worker expresses doubts and difficulties, the leader should not try to smooth over the facts. He should admit that the worker has problems and show concern. For most workers it is more helpful if a leader says, "I know that is a difficult task." The leader who says, "Oh, come on, it's not hard," may find himself rejected.

Excuses must not be accepted. Beginning in the Garden of Eden, people have had a tendency to make excuses and to blame other people, the devil, and circumstances for their problems and failures. Each time he makes an excuse, a person puts responsibility away from himself and therefore weakens his own position, especially in his own sight. Therefore, when we accept excuses we are not being kind. We are escaping from responsibility ourselves. A responsible leader will take upon himself what Glasser calls the greatest task of all mankind: teaching others to be responsible for their own behavior.

Each person needs to feel that he is capable of accomplishing some goal. Excuses allow him to avoid reality. In order to help him be successful, and thereby add to the success of the church, the leader must set standards for performance. If a person offers an excuse, the leader must not say, "That's all right." He must show love and respect for the person, and then help him to live up to the required standards. This takes patience and love, and a certain amount of risk on the part of the leader.

Give the person full credit for the success he has made. Point out to him that he has good qualities and has made improvements. Then explain exactly what is expected. Set goals and standards. Give specific instructions and be sure that he understands how he is to proceed. Pray with him and let him know that you are expecting him to accomplish the objectives.

12 Circle the letter in front of the correct answer. What is meant by a *realistic objective*?
a) One which proves the faith of the leader
b) One which can be attained with reasonable effort
c) One which is approved by everyone in the group

13 Circle the letter in front of the correct answer. How can a leader help his workers to achieve?
a) By telling them the work is easy
b) By expressing doubts and difficulties
c) By understanding their difficulties

14 Circle the letter in front of each TRUE statement.
a *Reality thinking* does not take into account the element of faith; therefore, when setting goals you can realistically claim what reasonable expectations would permit without faith.
b *Reality thinking* recognizes obstacles and difficulties, endeavors to explain them, and requests prayer and suggestions for ways to overcome them.
c *Reality thinking* refuses to accept excuses, recognizing that to accept excuses is to encourage others to be irresponsible for their own performance.
d *Reality thinking* demands that one establish performance standards for his followers and recommends that they measure up; however, he must accept their excuses and reassure them when they fail to perform appropriately.
e Reality thinking takes into account recognition of people's efforts, their good qualities, and their improvements in a positive and sincere way.

Leaders Face Their Own Reality

Objective 6. *Explain in a practical way the meaning of five facts of reality about leadership.*

There is a price to pay for leadership. All of our biblical examples have shown this. Only one fact can make the price seem reasonable and easy. That is the one goal toward which our efforts are directed. Christian leaders know they have a special place in the universal plan of God. Their purpose is His purpose.

Their goal is His goal. Even so, there are times of frustration and discouragement. Most of them can be overcome by prayerful application of reality thinking to our own lives. There will be problems and conflict. We cannot face these successfully unless we are willing to admit the absolute truth of the situation, just as Esther did. Here are some of the facts to be faced.

1. *Leaders are servants, not masters*. Even in the business world the leader is no longer considered to be a "boss" nor a "chief." He is considered an instructor, a guide, and helper to make plans and organize workers. Long ago Jesus instructed us in this style of leadership. Throughout Christian history the greatest leaders have followed His example, even to the point of giving their lives.

2. *Leaders work harder than those they lead*. A study was made to determine which factors were common to most successful leaders. It was found that leaders have very different sets of qualities, and very different personalities. Some are more authoritarian and some are more democratic. Only one fact applied to every successful leader in the study: they all worked hard. They kept longer hours, studied more, and put more effort into self-improvement than those who worked for them.

3. *Leaders are criticized and blamed*. It must be expected that some will not understand our motives nor agree with our methods. Also, we will make mistakes. We will offend people without intending to do so. If we accept this and do not resist nor try too much to justify and defend ourselves, criticism can be a blessing. We can judge ourselves realistically and look to the Lord to help us make needed improvements.

4. *Leaders suffer loneliness*. Leaders seem popular and privileged when we see them in public. But good leaders are more lonely than any class of people. Most of us like to talk things over with others and share our burdens and problems. We can do this to some extent in our work with people. But when major decisions are to be made and real responsibility is to be assumed, then we are alone with God. We must respect the confidence and the feelings of others. We must not involve our families and friends in

the business of the church. We must spend time and energy in ways that others cannot share or even understand.

5. *Leaders suffer stress*. We feel the pressure of time. There is so much to be done. We feel the pressure of expectations which others put upon us. Most people in leadership positions in the church, as we have seen, are middle leaders. They are supervised by pastors or other church officials, and they are responsible to provide leadership for other groups. This creates a double pressure as they are in the role of follower at one time and that of leader at another. We are subject to feelings of inadequacy and fear of making wrong decisions. We want people to like us, and yet we must be firm in leadership roles.

15 Explain in your own words the practical meaning of each one of the following facts about the realities of leadership. Write the answer to each question in your notebook.
a Leaders are servants, not masters.
b Leaders work harder than those they lead.
c Leaders are criticized and blamed.
d Leaders suffer loneliness.
e Leaders suffer stress.

What we have called *reality thinking* requires us to consider the importance of the Christian goals in relation to the real situation, with all its problems and obstacles. The conclusion of this experience is that we can accept leadership positions with full understanding of what is expected of us. Then we will never enter uncertainty or on an impulse into some position for which we are not qualified and to which we are not prepared to make the kind of commitment that Esther made: *For a cause this great I offer myself completely. I will take the consequences.*

16 Some of the five facts about leadership which we have just considered might also be called *hazards of leadership*: hard work and discipline are required; criticism, blame, and misunderstanding are to be expected; loneliness and stress will be experienced. Esther, as we have seen, made the ultimate sacrifice, choosing to take the possible dire consequences of her choice. In your notebook, tell why you are willing to face the hazards of leadership.

self-test

1 In the story of Esther we have an excellent example of leadership
a) arising because of great skill.
b) arising to meet a personal crisis.
c) emerging to meet a need.
d) arising on the basis of popular appeal.

2 Esther demonstrated which great principle of successful leadership when in a crisis hour, she said: "I will go to the king . . . If I perish, I perish"?
a) Leaders must be willing to identify with great causes.
b) Leaders must be willing to accept responsibility at any cost.
c) Leaders must be willing to work hard to reach their goals.
d) Leaders must be willing to stand alone in crises.

3 All of the following except one are sound leadership principles demonstrated by Esther. Which one is NOT such a principle?
a) The leader's position exists for the benefit of his people.
b) The leader involves his people, enlists their support, and keeps them informed.
c) The leader designs procedures appropriate for the situation he faces.
d) The leader, to act boldly and decisively, must always act quickly.

4 Esther's desire to see her people saved is the final goal for everything she did. Such a goal is referred to as an
a) institutional goal.
b) operational goal.
c) operational objective.
d) inspirational goal.

5 In order to reach her final goal, Esther initiated other goals or objectives that are called
a) terminal goals.
b) institutional goals.
c) organizational goals.
d) operational goals.

Leaders Accept Responsibility

6 Objectives, according to our lesson content, are important for all of the following reasons but one. Which reason is NOT one of the stated?
a) Objectives help conserve time, energy, and resources.
b) Objectives inspire cooperation and provide a basis for evaluation.
c) Setting objectives and goals is an easy task.
d) Stating objectives helps us discover gifts and talents.

7 We have seen that the primary effects of good objectives are these. They
a) help get the work done and they affect people's attitudes.
b) make the leader's work easier and require little follow-through.
c) make possible getting much more work done and they cut work time in half.
d) enable the leader to be impersonal and they eliminate problems with people

8 The term which describes the feeling of commitment a leader demonstrates when he perceives the true purpose of the church and understands its objectives plainly is
a) realism.
b) responsibility.
c) recognition.
d) reaction.

9 The term which describes the process leaders undergo when they consider the importance of the Christian goals in relation to the facts of the situation, with all its problems and abstracts, is
a) possibility thinking.
b) Christian idealism.
c) reality thinking.
d) evaluation consciousness.

10 When a leader accepts a follower's excuses for failure to perform his task according to the required standards, he is
a) demonstrating flexibility and Christian charity.
b) avoiding responsibility and permitting the follower to avoid it, also.
c) showing that kindness is more important than responsibility.
d) demonstrating that love enables him to avoid confrontations.

11 Place the number of each of the following facts of reality in front of the statement which explains how the leader must respond to each fact.

.... **a** The leader will become increasingly aware of his need to confide in the Lord and to keep his own counsel.

.... **b** The leader approaches the tasks as an instructor, guide, and helper.

.... **c** The leader recognizes the fact that his motives and methods will at times be misunderstood; therefore, he purposes to avoid being sensitive to his followers' reactions.

.... **d** The leader recognizes that his position will subject him to pressure; he also recognizes that it is the Lord's work and that the Lord will enable him.

.... **e** The leader understands that his commitment must be complete—that he must set the example in every way possible for his followers.

1) Leaders are servants, not masters.
2) Leaders have to work harder than those they lead.
3) Leaders are criticized and blamed.
4) Leaders suffer loneliness.
5) Leaders suffer stress.

answers to study questions

9 "If I perish, I perish" (Esther 4:16).

1 a 3) Goal.
  b 1) Leadership characteristic.
  c 3) Goal.
  d 2) Task.
  e 2) Task.
  f 1) Leadership characteristic.
  g 1) Leadership characteristic.
  h 1) Leadership characteristic.

10 Answers a) and c) are correct. (Answer b) is a contrast. Rebecca can't know real freedom because she has not truly committed herself to a goal. Her *impulse provides no basis for commitment, and her hope* will not give her any sense of freedom. Answer d) gives a classic example of making excuses to avoid responsibility. We should remember this: God doesn't call the qualified; He qualifies the called.)

2 There are people without a gospel witness.

11 If your score for these twelve questions is between 24 and 36, you tend to do the things required of successful leaders. If you score less than 24, reread the list and make a definite time commitment by the grace of God to begin doing the things you are not now doing.

3 He sees a need and seeks a leader to do a task.

12 b) One which can be attained with reasonable effort

4 Your answer. I have suggested the following: win people of that area to the Lord and provide them with a place of worship.

13 c) By understanding their difficulties.

5 Your answer might have included: 1) Have teams organized to do visitation in the area, and 2) have a committee to work on the building plans.

14 a False.
  b True.
  c True.
  d False. (He requires performance according to the standard. Also, he counsels them and helps them live up to the required standard.)
  e True.

6 b) One of our objectives is to repair six window frames.

15 Your answers may be different from mine. I've suggested:
  a I must consider myself a facilitator, not a spectator.
  b I must set an example for others by my own commitment to work, punctuality, standard of performance, and self improvement.
  c I must expect to be misunderstood at times, and I may be the subject of blame and criticism. Where I'm at fault, I must be willing to recognize my need of improvement, and I must seek the Lord's help to enable me to improve.
  d I can expect to be lonely; however, I can seek to fill this void by cultivating a deeper relationship with the Lord.
  e I must realize that my position will subject me to stress of many kinds. My relationship with the Lord must therefore grow to enable me to face stressful situations, permitting them to drive me to Him instead of to distraction.

7 Answers a) and c) are correct.

16 Your answer. Most leaders would probably agree that they have chosen to take up the mantle of leadership because they have caught a vision of the Lord's work: of reaching others and sharing their love. Having responded to the Lord's query, "Whom shall I send . . . who will go for us?" (Isaiah 6:8), they make a complete commitment to reach the goals to which God has called them *at any cost*. Having made the commitment, they experience satisfaction in spite of hardship, and they enjoy a true sense of freedom. Moreover, they know real self-confidence, for it derives from their confidence in the Lord.

8 c) Good objectives help get the work done.

for your notes

LESSON 8
Leaders Work Toward Objectives

While Michael was visiting his aunt in a village far from his home, he went with her to the market. There they met the pastor of the local church.

"I've heard you are a good speaker," said the pastor. "Would you bring a message at our church on Wednesday night?"

Michael was pleased, but he spoke with graceful humility: "I am not a great speaker, but I am glad to serve in any way I can for the glory of the Lord. I will speak, if you wish."

In his aunt's house Michael gathered his Bible and notebook and some books from a shelf. Once before he had prepared a message on the subject of worship and praise. It had been well-received. He decided to use it again. Of course he had to study and pray. He made a new outline. He found some illustrations. He practiced reading the Scripture portions. "These are strong points," he said. "With God's help I will preach a good message."

You know this is a very familiar incident, don't you? It happens so often that we do not find anything strange or remarkable in it. Yet there may be in the behavior of Michael and the pastor the indication of a serious error. It may be the error made most frequently by sincere and competent Christian leaders. Can you explain what it is?

In this lesson we will discuss this and other questions concerning how leaders establish objectives and work toward their achievement. Our Bible example in this lesson is the apostle Peter. There is so much to learn from him about Christian leadership!

"Would you bring a message ...?"

lesson outline

Peter—A Leader With Purpose
Christian Work as a System
Management by Objectives

lesson objectives

When you finish this lesson you should be able to:

- Describe leadership principles in the accounts of Peter, and recognize and apply these principles.

- Explain what is meant by systems approach in Christian work.

- Outline a plan for determining objectives and planning for their achievement.

learning activities

1. Read Luke 22:24-32; John 21:15-22; and 1 Peter 5:1-4.

2. Work through the lesson development and answer the study questions in the usual manner.
3. Take the self-test at the end of the lesson and check your answers carefully with those supplied at the back of this study guide.

key words

perpetuate
remorse

lesson development

PETER–A LEADER WITH PURPOSE

Peter Is Instructed by Jesus

Objective 1. *Recognize appropriate explanations of Jesus' instructions to Peter.*

The central truth of this course has been that Christian leadership is the process of helping people to accomplish God's purposes. Nowhere is this truth made so clear as it is in the relationships of Jesus Christ with His disciples. Almost every word he spoke to them had two meanings. One was for the disciples as persons, and the other was to help them teach others and so perpetuate the gospel. One striking example of this is found in our reading in Luke 22.

In the shadow of the cross, at the time of greatest heartache for Himself and His disciples, the thoughts of Jesus were for the future of His kingdom. Even as He reached out in tenderness and love to Peter, He could not let him forget his call to leadership. We feel sad when we read that at this sacred time, so near to the Last Supper, the disciples would dispute among themselves who would be greatest in this calling. On the other hand, we are glad for the clear revelation of the human qualities which God is able to use in His own way. We appreciate the beautiful way Jesus used Peter as an example of Christian leadership.

Evidently Peter felt very confident in his position. He declared his loyalty to Christ and may have given the impression that he loved the Lord more than the others did. Gently, but firmly, Jesus let Peter know that declarations of confidence do not constitute true strength. He let Peter know that he would face failure and yield to the temptation of the devil. "But I have prayed for you," said Jesus, "that your faith may not fail. *And when you have turned back, strengthen your brothers*" (Luke 22:32). In these few verses we find two great lessons in leadership. The first is a warning against over-confidence. The second is that personal experiences are to be used to help others. Even failure is a blessing, if it gives us understanding and leads to empathy and wisdom in our relationships with others.

Peter did fall into the trap of Satan, just as Jesus foresaw that he would. But in spite of this human weakness, he was devoted to Jesus. In shame and remorse he learned his lesson. His heart must have been longing for opportunities to express the faith and love which now possessed him. Jesus used this situation to teach Peter more about the nature of his calling. Recall or review John 21:15-17.

"Do you truly love me?" Jesus asked.
"Yes, Lord," Peter answered, "you know that I love you."
"Feed my lambs," said Jesus.

Jesus repeated the question three times. Each time the response of Peter was the same. And each time Jesus met the declaration of love by assigning Peter a task. "If you love me, feed my lambs. Feed my sheep."

"We must note what love brought Peter," says the Bible commentator, Barclay. "Love brought him a task."

We have discovered in each biblical example of a calling to leadership that a particular situation or need required attention in order that God's purpose could be accomplished. This was true in a special way when Jesus told Peter to feed the sheep. Jesus had completed His earthly part in the plan of salvation. As we have noted in earlier lessons, God's plan was to establish the church in order to continue the work of Jesus through human instruments. Jesus expressed His love to Peter by giving him a task in this great plan. Peter expressed his love by accepting the assignment.

Jesus spoke in what we call figurative language. That is, he used the words *lambs* and *sheep* to represent people, and the word *feed* to represent the work of teaching and helping the people. By using this figurative language He was able to communicate in only a few words the urgency and importance of His message. Let's think some more about the meaning of these words.

1–4 Circle the letter which represents the most appropriate answer to each of the following questions.

1 What did Jesus mean when He said, "Feed my sheep"?
a) Take care of hungry people
b) Teach and guide people with spiritual needs
c) Take charge of all church activities

2 Why did Jesus ask Peter to feed the sheep?
a) The people were in need, like hungry sheep.
b) Peter knew more of the Word than the others.
c) Peter loved Jesus more than the others.

3 Why would Peter be willing to feed the sheep?
a) He wanted to demonstrate his ability.
b) He wanted to make up for his failure.
c) He loved Jesus.

4 What goal did Jesus have in mind when He asked Peter to accept the task of feeding the lambs and sheep?
a) To keep His disciples happy and satisfied
b) To give Peter a position in church leadership
c) To carry out God's plan for the church

Peter Instructs the Elders

Objective 2. *Explain how Peter's instructions to the elders were based upon what he had learned from Jesus.*

While you undoubtedly read the recommended Scripture portions as part of your pre-lesson activities, please review 1 Peter 5:1-4.

Throughout the writings of Peter there is a tone of gentleness and deep concern for the needs of others. Bible scholars call his manner "warm" like that of an ideal pastor. We know that he understood very well the lessons he learned from Jesus, for he made them a part of his own ministry in many striking ways. One brief passage which illustrates this for us is his instructions to the elders. These few lines contain evidence of his obedience to the words of Jesus and his understanding of Christian leadership.

1. *Personal humility.* Peter was an apostle and is generally called the chief of the apostles. But he did not hesitate to call himself a "fellow-elder" thus placing himself not above, but among, those to whom he gave instructions. This concept is involved, also, in his instructions to the elders to be examples to the flock. The purpose of being an example is to help others to be as the leader is. The leader must be what he expects others to be. This places the leader very close to those who follow him.

2. *Understanding of the needs of others.* The functions of elders, in both Hebrew and Greek societies, were concerned with the needs of people. Elders were overseers of community affairs and matters of justice and finance. They were managers and teachers. This type of office was incorporated into the church at an early date. When Peter called himself an elder, he placed himself among those whose office was to meet the needs of others. We know that Peter lived in a time when persecution was great and teachers were few. The need was for leaders with a pastor attitude—diligent, but gentle. "Be shepherds of God's flock that is under your care," he instructed the elders.

3. *Understanding that the flock belongs to God.* Peter was called to emphasize the fact that the people were God's flock, placed by God under the care of elders. It was as if he were saying to the elders, "You feel a special tenderness and responsibility toward people when you think of them as the ones for whom Christ gave His life." We should note also the words *those entrusted to you.* Peter meant by this that God entrusts his people to the elders for the care they need. He wants the elders, and us, as leaders to care for the flock *as God wants.* Barclay says, "God has allotted us a task

to do and we must do it as God Himself would do it. This is the supreme ideal of service in the Christian church."

4. *Motivation, or the reason for Christian service.* Then Peter told the elders that they should serve willingly. He gave them three rules of motivation: First, they were not to avoid service because it was too demanding. Second, they were not to serve as though it were an unpleasant duty forced upon them. Third, they were not to grab for positions because of any gain that might come from them.

Peter's words indicate that a leader must not be greedy for financial gain, nor for power, popularity, and special privilege. Sometimes greed for personal success is a greater danger to a leader than is greed for financial gain. When a leader has his mind too much upon gaining approval or popularity, he forgets that his objective is to meet the needs of people. Leadership is not for personal gain. It is not something we deserve as an honor or have earned as a right. It is allotted to us by God. It is the practical expression of love.

5. *Consciousness of their goal.* Throughout the writings of Peter there is continuous consciousness of the ultimate goal—to be ready for the return of Christ to claim His own. "When the Chief Shepherd appears" He will claim His flocks from the faithful care of those to whom He has entrusted them. Then "you will receive the crown of glory that will never fade away."

5 Match the principles of leadership (right) with facts from the teachings of Jesus (left).

.... **a** Jesus told Peter to feed the sheep.

.... **b** Jesus asked Peter, "Do you love me?"

.... **c** Jesus said, "Be ready ... the Son of Man will come" (Matthew 24:44).

.... **d** Jesus used the words, "My sheep."

.... **e** Jesus warned Peter that he would fail.

1) Personal humility
2) Understanding the needs
3) The flock belongs to God
4) Proper motivation
5) Consciousness of goal

Leaders Work Toward Objectives

6 Jesus taught Peter the true purpose of leadership by using figurative language. He did not say to Peter, "Be a great leader." He said:

a ....
b Peter used the same figurative language when he told the elders:

....

CHRISTIAN WORK AS A SYSTEM

Objective 3. *Select true statements concerning the systems approach.*

You have seen the terms *objectives, goals*, and *needs* often in these lessons. Now that we are somewhat familiar with the way they are used in studies of leadership, we will look at them more closely. We will see how they relate to one another in the total activity or *system* of Christian work. In Lesson 7 we discussed the nature and importance of objectives. In this lesson we will see how leaders establish objectives and use them in planning and working with people.

The Systems Approach

We may think of the systems approach as a systematic, or orderly, way of looking at what goes on in an organization or a leadership situation. The idea grew from the desire of leaders to understand the total processes of their activities. Most leaders were engaged in planning programs and trying to get people to work at various tasks. Some of them began to ask: "What do we really accomplish?" "How can we tell if we are getting the most benefit from the effort we are investing?"

These leaders realized that organizations are busy doing two different jobs. They are keeping themselves going as institutions, and they are producing some kind of product or outcome. Church leaders were sometimes confused because it was difficult to tell which part of their work was to maintain the organization and which was to do something for other people. Sometimes they would begin new projects or order new Sunday school literature and find that these were of little or no help to the church. Why? Their conclusion was that each activity was considered separately without asking how it fit with the others or what real purpose it would be expected to accomplish.

Some of these leaders began to feel that if they could look at the activities of the church as a complete system, made up of various parts, they might understand how to make their work more successful. They found that studies, called *systems analysis*, were being made for organizations in business, government, and education. The purpose of these studies was to analyze the parts of an organization and see how they relate to each other and to the whole.

More recently, several such studies have been made to analyze Christian organizations. The results are very similar in each case. The main conclusion is that every activity requires that something be started, or put into action. Sometimes this is called *input*, or literally, that which is put in. This input goes through some kind of operation or handling. This is called the *process*. Then something is produced. Something results or is realized from the process. This is called *outcome*. From this approach, or viewpoint, every organization is a *system*, made up basically of input, process, and outcome.

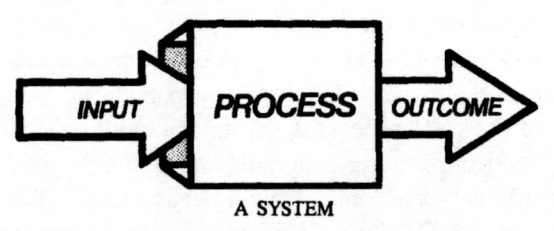

INPUT → PROCESS → OUTCOME

A SYSTEM

When we look at a system this very simple way the first conclusion seems clear: In order to have a good outcome, it is necessary to have the right input and the right process. The next conclusion might be that a leader must be sure of what outcome is desired, or he will not know how to manage the input and the process.

Let's make an illustration from an everyday activity—cooking. Ingredients are put in, the processes of mixing and heating are carried out, and the prepared food is the outcome. It is obvious to us that the cook must know what food is desired before the ingredients and the processes can be selected. Bread would be the outcome only if certain ingredients were used and certain processes followed. Soup would require an entirely different set of ingredients and processes.

Most cooks know what the desired outcome is. They know their objective, whether it is bread or soup. Therefore they use the correct ingredients and the correct processes. But it is a sad truth that sometimes leaders do not understand their objectives well enough to choose the correct input and processes. They put in ideas and plan activities without stating clearly in advance what outcome is expected.

Think of Michael, the example with which we started this lesson. His input was good material and study. He planned a process—the presentation of a message. But he did not have in mind any specific outcome. He put his attention on the message but did not seriously consider the people for whom the message was intended. By thinking of Christian activity as a system we can avoid this mistake. We can learn to establish clear objectives and then select or provide what is appropriate to attain those objectives.

Now let's go more deeply into our examination of Christian work. There is a better and more complete way to describe it as a system. The parts are as follows:

1. *A supreme goal.* The goal is to accomplish the ultimate purpose of God, through His church.

2. *Relationships.* Christian leadership involves relationships with people. Out of our relationship with Christ we are motivated to develop relationships with other leaders, Christian believers, and the people we are called to reach for Christ. A leader must establish and maintain working relationships with and among his people.

3. *Needs.* The difference between the present condition and the objective toward which we are working is defined as the

need. Leaders are called because there are needs. When a leader plans an activity, he should be able to state specifically how it relates to the needs of people. What are the needs? How will this activity meet them?

4. *Objectives*. The outcomes which we wish to see accomplished are defined as objectives. Objectives are stated in terms of what we desire to be the result of our work, rather than what we intend to do. For example, the objective is not to have a meeting. The objective is what we expect to be the result of the meeting, such as a decision on a certain issue.

5. *Tasks*. The tasks are what we do in order to reach the objectives. They are the processes, including the planning. There are tasks for the leader and those he assigns to others.

6. *Evaluation*. In every complete system there is planned evaluation. This is measurement of the results. Were the objectives achieved? Were the needs met? Have good relationships been maintained? Were the tasks assigned to the right people? Could they have been done better some other way? The leader finds answers to questions like these and learns how to make improvements. The evaluation probably will lead back to improving relationships, stating new needs which have emerged or been discovered, establishing new objectives, and making adjustments in task assignments.

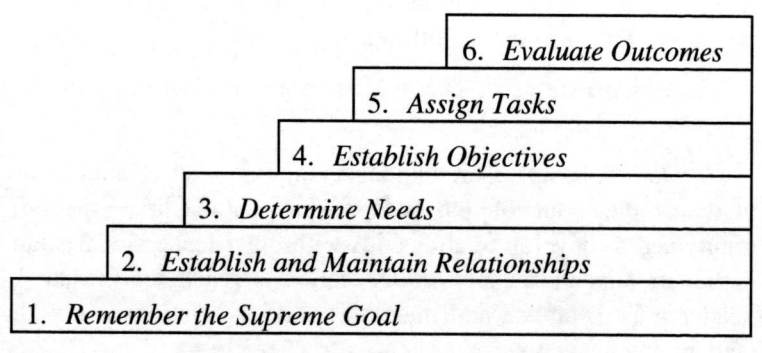

|6. *Evaluate Outcomes*|
|5. *Assign Tasks*|
|4. *Establish Objectives*|
|3. *Determine Needs*|
|2. *Establish and Maintain Relationships*|
|1. *Remember the Supreme Goal*|

A System for Christian Leadership

In the conversation between Jesus and Peter there is an example or an indication of most of these parts of a Christian

Leaders Work Toward Objectives

work system: The *supreme goal* was to carry out the will of the Lord. The *relationship* between Jesus and Peter was that of a loving teacher and a student who returned His love. The *need* was that people were spiritually hungry, or unfed. The *objective* was spiritually nourished people. The *task* was to feed the people—supply the food and the action.

7 To summarize what we have learned about the systems approach, circle the letter in front of each TRUE statement.

a The systems approach is a systematic way of looking at organizations and leadership situations.
b The main characteristic of a system is that it is composed of parts which have specific relationships to one another.
c The systems approach means that an organization works like a machine.
d The systems approach can help leaders to understand their place in the total organization and their relationships to other leaders and workers.
e The systems approach can help leaders to establish appropriate objectives.
f The main reason we learn to use the systems approach is so that we can discover ways to improve our work.

8 Think of your own organization or project or one with which you are familiar. How would you analyze it, using the methods discussed in this lesson? How do the people relate to one another? Are there problems which result from misunderstandings among the workers and leaders? What are some of the specific needs of the people? Remember needs are related to the age group, the spiritual background, social and economic problems, and other life conditions. Can you state some objectives? What kind of tasks would be involved in achieving the objectives? How would you evaluate, or measure, the outcome? Write in your notebook some of your ideas to keep for future reference.

Understand the Needs of People

Objective 4. *Select true statements concerning needs assessment.*

Remember we said that the behavior of Michael and the pastor illustrates a serious error which is made by many sincere and competent Christian leaders. Turn back to the first page of this lesson to review the story to see if you can detect the error.

9 Write a brief statement telling what error you believe is demonstrated in the behavior of Michael and the pastor. Use your notebook for this answer.

Do you see how your answer is related to our lesson on communications? In order to reach people with a message, you should know something about them. Neither the pastor nor Michael mentioned the characteristics nor the needs of the people who were to receive the message.

In Christian work we have an advantage over those who try to communicate in the business world. We have the guidance of the Holy Spirit. He knows the people, and He is able to guide us as we study and pray. Many sincere and competent Christian leaders depend entirely upon this truth. However, it is inconsistent to believe that we should spend time and effort working out an outline and making a good delivery and then say it is not necessary to think about the objectives of the message or the needs of those for whom it is intended.

Probably the most neglected part of our Christian work system is the part we have called *needs*. This is a serious error because, as we have seen, the parts of the system are interrelated. If we do not understand the needs of people, we cannot establish appropriate objectives.

It is characteristic of Jesus that he spoke in terms of the people more often than in terms of the message. We have seen that He did not tell Peter just to learn a lesson from his failures but to pass on to others what he learned. He did not tell Peter to be a good leader, but to feed the sheep. In His own ministry Jesus considered the needs of people of various ages and conditions. He knew, of course, that they all needed salvation. But He did not rely on a basic "salvation message." He offered water to the thirsty, healing to the sick, and food to the hungry. Peter, following His pattern, speaks with an awareness of the suffering and persecution experienced by his particular audience.

It may be that we overlook the importance of finding out what the needs are because we take for granted the divinity of Christ. He did not have to make surveys in order to find out needs. Our own position is different only in that we are required to use the implements available to us, just as Jesus used those available to Him.

Needs Assessment Methods

In addition to informal ways of finding out the needs of people, there are formal needs assessment methods which have been designed by scholars in the fields of leadership and management. Some of these have been used with great success in Christian work. You should be aware of them and understand the basic principles. Then you can adapt them in ways appropriate to your own situation. We will describe briefly here four types of needs assessment.

1. *Initial activity.* In an unfamiliar situation, such as taking a position in a new area, starting a church, starting a class, or planning a series of meetings, you know little or nothing about the needs of the people. Without making assumptions in advance, the leader asks the people to state how they perceive their own needs—what they think their needs are. This can be done by surveys and questionnaires or by personal interviews. The leader may feel that the people do not understand their own needs, and this may be true. But for the initial needs assessment the point is to find out how the people perceive their own needs. This is a type of listening and can be very useful in helping a new leader to work efficiently and be accepted by a group.

2. *Perceived needs.* This method begins with the needs perceived by those in charge. The leader has observed or received information from others that needs exist. A list is made of these perceived needs, and the people are asked to indicate whether or not the needs exist or to what degree they are being met by the organization at the present time. In this way a leader can understand how the people feel about the success of an activity or procedure. If needs are not being met, changes can be made.

3. *Known needs.* It may be that there has been a failure to accomplish objectives. The leader must face reality and help his group to face reality. The leader must see that the needs are described more accurately so that the entire group understands them in the same way as the leader. In Christian work some needs are common to all and cannot be questioned. The leader must guide the group in stating the objectives clearly and finding ways to accomplish them.

4. *Comparison of needs.* The activity of comparing the importance of needs and setting priorities for action is essential in most organizations. The leader must decide how to allot personnel, time, and money to meet the needs. He does this by asking his people to rank the needs according to their importance.

10 To summarize what we have learned about needs assessment, circle the letter in front of each TRUE statement.
a The needs of people are neglected because leaders do not care.
b We must understand needs in order to set appropriate objectives.
c The idea of needs assessment is supported by Scripture.
d Asking people to state their needs is one way for a leader to become more efficient in his own work.
e A leader must understand needs in order to set appropriate priorities for the use of time and money.

MANAGEMENT BY OBJECTIVES

Objective 5. *Define the term objective as it is used in the systems approach and explain how to manage by using objectives.*

We have seen that needs and objectives are interrelated parts of the Christian work system. We must know the needs of the people in order to minister to them in effective and appropriate ways. When we have determined the needs of the people and stated them clearly, then we can establish our objectives. We define objectives as the desired outcome of our work. In Lesson 7 we learned something about the importance of objectives. Now we can understand this importance more clearly because we see objectives as a part of the total system.

Leaders Work Toward Objectives

Leaders are responsible to take care of the work or get the job done. This is what we mean by *management*. When we say *management by objectives* we mean that you must identify your objectives and then handle the work in a way which will lead to the accomplishment of the objectives. This is probably the most efficient way to handle any kind of work. Most of the problems in Christian work result from the fact that leaders have not established objectives, or do not understand the difference between an objective and an activity. They have given attention to having meetings and projects. They have an idea that these activities are for the glory of the Lord, but they do not know how to judge whether or not they have been as successful as they could be.

You learn to *manage by objectives* by seeing your work, or your organization as a whole, with definite purposes which you understand. Then you and those who work with you establish objectives which can be achieved and measured.

Think again of Esther. Her goal was the salvation of her people. Everything she did was for the purpose of saving them from death. In order to achieve her purpose—reach her final goal—she had to achieve other objectives, such as gaining the attention and the approval of the king.

Think of the preparation and delivery of a sermon. Let's say the final goal is to have decisions for Christ. In order to achieve this we set for ourselves the objective: an effective sermon. In order to achieve this, we must have good content and good delivery. Each of these, then, becomes an objective. In order to have good content, we must know how to study the Bible. This may mean learning how to use tools such as the concordance and the commentary. This means, of course, that we must know how to read. In order to have good delivery we may take a course in preaching. We need to know something about grammar and vocabulary. We see that in order to achieve a final goal we must achieve a number of objectives. A leader must understand this and must be able to explain it to his workers. This is management by objectives.

How to Manage by Objectives

1. *Consider the past and present situations.* Really study your own organization and see what has been accomplished in the past. Try to evaluate honesty the present state. How successful are you? What parts of the work have been successful, and what parts need improvement? What would you like to see accomplished?

2. *Set realistic objectives.* What do you feel could be accomplished that would meet the needs of the people you wish to serve? Depending upon the guidance of the Spirit, decide what outcomes you expect to see within a specific period of time. Set your objectives high, but do not be afraid to be realistic. Your people need to feel that they are challenged and that you have faith in the Lord, but if the objectives seem too far out of reach, the people will be discouraged.

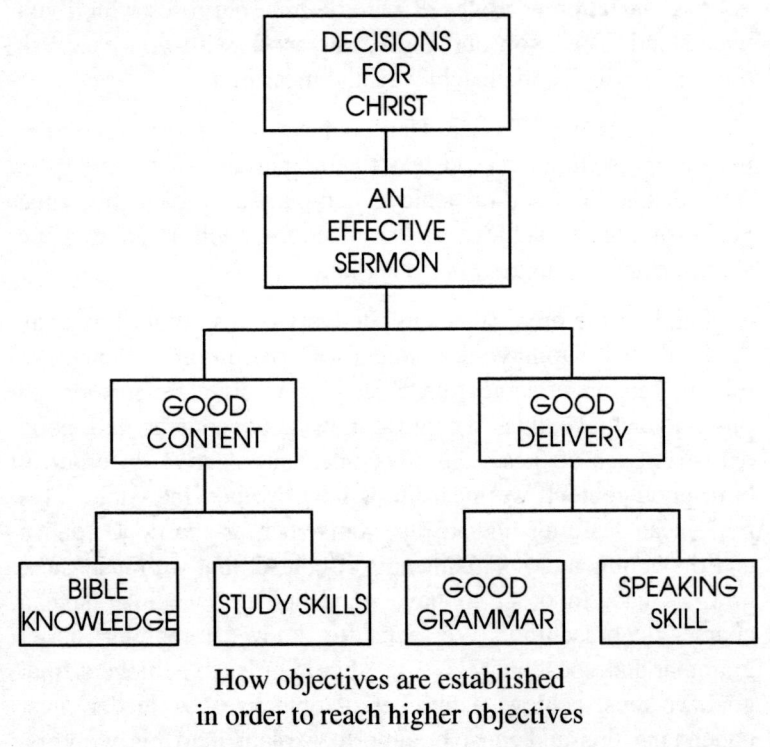

```
              DECISIONS
                FOR
               CHRIST
                 |
                 AN
              EFFECTIVE
               SERMON
              /        \
          GOOD         GOOD
        CONTENT      DELIVERY
         /    \        /    \
     BIBLE   STUDY   GOOD   SPEAKING
  KNOWLEDGE  SKILLS GRAMMAR  SKILL
```

How objectives are established
in order to reach higher objectives

3. *Be sure your objectives are measurable.* A time limit and a way of measuring success must be decided upon in advance.

Otherwise it will not be possible to know whether or not an objective has been reached. Make a clear statement of what should be accomplished by a certain date.

4. *Be sure the objectives are understood by those who work with you.* A leader must share his vision and his sense of mission with the people. We will see in our next lesson that people are challenged or motivated to work toward the goals of the organization when they are sure what those goals are.

5. *Make a plan to reach the objectives.* Show the workers how you intend to accomplish what you have set out to do. Assign definite tasks and responsibilities to individuals. Let your people know that they are important and how they relate to one another in the work. Share your ideas, your enthusiasm, and your faith.

6. *Get activity started in the right direction.* A leader is expected to make things happen. It is not enough to preach and explain. You must see that there is action and that the action is appropriate for the situation. If there is too much delay between making a plan and putting it into effect, people tend to lose interest. As soon as you have made a plan, get it into action.

7. *Keep the activity directed toward the objective.* People tend to keep on doing what they are accustomed to do and so lose sight of their reason for doing it. A leader cannot announce a list of objectives and then forget about it. He must see that the people are constantly reminded and encouraged to work toward the objectives. Inspiration and enthusiasm must be provided consistently.

8. *See that the results of every effort are evaluated and recorded.* When results are evaluated the leader has an opportunity to decide whether the procedure has been appropriate, whether the right people have been assigned to a task, and whether the objective should be changed in some way. Failure to reach an objective is not necessarily an indication of inadequate dedication or incompetent work. The leader must take the risk of making honest evaluations. This is his best insurance that the work can be improved and the ultimate goals reached.

9. *Recognize and reward those who help to accomplish objectives.* Recognition should be given on the basis of

accomplishment of objectives rather than upon personal factors. In this way the people are made to see the importance of the goal and to enjoy the satisfaction of working toward goals, rather than making less meaningful contributions of their resources.

10. *Demonstrate that personal objectives are reached by those who work toward the objectives and ultimate goals of the institution.* In business management much thought and effort are given to making workers feel that they can attain personal advantages and reach personal objectives by helping the company or institution to reach its objectives. In Christian work the problem is not so great. All true Christians have the same basic objectives. All wish to please God, and most are very anxious to serve Him in some definite way. It becomes the duty of the leader, then, not to prove that working for institutional goals is to their personal advantage but to show them how this can be done in the activities of the church. Christians need to be supplied with structure, or plans, to guide them in doing the Lord's work. This is the really marvelous aspect of management by objectives. It helps a leader to guide workers into the paths they deeply wish to follow. It helps them to see the order, the reason, and the purpose of Christian service. Your greatest reward as a leader is to see people finding their own needs met, and achieving their own spiritual goals, as they work toward the supreme goal, according to God's plan.

11 We may define the term *objective*, as it is used in the systems approach, most accurately as
a) what we intend to do.
b) the desired outcome of our work.
c) the planned evaluation of the work of the complete system.

12 In your notebook write two objectives suitable for some situation with which you are familiar.

13 Write in your notebook two personal objectives which you could achieve while working toward the goals of the church.

14 Explain briefly what it means to manage by objectives.

....
....

Leaders Work Toward Objectives

self-test

1 The leadership principle we recognize in Peter's words "Lord, I am ready to go with you to prison and to death" is this:
a) One must be slow to make any great spiritual commitment.
b) One should never express openly his feelings of loyalty.
c) Actions are important; words are meaningless.
d) One must guard against overconfidence.

2 We learn a second major leadership principle from Jesus' words to Peter—"Satan has desired to sift you . . . when you have turned back, strengthen your brothers"—which is that personal experiences
a) must never be used to illustrate biblical truths.
b) are to be used to help others.
c) always weaken one in spirit, soul, and body.
d) which don't produce major spiritual victories are wasted.

3 Peter's greetings to the elders, "To the elders among you, I appeal as a fellow elder," demonstrates his knowledge of an important quality of leadership:
a) understanding the needs of others.
b) personal humility.
c) consciousness of a goal.
d) motivation for Christian service.

4 An important leadership principle is bound up in Peter's exhortation to the elders in which he describes the flock as "those entrusted to you." By this Peter means that
a) the people under a leader's care are God's people.
b) people resemble sheep and are incapable of assuming responsibility.
c) people are like children (irresponsible); therefore, leaders are entrusted with what needs to be done.
d) once a responsibility is assumed by a leader as a sacred trust, it can't be laid aside.

5 Peter's reference to the appearing of the Chief Shepherd reveals yet another principle of Christian leadership: To keep motivated and remain effective, a leader must
a) be concerned about pleasing the "sheep."
b) fear lest his best efforts fall short of acceptance.
c) develop more short-term goals, since time is so short.
d) be continually conscious of the ultimate goal.

6 Which one of the following statements explains best what is meant by the systems approach according to your lesson? A Systems approach
a) views the process of management as a mechanical device.
b) is an orderly way of looking at what goes on in an organization.
c) eliminates much work because it relies on computers instead of people.
d) simply relies on two main parts: setting and evaluating objectives.

7 Studies called systems analysis have been developed in order to analyze the parts of an organization and see how they
a) function and why they don't function more efficiently.
b) handle input, evaluation, and feedback.
c) specify objectives, assess needs, and select activities.
d) relate to each other and to the whole.

8 In the systems approach the three primary ingredients are
a) input, process, and outcome.
b) input, evaluation, and feedback.
c) to specify objectives, assess needs, and select activities.
d) to specify objectives, select activities, and provide evaluation.

Leaders Work Toward Objectives

9 All but one of the following statements are true concerning *needs* assessment. Circle the letter in front of the one that is NOT a true statement.
a) One must understand needs in order to set appropriate objectives.
b) Asking people to state their needs is one way for a leader to become more efficient in his own work.
c) A leader must understand needs in order to set legitimate priorities for the use of time and money.
d) The needs of people are neglected because leaders do not care.

10 If you were asked to outline a plan for determining objectives, you would follow which one of the suggested approaches?
a) Determine the ultimate goal and set the objectives necessary to help reach the final goal.
b) Determine goal, plan activities, review activities, make adjustments, and evaluate.
c) State the outcome you wish, gather information, consult people, plan activities, and initiate your program.
d) State your goal, reconcile your goal and that of your organization, plan activities that will keep your people occupied, review the effectiveness of your plan, and change activities as need requires.

11 Match each part of the system (right) with its appropriate description (left).

.... **a** What we desire to result from our work
.... **b** The bond which the leader develops with and among his people
.... **c** The measurement of the results
.... **d** The ultimate purpose of God through His church
.... **e** What we do in order to reach objectives
.... **f** The difference between the present conditions and the objectives toward which we are working

1) A supreme goal
2) Relationships
3) Needs
4) Objectives
5) Tasks
6) Evaluation

answers to study questions

7 a True.
  b True.
  c False. (By approach we mean a viewpoint, to help the leader understand his work. The work is not done in a mechanical way, but is examined by a careful method.)
  d True.
  e True.
  f True.

1 b) Teach and guide people with spiritual needs.

8 Your answer.

2 a) The people were in need, like hungry sheep.

9 Your answer might be slightly different from mine. I've suggested the following. Neither one of these brethren appears to be primarily concerned with the ones who are to be the recipients of the message. The pastor may have believed he was doing Michael a favor by letting him preach. Or he may have preferred to relax while the younger man ministered. Michael was so intent on the preparation and presentation of his message that he did not have a goal beyond the delivery of the message. He did not have in mind a specific outcome.

3 c) He loved Jesus.

10 a False. (Leaders may be very caring, but do not know the importance of finding out what the needs are before planning their activities.)
  b True.
  c True.
  d True.
  e True.

4 c) To carry out God's plan for the church.

11 b) the desired outcome of our work

5 a 2) Understanding the needs.
  b 4) Proper motivation.
  c 5) Consciousness of goal.
  d 3) The flock belongs to God.
  e 1) Personal humility.

12 Your answer. An example might be as follows: My goal is to see my church people gain a good, general knowledge of the Word of God. My first objective is to design and implement Phase I of a curriculum for each age group so that within the next three years each will study the Old Testament in depth. As a result each person will be able to demonstrate his knowledge of the material by scoring at least 70% on a general knowledge exam on the Old Testament. My second objective is to initiate Phase 2 of the curriculum so that each age level will study the New Testament in depth for the next two years. As a result each person will be able to demonstrate his knowledge of the material by scoring at least 70% on a general knowledge exam on the New Testament.

6 a "Feed my lambs (or sheep)."
  b "Be shepherds of God's flock."

13 Your answer. Two personal objectives one could set and achieve while working toward the goals of the church might be: 1) To become more sensitive to the Lord's leading as opportunities for witnessing present themselves, and 2) to cultivate a deeper personal relationship with the Lord as demonstrated in more consistent Bible study and time in prayer.

14 Your answer. I've noted that in order to achieve a final goal, we must achieve a number of objectives. We must understand this and be able to explain it to our followers also.

LESSON 9
Leaders Are Motivated and Motivate Others

Two Bible school students were looking at a notice on the bulletin board. It said: "All Christian workers are invited to attend a special conference on BURN-OUT. A Christian psychologist will give help and advice from the Bible and from his many years of experience."

"What does that mean?" asked the young man.

"I was reading a book about it," the young woman answered. The word *burn-out* is used to mean apathy, to give up, become languid and depressed, just generally lose interest in your work. The author of this book says it is hard to keep workers motivated. They start out with enthusiasm, and then they seem to lose interest or get tired and depressed. The conferences or seminars are to help Christian workers who have this problem."

"I can't believe such a thing," the young man declared. "How could anyone get tired of doing the Lord's work? It is the greatest privilege we have! Besides it is a calling. We know the prophet Isaiah says: 'Those who hope in the Lord will renew their strength. They will soar on wings like eagles; they will run and not grow weary, they will walk and not be faint'" (Isaiah 40:31).

"How could anyone get tired of doing the Lord's work?"

How do we feel about this subject? Have you ever felt weary and depressed, while at the same time you sincerely wanted to do the will of the Lord? Have you, in a position of leadership, found workers starting out well on a project and then leaving it unfinished?

These questions are related to what is generally called motivation, which is the topic of this lesson. We will look at the example of the apostle Paul, and then consider some theories and ideas of modern scholars.

lesson outline

Paul–Committed and Consistent Leader
Dangers and Depressions in Christian Work
Motivation—Key to Successful Leadership
How Leaders Motivate Others
The Goal Is Worth the Race

lesson objectives

When you finish this lesson you should he able to:

- Describe leadership principles in the accounts of Paul, and recognize and apply these principles.

- Recognize dangers which keep leaders and workers from reaching their goals, and be prepared to avoid these dangers.

- Explain the concept *motivation*, and describe some major theories of motivation as they relate to leadership.

- Motivate others to work with you toward objectives and goals in Christian service.

learning activities

1. As background for this lesson, read the following Scriptures: Numbers 11:26-29; Isaiah 40:28-31; 50:4; Luke 22:31-34; John 21:20-22; Acts 14:11-15; 20:22-28; 21:37-22:10; 27:1-2, 13-44; Romans 8:35; 1 Corinthians 9:27; 11:2; 12:4-11; 2 Corinthians 7:14; 11:25-29; 13:10; Galatians 6:1-10; Philippians 3:13-14; 2 Timothy 4:7-8; 1 Peter 5:1-11.

2. Work through the lesson development and answer the study questions in the usual manner. When you have finished, take the self-test and check your answers.

3. Carefully review Unit 3 (Lessons 7–9). Then complete the unit student report for Unit 3 and send it to your instructor.

key words

ambition	environment	mystical symbols
apathy	favoritism	panic
centurion	indulge	poise
chants	internalize	rank
compromise	languid	sensation
custody	martyr	serene
depressed	morality	
depression(s)	morals	

lesson development

PAUL—COMMITTED AND CONSISTENT LEADER

Objective 1. *Choose a statement which explains the importance of leadership behavior in the experiences of Paul.*

The writer of the book of Acts says that in his former book he wrote about all that Jesus began to do and to teach. In Acts he would tell some of what Jesus continued to do and teach, through the Spirit-filled followers of Jesus. Acts is chapter one in the history of this carrying out of the commission Jesus gave. As Jesus had said, it was better for Him to go away, after His earthly part of the work was done. Then the Holy Spirit, with no limitation to one earthly body, would work through the many who make up the universal body which is the church. With what joy and dedication those first disciples went forth! And because their purpose was to accomplish God's purposes, working with and through people, their qualities and behaviors were in every case, as we have seen, those of effective leadership.

One of the most remarkable examples of the nature and importance of leadership behavior is the account of Paul's arrest in Jerusalem and his journey in chains to Rome. Can we begin to imagine the degree of faith, commitment, and poise demonstrated that day Paul was seized? Dragged from the temple by rioters, arrested by soldiers and bound with two chains, he had to be carried by the soldiers to escape the violence of the mob. And calmly he asked, using the best of speech and dignity of manner, "May I say something to you?"

Then, when he had received permission from the commander, he stood on the steps and motioned to the crowd to be quiet. Complete silence resulted. This was neither a mere show of courage nor the resignation of a martyr. This was the presence of a leader chosen by God, acting in the power of God to influence the behavior of people. God could have struck the people dumb or even struck them dead. But He chose to have a human instrument, whose behavior could be recorded for all of us as a pattern.

Paul did not begin to scold or threaten the people. He did not preach a sermon nor demand to be recognized as God's messenger. First he sought to identify with the Jews, and then he gave his own testimony of conversion. He was fearless in his presentation of the truth, but objective and serene in his manner.

It will be to your advantage to read the entire account from the Bible, but here we will mention only a few more major points. As Paul defended himself, rulers and chief officials listened to him with respect, even though he was their prisoner. He continued to state facts forcefully, and to repeat his conversion experience with power that deeply affected his hearers. He demonstrated knowledge of the law and his rights as a citizen without any loss of self-control or show of bitter self-pity.

Finally, on the ship starting for Rome, Paul was placed in the charge of a centurion who seemed to treat him more as a co-worker than a prisoner. Imagine again: Paul standing in that storm-tossed ship, giving advice to those who held him in custody. He assured them of God's protection.

Why did they respond to him? He did not speak of God in exotic ways nor use mystical symbols or chants. He did not cry out to God in a dramatic fashion. He simply acted in the role of a Spirit-guided leader. He spoke in terms men understood, with an authority they could not resist. He kept some of them from abandoning the ship. He used practical wisdom, telling them to eat so they would be physically able and have a more cheerful outlook in the time of danger. Throughout the experience he showed concern for their needs; he kept them working together toward the goal of saving all their lives.

And they all made it safely to a shore. They built a fire and warmed themselves from the cold rain. We are not told that anyone said, "Thank you, Paul." But to us it is clear that the Lord had preserved their lives, and Paul had been His instrument. It is obvious, too, that the method God used was a demonstration of magnificent leadership.

Once again we are taught the thrilling lesson of God's ways with His people. He could have saved the ship with a miracle of

Leaders Are Motivated and Motivate Others 231

calming the sea or guiding the vessel through the rocks to a quiet landing on the sand. When you think about this, how do you feel about the privilege and the responsibility of being in a position of Christian leadership? In what respect does it make you feel uplifted? In what respect does it make you feel humble?

1 Consider seriously the questions we have just asked. Ask the Lord to open your understanding and your appreciation. Then write your answers in your notebook.

2 Turn back to Lesson 1 and review the section "What A Leader Is Like." Then find in the experiences and words of Paul examples of each of the traits or qualities mentioned below and cite the appropriate Scripture reference(s) for each.

a Empathy ....

b Goal achievement...

c Competence..

d Emotional stability ....

e Group membership...

f Ability to share leadership ....

g Consistency and dependability ....

3 The importance of leadership behavior in the experiences of Paul is expressed correctly by which of the following statements?

a) Paul's behavior as a leader is important because the authority he wielded and the uses of power he employed opened doors that would not have opened to any other approach.

b) The apostle's greatest asset as a leader is seen in his ability to manipulate people, for it enabled him to achieve his goals.

c) The importance of Paul's behavior as a leader is this: God used Paul's behavior to influence people positively toward the claims of the gospel.

DANGERS AND DEPRESSIONS IN CHRISTIAN WORK

Objective 2. *Recognize examples of behavior and attitudes which endanger effective leadership.*

We have had a glimpse of Paul as a leader while in prisoner's chains. This gives us a view quite different from the usual image of the leader as a strong and popular figure. Elsewhere in his writings Paul lets us know that his position brought with it many dangers and discomforts. He does not complain about this. On the contrary, his attitude is that to mention his trials is to "boast" of what he is privileged to suffer for the sake of the ministry God has given him (2 Corinthians 11:25-29). The lesson for us at this time, however, is that we must be aware that dangers and discouragements exist in the life of every leader.

The dangers we face usually are quite different from those mentioned by Paul. There may be some physical threats to us in times of war and persecution. But more often we are threatened with dangers to our spiritual lives, our joy in the Lord, and our success in reaching Christian goals. Most of these dangers can be placed within one of two classifications. The first classification involves too much self-interest and personal ambition. This is a problem of *wrong motives*. The second classification involves too much self-doubt, self-criticism, and discouragement. This leads to depression, apathy, and what the psychologists call *burn-out*. It is a problem of *insufficient motivation toward the goal*.

Dangers Involving Wrong Motives
Review 1 Corinthians 3 and 1 Peter 5:1-11.

1. *The ego–personal pride.* Almost any position of leadership brings with it the condition of being elevated over other people. Instead of keeping their attention centered in the work, some leaders begin to compare themselves with others. They begin to speak as though the work belonged to them. They speak of themselves, saying, "My project," "My office," "As your leader I must insist that you . . . ."

They become very sensitive to criticism and tend to ridicule or ignore opinions which are different from their own. They expect to be given special privileges and public honors. Sometimes they even become proud of their spiritual gifts. We notice that both Peter and Paul give us strong warnings against the awful spiritual shipwreck that can result from personal pride.

2. *Overconfidence.* We learned from Peter of this danger, also. It is related to pride but is different in that a leader may believe he is exercising faith. He may know that he has more experience, both as a servant of the Lord, and in regard to the task, than anyone else in the group. He expects others to accept his decisions and rely upon his judgment. This is required to a degree in leadership. But when a leader refuses to admit that he may be wrong and insists upon doing everything his own way, he is in danger of losing his effectiveness. We must remember that standing up for our convictions is not the same as being stubborn.

3. *Popularity and praise.* Paul became extremely upset at the prospect of himself, or any man, receiving praise that is due only to God. "Do not deceive yourselves," he exhorted the Corinthians. "No more boasting about men!" (1 Corinthians 3:18-23). We remember, also, that Paul and Barnabas tore their clothes and rushed into the crowd at Lystra vigorously rejecting the praise of those who would call them gods (Acts 14:11-15). When a leader is motivated by desire for popularity, the result is more than the danger to his personal morality. There is danger to the work, too, for he may be tempted to compromise in order to please people. There is the danger that he will indulge in favoritism and fail to uphold Christian standards. Perhaps there is no person weaker than one who believes that he is strong because he is popular.

Many innocent and well-meaning people are always on hand, as they were in Lystra, to offer praise to those in leadership positions. It is the responsibility of the leader to control the tendency to enjoy such attentions. As churches become more organized in formal ways, with ranks of leadership, it seems that more honor is given to men for their special talents and gifts. The church must teach its members to respect leadership that is ordered by the Lord. We should honor our leaders in reasonable ways and care for their needs. But we must refrain from treating them as though they were popular musicians and sports heroes. It is for the leader, in the spirit of Paul, to absolutely reject personal praise for spiritual accomplishments, God-given talents, and service to the church.

4. *Jealousy.* Suppose you have worked very hard and have refused to accept praise for your accomplishments. Then someone else takes the credit and is given public praise. How do you feel? The natural response is to feel resentful toward the other person. This is a grave spiritual danger which most leaders face, for it leads beyond a normal degree of resentment into the ugliness of jealousy. Again, this is not merely a matter of personal morals. The work of the Lord suffers because jealous leaders are afraid to delegate responsibilities to competent people. They do not want to share credit. They are afraid others will receive more credit than they. Did you notice that Peter almost fell into this dangerous trap of Satan's? You may wish to look back at John 21:20-22. Moses refused to be weakened by this danger (Numbers 11:26-29).

5. *Power.* Most of the dangers of leadership are associated in some way with the original sin of Satan—a desire for power. It is terrifying to a sensitive Christian to realize how great and universal this danger is. We have learned that even the disciples of Jesus, in some of their last contacts with Him, were asking, "Who will be the greatest?"

In this world, judgments most frequently are made, not upon the basis of true quality, but upon the basis of comparison with other people. To be "good" means, in many cases, to be ahead of others. The writer of this study course has tested the principle on a number of occasions by asking students in a class, "If you receive an 'A' grade, what does it mean to you?" Only a few students answer that the grade indicates they have gained valuable knowledge. Most answer in terms of how high they stand in the class. In most commercial and social organizations the rate of pay is not based upon skill but upon how many people rank above and below you. Achievement has come to mean, in many of our social systems, that we are ahead of others. This is not the system that the Lord desires for His church. (See Galatians 6:3-4.)

Leaders Are Motivated and Motivate Others 235

4 What dangers to effective leadership are indicated in the following examples? From the five dangers we have just discussed, list those which apply to each example.

a The director of the meeting said, "We want Brother X to come to the platform to lead us in prayer. He is a great man of God who has won many souls, has a college degree, and has preached in many large churches.

....

b "Why was she chosen to that high position?" Sister Y asked. "After all, I've been here longer and worked harder than she."

....

c Chairman Z wanted everyone to know that he had been elected by a very large majority.

....

d Leader Q felt that the youth project was not really suitable, but he decided not to say anything. It was almost time for the election of new officers, and he wanted to be reelected.

....

e Leader M was hurt because no one asked him to sit on the platform.

....

f Leader F announced that he had made the only possible decision and was very sure he could handle the task without any help from others who had offered their services.

....

Depression and Apathy

Objective 3. *Select true statements concerning depression and apathy among Christian workers.*

"Let us not become weary in doing good, for at the proper time we will reap a harvest if we do not give up" (Galatians 6:9).

These words indicate that Paul was aware of the danger of apathy. He understood, long before studies were made of motivation and *burn-out*, that people can get tired and discouraged when they are "doing good." He reminded them of the goal toward which they were working. This was to encourage or motivate them. He knew that the best way to succeed is to have a clear purpose in mind. He asked Christians not to give up trying to help people.

Sometimes Christian workers do feel like giving up or quitting. Great demands are made upon them. They are expected to be helpful to others even when they are tired and have problems of their own. Sometimes they make careful plans and then everything seems to go wrong. People they are trying to help may not seem to make any progress. No one ever says, "Thank you."

"What's the use?" a discouraged leader may say. "I'm not getting anywhere with this. Maybe I really don't have what it takes."

In Lesson 7 we discussed *reality thinking*. The same principle is useful to us as we consider the problem of depression. Since we are Christians we feel guilty about the very idea of being discouraged. We blame ourselves and feel ashamed that we do not have stronger faith. It is helpful to admit our human weaknesses and examine some of the reasons why Christian workers get depressed.

1. *We have high ideals and expectations*. Most Christians begin a project or accept a position with great emotional dedication and high hopes. We know our God does not fail. Therefore, when problems arise we tend to blame ourselves and doubt our spirituality or our calling.

2. *We see much human pain and trouble*. People come to us with their problems. We try to help them. Sometimes we think we have helped them, and then we see them fall back into the old conditions. Sometimes they refuse our help. Some we know we cannot help at all.

3. *We work without adequate resources*. Often we must try to accomplish our tasks with little or no money. There may be too little

space for our needs. The equipment is worn out. We must use odds and ends of materials which are not really suitable. The workers are few. All this may lead us into feelings of panic and frustration.

4. *We become disillusioned by watching people.* Christian work is work with people, and people do not always live up to our expectations of them. We feel betrayed and hurt. We tend to judge people by some standard or idea of our own instead of leaving all judgment to the Lord.

5. *We become physically and emotionally exhausted.* The prophet Elijah is an example of how even a powerful man of God may be driven to depression (1 Kings 19:3-5, 10, 14). We work hard, and spend all our energy, and yet so little seems to be accomplished. Even after the joy of a victory in the Lord's work, we are sometimes crushed to realize how much more there is to do. If this emotion is allowed to continue it brings apathy. Like Elijah, we feel we might as well die. Finally, we give up, and say, "What's the use? I think I will quit." This is the dangerous condition which threatens nearly all dedicated Christian workers at one time or another.

5 Following are some questions for meditation and self-analysis. Read them over carefully and then write your response in your student notebook. Can you think of times when you experienced feelings of depression and discouragement? What do you believe caused these feelings?

6 Circle the letter in front of each TRUE statement.
a Christian workers should be able to avoid all depressions.
b God scolded Elijah for wanting to give up.
c The physical condition of the body may lead to depression.
d Self-doubt and self-blame are not the same as humility.
e It is depressing to a good Christian to want to help someone and not be able to do so.
f Judgment of others may lead to depression for ourselves.
g Dedicated workers may become depressed after they have experienced great success in the Lord's work.
h Good Christians never get concerned about material things such as equipment and buildings.

MOTIVATION—KEY TO SUCCESSFUL LEADERSHIP

The Concept of Leader Motivation

Objective 4. *Identify a statement which explains correctly the concept motivation.*

We say that motivation is a concept because it is something we know about but cannot see directly nor fully explain. Like the concepts *love* and *ambition*, motivation can be understood from behavior but not really defined. We know it is there because of the way people act. In fact, the best way we can define motivation is to say that it is the process behind the action or behavior which we see.

All people are motivated in some way. When we say a person is *not motivated*, usually we mean we do not see in him any action which shows he is interested or eager to move in a certain direction or do a certain thing. We have seen that Christian workers who are discouraged and depressed lack motivation. That is, they have lost their eagerness to work toward the goals which once seemed very important to them. We have read the words of the apostle Paul telling Christians the importance of keeping their minds on the goal. He wanted them to remain highly motivated.

There are several practical steps Christian leaders can take to renew their own motivation and avoid the dangers of depression and apathy. Here are a few suggestions:

1. Remember that leadership is a calling.
2. Give thanks continually for spiritual gifts and exercise them.
3. Set aside time for private devotions.
4. Read the Bible daily and use study helps to increase knowledge.
5. Read helpful and inspirational books and publications.
6. Attend worship services faithfully.
7. Attend conferences and seminars which are appropriate.
8. Share pleasant times with family and friends.
9. Give appropriate attention to health and personal grooming.
10. Do not expect to be perfect, except in faithfulness to the Lord.

7 For your own meditation and self-analysis, consider the following questions carefully. Then write your response to each in your notebook.
a How have you overcome feelings of depression in the past?
b What new steps can you take now to help you avoid becoming depressed and discouraged in the future?

8 The concept *motivation* may be explained correctly as the
a) organizational genius behind one's actions which helps him to do his work easily.
b) interest or eagerness one demonstrates as he moves in a certain direction or does a certain thing.
c) power or ability one can bring to bear on a task because of his natural ability, acquired skills, and his training.

Theories of Motivation

Objective 5. *Classify examples of major theories of motivation.*

We have seen that the Christian leader must have the right motives and must be strongly motivated toward Christian goals. But this is only the beginning. Next he must see that others are motivated. In order to do this he must have some understanding of motivational theories or explanations of why people behave as they do.

Often people do not respond to leadership in the expected ways. For example, workers are absent, come late, do not prepare well, fail to follow instructions, or do not get along well with fellow workers. The leader says: "They're not doing it right. They don't have the right attitude. They're not dedicated to the Lord."

Then the preaching begins. The leader urges everyone to do better. He reminds them of sacred Christian duties. He may assume that the people who do not do better are simply unwilling to cooperate. But this may not be true.

Failure of the workers to respond to the leader may be caused by lack of ability, lack of information, personal problems, or some other obstacle. Part of the leadership responsibility is to find out why workers are not responding and objectives are not being accomplished. The mistake is to believe that all problems can be solved by preaching or by changing workers. It is more likely that problems can be solved by finding out how people can be motivated and then providing the proper motivation for each situation.

There are several theories of motivation. Probably none is altogether correct. But they all help us to a better understanding of this interesting and complex subject.

The Need Theories

By *need theories* we mean explanations of behavior based upon the idea that there are in each human being certain needs which must be satisfied. Probably the best known is Maslow's levels of needs theory. It states that people have five kinds of needs: 1) basic physical needs (such as for food); 2) the need for physical safety; 3) social needs; 4) the need for self-esteem and respect from others; and 5) the need for self-fulfillment, or opportunity to be creative.

According to this theory, people are motivated to satisfy these needs. The most basic need, such as hunger, must be satisfied before a person can be motivated to work for the satisfaction of some other need. For example, if a person is very hungry he may not be highly motivated to work on a creative project. If a person feels hurt or misunderstood by his companions, he may show a lack of interest in what the leader is saying about institutional goals.

Another need theory is that of F. L. Herzberg. Its main principle is that people have two types of needs in relation to their work. One type is for satisfaction in the work. This means people are motivated toward the work goals when they are given opportunities for personal achievement and responsibility and are given recognition for what they have done. The other type of need is for acceptable conditions surrounding the work. In the business world, this would mean the wages and working conditions. In Christian work it includes such items as relationships with the leader and other workers and being provided with materials for doing an assigned task.

Reward and Punishment Theories

The reward and punishment theories are based upon the work of B. F. Skinner. The central concept is that people will do that which brings them some kind of pleasure, or reward, and will avoid actions which bring some kind of pain, unpleasantness, or punishment. In work situations the application of this theory usually is to reward desired behavior and simply ignore, or fail to reward, behavior which is not approved.

Goal Theory

Goal theory is closely related to what we have already studied concerning management by objectives. It has been most formally stated by E. A. Locke. His findings are as follows: People are motivated to better performance if goals are specific, if they are fully understood, and if they are accepted by those who are expected to work toward their achievement. Goals which challenge the workers—that is, seem somewhat difficult—are more effective in motivation than easy goals. On the other hand, goals must be realistic in order to be effective.

Further research has shown that goals provide stronger motivation if the results of the workers' efforts are reported to them as soon as possible (this is *feedback*). Also, the strong support and participation of the leader motivates workers toward better performance.

Theories Involving Perception

It has been stated by numerous scholars in the field of human behavior that all behavior is the result of interaction of the person with the environment. This sounds simple and obvious. We realize that it is not simple when we think how distinctive the *perceptions* of individuals are. That is, different persons will see the same environment in different ways. (You may wish to review the material on perception in Lesson 5.)

A rather humorous example of different perceptions is an event which happened to a North American woman and a child from a rural environment in a tropical country. The woman took the child to the city. She wanted to please the child, so she bought a food that is considered a treat for children in many places. It was a mixture of milk and sugar, frozen nearly hard. "Have some ice cream," she said, smiling, watching for the child to smile in pleasure. The ice cream was a pretty color. The child took it and filled her mouth. But she did not smile. She screamed and spit out the food. "Hot!" she cried, "It burns me! It's hot!" In the rural tropics the child had never felt anything really cold; to her the sensation was that of burning. What the woman *perceived* as a cool treat was *perceived* by the child as an unpleasant burn.

You would not scold the child and say she was ungrateful. You would not say she was stupid because she didn't know hot from cold. Yet many leaders make similar mistakes. They scold and preach when they should be trying to understand why people respond as they do. Again we see the importance of the quality *empathy*. We must try to consider how the environment or the situation seems to others.

When we say *environment*, we are, of course, including other people. The child might have perceived that the woman was trying to hurt her. Then she would have been angry or insulted So we are reminded again of the importance of the way we communicate (how we speak and how we listen).

In addition to all this, there is the fact that people may perceive themselves in ways we do not immediately understand. A person may perceive himself as useless, when we think of him as very capable and important in his position. Or another may think he is being helpful to the leader when actually he is causing problems. In order to work effectively with people the leader must be aware of the importance of perception of these three types: perception of the environment, perception of other people (including the leader), and perception of self.

9 Write the number of each theory of motivation in front of its appropriate example.

.... **a** The teacher with the best attendance record for his class received an honorable mention in the church bulletin.

.... **b** Maria refused to take the assignment because she thought she was not as qualified as the others.

.... **c** The leader appointed a new convert to the committee in order to help him feel more accepted by the group.

.... **d** The leader said, "If we all work hard we can have 300 in Sunday school before Christmas."

1) Theories involving perception
2) Reward and punishment theories
3) Goal theory
4) Need theories

HOW LEADERS MOTIVATE OTHERS

Types of Response to Leadership

Objective 6. *Explain three types of response to leadership.*

As we have seen, it is important in the work of the Lord not only to be successful in getting the work done but also to do it for the right motives. Leaders must work because they are motivated by the love of the Lord and the knowledge of their calling. Then they must help their workers to act from similar motivations. In order to do this, it is necessary to understand the three kinds of response that people may give to leadership.

1. *Compliance.* Most persons wish to do the right thing and be accepted by the group. They want the leader to approve of them. Therefore, they will try to obey directions in order to be cooperative and to avoid unpleasantness or inconvenience. They will do whatever a strong leader tells them to do. This is obedience without personal commitment. Leaders who are satisfied with this type of response think they are strong. They give orders and people obey. The work is done. And of course there are situations in which this kind of response is necessary. People do not always understand the motives of the leader. Sometimes they must trust him and comply, or do as he says, simply because he is the leader. But this is the

response which is least effective for the work and for the persons who comply. It is a childlike response. Good leaders are not satisfied to have people respond in this fashion. The result is that a leader becomes surrounded with people who agree with anything he says. They do not help him grow and develop. The leader feels powerful, but his work is built upon a weak foundation when he requires only compliance of those who work with him.

2. *Identification.* A second type of response to leadership is identification. This term describes the response of individuals who do not perform because they are interested in the project, but rather because they have genuine admiration for the leader. They want to be like him and copy his actions. They want to establish a friendship relation with him. This differs from compliance in that the response is given in sincere respect and a desire to live up to the expectations of the leader. They work for the leader and not for their dedication to the purposes and goals. There is a temptation for leaders to encourage this type of response, but in the long run the work is weakened. Both the leader and the worker are turned from the true meaning of the work.

3. *Internalization.* The best type of response, that which is most effective for the work, the worker, and the leader, is that in which the worker sincerely claims the leader's goals as his own. The purpose of the work is a part of the worker's own value system. The worker perceives the project as an expression of his own love to God and an exercise of his own gifts and commitments. The leader gives directions and suggestions. The worker follows them because he believes in the work itself and is glad to have guidance in reaching his own Christian goals. When a person is successful in bringing about this attitude in a group of workers, he can call himself a true Christian leader.

10 In your notebook write, in your own words from memory, a brief explanation of the three types of response to leadership which we have just discussed. If you cannot do it easily, go back, read the section once more, and try again to write your explanation. This exercise will help you *internalize* the knowledge. Then you will have something more than words from a lesson. You will have your own living ideas, which you can easily share with others.

Practical Applications of Theoretical Knowledge

Objective 7. *Select examples of leadership behaviors which are effective in motivating workers.*

The reason we study theory is that it gives us a basis for practical action. Theoretical knowledge helps us to predict what outcomes might be expected under certain circumstances. If we know, for example, that people are motivated by the satisfaction of their needs, then we try to find out what the needs are and how we may help them to be satisfied through Christian service. If we know that people tend to be motivated by realistic goals, but discouraged by goals that are too difficult, then we can make appropriate plans.

Our understanding of motivational theories and types of response to leadership help us decide what kind of action, or behavior, on our part is most likely to motivate workers to do the tasks necessary that the goals may be achieved. Following is a summary of leadership behaviors based upon our theoretical knowledge. These are practical applications which leaders have found to be effective in the business world and also in Christian work.

1. *Competence.* The leader must know his job and behave in ways which indicate competence. This does not mean that the leader must be perfect. The leader must show confidence without a display of human pride. Workers are motivated to follow a person who has ability and can provide help and information to others.

2. *Purpose.* People will not work well without specific objectives. The leader must have objectives in mind and be able to arrange them, as we have learned, so that they lead to higher objectives and goals in a reasonable and realistic manner.

3. *Delegation and opportunities for participation of workers.* From our study of needs we know people need to feel accepted and creative. They must be given opportunities to participate in decisions concerning objectives and tasks. The leader must delegate, or make assignments to certain workers, and allow them to have full responsibility in certain situations.

4. *Training and growth opportunities.* People work better if they are learning and growing personally. When they feel that they know how to do a task well, they take more interest in it. Thus the leader who offers training or provides learning opportunities is working in two ways toward the final goals.

5. *Reward, recognition, and appreciation.* All people work for rewards of one kind or another. As we have found in the words of Paul, the Bible encourages us to keep our minds upon the eternal rewards. Good Christian leaders act in ways that make people feel constantly rewarded in the service of the Lord.

From our studies of burn-out, or apathy, and the perception theories, we know that people get tired and discouraged. They begin to think they are worthless or not appreciated. This causes them to lose sight of the goal. The good leader truly appreciates the workers and tells them freely. You have noticed in several of our Scripture readings Paul's words of appreciation to those who worked with him. Remember how he said that his authority was for building up, not for tearing down (2 Corinthians 13:10).

We have learned that the right kind of motivation can be encouraged by the right kind of reward. Too much personal praise and attention lead to human pride, but honest recognition of service and skill motivates people to work toward a meaningful objective.

6. *Feedback and renewal.* People work best when they are made aware of the results of their efforts and when they see the beginning and the end of specific tasks. A good leader knows that time schedules and reports frequently are more effective in motivation than inspirational speeches. If a task is worth doing, the worker should be given some kind of concrete evaluation of the outcome. Assignments and appointments to positions must be made with time frames, so that the worker feels periodically that he has finished something. Then he can start over with renewed interest. Much burn-out comes because people feel they have dragged on in the same old job so long that it has lost its meaning and nobody cares whether they do it or not.

11-14 Circle the letter in front of the correct answer to each of the following questions.

11 People are motivated to follow a person who
a) is perfectly competent in every respect.
b) explains that he is not very competent at a task.
c) expresses complete confidence in all he does.
d) shows he is competent without being proud.

12 People are best motivated by goals which
a) show the leader has great faith.
b) are difficult but realistic.
c) are easy to achieve.
d) are stated by inspirational leaders.

13 Need theories indicate that leaders should
a) supply every need for all the workers.
b) give every worker an equal amount of work to do.
c) give workers opportunities to meet their needs as they work.
d) delegate all the most difficult tasks to the best workers.

14 Time schedules and reports are important because
a) they provide feedback and opportunities for renewal.
b) they prove that the leader is efficient and dedicated.
c) assignments must be made according to the church calendar.
d) appointments to positions must be made in time frames.

15 Match each leadership behavior (right) with its appropriate description (left).

.... **a** People work best when they are made aware of the results of their efforts and when they see the beginning and end of specific tasks.

.... **b** The good leader truly appreciates the workers and tells them freely.

.... **c** Workers are motivated to follow one who has ability and can provide help and information to others.

.... **d** People work better if they are learning and growing personally. When they feel that they know how to do a task well, they take more interest in it.

.... **e** The leader must make assignments to certain workers and allow them to have full responsibility in certain situations.

.... **f** People work much better when they have specific objectives which lead reasonably and realistically to the goals established.

1) Competence
2) Purpose
3) Delegation and opportunities for participation of workers
4) Training and growth opportunities
5) Reward, recognition, and appreciation
6) Feedback and renewal

THE GOAL IS WORTH THE RACE

Paul never suffered from burn-out. This was not because he became relaxed and took his work less seriously, but because, as his words indicate, he was literally *racing* toward a worthwhile goal. His objectives were not easy, as we know, for he spoke of a good fight. But he was sure the reward at the end was worth whatever the cost might be, so he never lost his enthusiasm (Romans 8:31-39; and 2 Timothy 4:7-8).

We have seen in the life and work of Paul, as in the life and work of each of the Bible characters throughout this course, that God's plan requires human leaders. In no case has prayer alone, nor miracles alone, ever accomplished the purposes of God. The awful responsibility for and the glorious privilege of carrying out His plans, God placed in the hands of those creatures He made from the dust of the earth. And, in almost every event, there has been a chosen leader, who never worked alone, but charged ahead, empowered by the Holy Spirit, inspiring others with some form of the Pauline battle cry: "We are more than conquerors!"

self-test

1 Paul's response to a crisis situation such as his arrest demonstrates the importance of leadership behavior to influence people's behavior positively in all of the following statements but one. Which facts are NOT statements of Paul in this situation.
a) Paul used every opportunity to preach against people's sins, prejudices, and spiritual blindness.
b) He remained calm, was courteous in manner, and conducted himself with dignity.
c) Paul's response was geared to inspire confidence in the reasonableness of the gospel's claims, for he demonstrated knowledge of the Law, the rights of citizens, and basic human nature.
d) Paul sought to identify himself with his audience and gave his own testimony of conversion fearlessly and reasonably.

2 In his trip to Rome, Paul revealed some choice qualities of leadership:
a) He assumed control of all decision-making processes after the centurion and the captain proved their inability to make good decisions.
b) He offered practical advice, remained cheerful in the time of danger, showed concern for his fellow-travelers' needs, and kept them working toward a common goal.
c) He waited until the official leaders had demonstrated their inability to lead, then he mapped out his strategy for success.
d) He remained aloof from the events which went from bad to worse, waiting for them to come to him for advice.

3 In Paul's shipwreck crisis, God chose to speak to all those concerned by means of
a) a miraculous sea rescue.
b) suspending natural laws, calming the sea in the midst of the storm.
c) providing supernatural guidance of the ship past the dangerous rocks.
d) Spirit-anointed and directed leadership.

4 The five dangers we considered which often keep leaders and workers from reaching their goals are listed in three of the four choices which follow. Which choice does NOT name danger we considered in this lesson?
a) Ego—personal pride
b) Popularity and praise
c) Political turmoil and religious prejudice
d) Jealousy and power

5 A spirit of competition is encouraged by our world, because it evaluates people on
a) their inherent value as individuals.
b) the basis of their performance.
c) their relative potential based upon their family status and training.
d) the basis of comparison with other people.

6 Since Paul recognized the fact that people can become weary in doing good, he endeavored to
a) shock them into the realization that they had missed the mark.
b) encourage or motivate them to keep their purpose in mind and to keep helping people.
c) have them repent of their defeatist attitudes and renew their dedication.
d) purge their ranks by getting rid of all those who were expressing feelings of discouragement and depression.

7 All of the following choices but one give reasons why Christian workers get depressed. Which one does NOT give reasons named in this lesson?
a) Christian workers are undermotivated and overworked.
b) Christian workers see much human pain and trouble and they often become physically and emotionally exhausted.
c) Christian workers frequently work without adequate resources and they become disillusioned by watching people.
d) Christian workers are optimistic and have high ideals and expectations.

8 Motivating leaders and workers is one of the most important steps to successful leadership. Motivation, as it is described in this lesson, is defined best as
a) intense human desire.
b) the task of getting workers to obey the leader and getting the task done.
c) the process behind the action or behavior which we see, the eagerness and interest shown in doing something.
d) the reason a person gives to explain why he accepts a responsibility.

9 The theory of motivation which says that people are motivated by the satisfaction of certain basic requirements is the
a) goal theory.
b) need theories.
c) reward and punishment theories.
d) theories involving perception.

10 The motivational theory which holds that people will do that which brings them some kind of pleasure and avoid whatever brings pain, unpleasantness, or punishment is the
a) theories involving perception.
b) need theories.
c) goal theory.
d) reward and punishment theory.

11 The motivational theory which holds that people are motivated to better performance if ultimate objectives are specific, fully understood, and accepted by those who are expected to work toward their achievement is the
a) goal theory.
b) need theories.
c) theories involving perception.
d) reward and punishment theories.

12 The theory of motivation which concerns the way people look at their total environment is the
a) reward and punishment theories.
b) goal theory.
c) theories involving perception.
d) need theories.

13 The kind of response that people give to leadership which is a childlike acceptance of what is done and involves doing the right thing to be accepted by the group and the leader is called
a) compulsion.
b) compliance.
c) counterproductive.
d) coercive.

14 A second kind of response to leadership involves those who don't particularly care about the project but who greatly admire and want to be like the leader is called
a) compliance.
b) solidarity.
c) internalization.
d) identification.

15 The best type of response for all concerned is that in which the worker sincerely claims the leader's own goal as his own. It is called
a) identification.
b) compliance.
c) intensification.
d) internalization.

16 Match each of the dangers involving wrong motives (right) with its appropriate description (left).

.... **a** Reveals itself in the attempt to demonstrate how one is ahead of others by comparison of oneself with others

.... **b** Is revealed when one refuses to admit he may be wrong and insists on doing everything his own way

.... **c** Behavior demonstrated by one who is very sensitive to criticism, expects special privileges and public honors, and is arrogant about his spiritual gifts

.... **d** The kind of behavior rebuked by Paul in these words: "No more boasting about men!" Is the motivation of a leader who seeks glory from people and loves it

.... **e** Because of this danger leaders often fail to delegate responsibilities to competent people; it also reveals itself in feelings of resentment toward others who are commended for doing a job on which a leader has worked hard

1) Ego–personal pride
2) Overconfidence
3) Popularity and praise
4) Jealousy
5) Power

Be sure to complete your unit student report for Unit 3 and return the answer sheet to your GTN instructor.

answers to study questions

8 b) interest or eagerness one demonstrates.

1 Your answers.

9 a 2) Reward and punishment theories.
  b 1) Theories involving perception.
  c 4) Need theories.
  d 3) Goal theory.

2 Your answers may be any of the Scripture references from Pauline writings, as mentioned in Lesson 1 or Lesson 9, or any example given in your own words from the account in this lesson. I've suggested the following:
  a Galatians 6:2
  b Philippians 3:14
  c 1 Corinthians 9:24-27; 2 Timothy 2:15
  d 2 Timothy 4:5
  e Ephesians 4:16; 1 Corinthians 12:4-12
  f Philippians 4:1-3; Colossians 4:7-14
  g Luke 9:62; 1 Corinthians 15:58; Ephesians 4:14.

10 Your answer.

3 c) The importance of Paul's behavior as a leader is this.

11 d) shows he is competent without being proud.

4 a Praise.
  b Jealousy.
  c Pride, popularity, ego, and power.
  d Desire for popularity, power.
  e Pride, jealousy, and ego.
  f Overconfidence, pride, and power.

12 b) are difficult but realistic.

5 Your answer. Were your feelings caused by some of the things listed in this lesson? I trust you will learn to look beyond the times of temporary discouragement to the final goal. Remember: We will certainly reap if we don't faint or give up (Galatians 6:9).

13 c) give workers opportunities to meet their needs as they work.

6 a False. (No human being can avoid all depression.)
  b False. (No, the Lord saw that he was strengthened in body and soul, giving him rest, nourishment, and encouragement.)
  c True.
  d True.
  e True.
  f True.
  g True.
  h False. (These are normal concerns, but we should trust the Lord to help us with them and not allow them to worry us too much.)

14 a) they provide feedback and opportunities for renewal.

7 Your answer. I trust that you have found help in the Word of God, in prayer, and in the fellowship of other believers. And I hope you have gained new perspectives for coping with future times of difficulty from the list of suggestions given. Paul obviously gained consolation from his ability to forget the mistakes of the past. He bids us all to follow his example in this Phillippians 3:13, 15).

15 a 6) Feedback and renewal.
  b 5) Reward, recognition, and recall.
  c 1) Competence.
  d 4) Training and growth opportunities.
  e 3) Delegation and opportunities for participation of workers.
  f 2) Purpose.

for your notes

Appendices

Appendix A — Checklists

SELF-DEVELOPMENT CHECKLIST

.... Keep up personal spiritual life-Bible reading, church attendance.

.... Recognize exact responsibilities.

.... Enjoy working with others.

.... Get pleasure from accomplishments of others.

.... Keep informed-study and read.

.... Ask for advice and information when needed.

.... Use the experience and talents of others.

.... Have a clear understanding of policies and procedures.

.... Be willing to take risks.

.... Learn to do the best you can with what you have.

.... Make prompt but not hasty decisions.

.... Accept full responsibility for decisions.

.... Schedule personal time.

.... Adjust to new conditions.

.... Control temper.

. . . . Maintain sense of humor.

. . . . Support memory with written notes; use checklists.

. . . . Set personal goals and work to reach them.

. . . . Exercise spiritual gifts in appropriate ways.

HUMAN RELATIONS CHECKLIST

. . . . Give instructions clearly.

. . . . Explain why things are done as they are.

. . . . Explain the importance of every assignment and task.

. . . . Encourage people to do their best, and improve their skills.

. . . . Show respect for all workers.

. . . . Use workers' suggestions whenever possible.

. . . . Help others to set their own goals and reach them.

. . . . Recognize good work and show appropriate appreciation.

. . . . Learn to criticize in a constructive, helpful way.

. . . . Share information.

. . . . Encourage teamwork and sharing rather than competition.

. . . . Accept criticism and blame when appropriate.

. . . . Consider the feelings of others; never embarrass anyone publicly.

. . . . Give attention to shy, lonely people.

. . . . Express high expectations and confidence in people.

. . . . Share yourself and set the example whenever possible.

. . . . Listen and provide appropriate feedback.

COMMUNICATIONS CHECKLIST

. . . . Explain clearly, and allow others to ask questions.

- . . . Show and demonstrate whenever possible and appropriate.
- . . . Answer the questions: What? When? Where? Who? How? and Why?
- . . . Encourage others to express themselves.
- . . . Check back to be sure you are understood.
- . . . Explain changes before making them.
- . . . Explain decisions made by others over which you have no control.
- . . . Give reasons for all policies and procedures.
- . . . Keep superiors informed; work through proper channels.
- . . . Have a purpose for everything that is done.
- . . . Give progress reports.
- . . . Do not rely upon written bulletins and memos.
- . . . Listen carefully to complaints and suggestions.
- . . . Use language and illustrations appropriate for the group.
- . . . Learn to conduct interesting and effective meetings.

TASK SUPERVISION CHECKLIST

- . . . Develop and use checklists, work sheets, calendars.
- . . . Learn to manage time and set priorities.
- . . . Anticipate personnel and materials needs and costs.
- . . . Select and train workers.
- . . . Make specific assignments.
- . . . Establish objectives and set standards.
- . . . Keep accurate records.
- . . . Delegate responsibility and authority appropriately.
- . . . Make realistic requirements.

- .... Coordinate people, materials, time, place, method to reach goals.
- .... Provide a continuous plan for evaluation and improvement.

LEADING A GROUP CHECKLIST

Preparation

- .... Members notified about meeting time, place, topic, or purpose.
- .... Meeting place arranged-appropriate space; seating; physical comfort of members, such as heating and lighting.
- .... Outline or agenda prepared.
- .... Information, facts for the discussion, background data.
- .... Materials, notes, visual aids ready for use.
- .... Plans for developing a friendly atmosphere.
- .... Plans for spiritual activities.
- .... All participants notified and informed of the procedures.

Leading the Meeting

- .... Opening moments should be well-prepared.
- .... Members should be made to feel involved.
- .... Everyone should understand the purpose of the meeting and subjects or issues to be discussed.
- .... The meeting should open and close on time, unless there are very special circumstances.
- .... Every member should feel free and be encouraged to participate in open discussions.
- .... Discussions should be kept on the subject.
- .... Members should be given enough time to express themselves, but not allowed to monopolize the time.

.... Opportunities should be allowed for questions and suggestions.

.... Discussion should be summarized and clarified when needed.

.... Enthusiasm and good humor should be encouraged.

.... Members should be made to feel that their attendance and participation was appreciated and the meeting was worthwhile.

Evaluation of the Results

.... Did the group work well and seem satisfied with the meeting?

.... Were there any special problems? What can be done about them?

.... Did some members fail to participate?

.... Were any important aspects of the topic overlooked?

.... What were the most positive outcomes of the meeting?

.... What conclusions were reached?

.... What could have been done better?

Notes to remember in preparation for the next meeting:

Appendix B — Worksheets

DAILY REMINDER WORKSHEET

MY DAILY REMINDER　　DATE _____

Appointments　　　　　　　To Do

Name　　　Time　　　　　_____
_____　　_____　　　　_____
_____　　_____　　　　_____
_____　　_____　　　　_____
　　　　　　　　　　　　　_____

Phone Calls　　　　　　　Material Needed

Name　　　Number　　　　_____
_____　　_____　　　　_____
_____　　_____　　　　_____
_____　　_____
_____　　_____

MY DAILY REMINDER　　DATE _____

Appointments　　　　　　　To Do

Name　　　Time　　　　　_____
_____　　_____　　　　_____
_____　　_____　　　　_____
_____　　_____　　　　_____
　　　　　　　　　　　　　_____

Phone Calls　　　　　　　Material Needed

Name　　　Number　　　　_____
_____　　_____　　　　_____
_____　　_____　　　　_____
_____　　_____
_____　　_____
_____　　_____

GOAL PLANNING WORKSHEET

The goal for which we are praying and planning is: _____

QUESTIONS FOR PLANNING	TASKS TO BE ASSIGNED
WHY IS THIS GOAL IMPORTANT? (It is important to write down the spiritual motivation.)	

WHAT WILL IT TAKE TO ACHIEVE THE GOAL?

1. How many people?
2. Which plan or program will be used to achieve the goal?
3. How much time is needed?
4. How much money?
5. What materials, tools?
6. What facilities?
7. Will training be required? If so, what type of training?

WHO MUST BE INVOLVED IN ORDER TO ACHIEVE THE GOAL?
(List persons, leaders, groups, etc.)

WHEN WILL ALL RESPONSIBILITIES BE DONE?

HOW WILL WE KNOW WHEN THE GOAL IS MET?

ARE WE PREPARED FOR SUCCESS?
(Physical needs, teachers, materials, space, etc.)

From **The Effective Pastor**
Edited by Zenas Bicket

PLANNING MEETING WORKSHEET

Name of Committee or Group _____
(Attendance list may be made on reverse side of this sheet.)

Date _____ Leader or Chairperson_____

PROGRESS REPORTS ON WORK BEING DONE
(Is the work on schedule? Are there any problems?)

Project	**Comments**
_____	_____
_____	_____
_____	_____

PLANS FOR NEW WORK: Name of Project _____

Task to be Done	Persons Assigned	Due Date
_____	_____	_____
_____	_____	_____
_____	_____	_____
_____	_____	_____

EVALUATION OF COMPLETED WORK
(How well was it done? Was it done on time? How could it be improved?)

Project	**Comments**
_____	_____
_____	_____
_____	_____

OTHER NOTES

Appendix C — Pointers on Parliamentary Procedure

FIVE ESSENTIAL PRINCIPLES OF PARLIAMENTARY LAW

1. Courtesy and justice to all.
2. Consider one item at a time.
3. The minority must be heard.
4. The majority must prevail.
5. The purpose of rules is to facilitate action, not obstruct it.

FIVE ESSENTIAL RULES OF DISCUSSION

1. Each member is entitled to speak once to a question; however, if there is no objection, he could speak twice or more.
2. Members must remain impersonal, avoiding reference by name.
3. Members must make inquiries through the chairperson.
4. The member who makes a motion has the privilege of opening and closing debate.
5. The chairperson must remain strictly neutral. Should he wish to debate, he must call the vice-chairman to preside until the pending question is voted upon.

ESSENTIAL RULES OF VOTING

1. Methods of Voting

Voice Vote: "Yes" or "No" majority vote

Rising Vote: "Affirmative" and "Negative" for two-thirds vote

Show of Hands: "Affirmative" and "Negative" (for small groups)

Roll Call: Gives a check on attendance as well as vote

Ballot: Assures voter secrecy; preferred for elections

Secretary to Cast One Ballot: If specified in the by-laws

By Mall or Proxy: If specified in the by-laws

By General Consent: For routine decisions the chairperson states,

"If there is no objection we will "

2. Types of Voting

Majority: A majority is a number greater than half the votes cast

Plurality: A plurality is the most votes cast regardless of majority

Two-Thirds Vote: Simply refers to two-thirds of the votes cast

Tie Vote: A tie vote occurs when the same number of votes is cast *for* and *against* the motion. (Should this happen, the motion is lost.)

THE CHAIRPERSON OR PRESIDING OFFICER

The chairperson administers operation of the organization and presides at all meetings.

The chairperson avoids the use of "I," and says, "The Chair," and when reporting says, "Your Presiding Officer" or "Your Chair-person."

The chairperson does not say, "You are out of order." Instead, "The motion is not in order." Remember: Make it the rule, not the person.

The chairperson organizes, delegates, and supervises but does not interfere. He must always be impartial.

The chairperson should not say, "Those contrary, say no." Remember: Members may be opposed to a motion, but they are not necessarily contrary.

The chairperson must remember that all members have the right to make requests of the Chair, ask for parliamentary information, withdraw their own motions if there is no objection, ask for a recount on a vote, or question the quorum.

The chairperson must prepare an agenda for each meeting. He should also bring to the meeting a copy of the by-laws, a reference book of the parliamentary authority, a list of committees, a timepiece, a calendar, paper, and a pen.

ESSENTIAL AGENDA FOR THE CHAIRPERSON OR PRESIDING OFFICER

1. *Call to Order.* Using one tap with the gavel, the chairperson says, "The meeting will please come to order."

2. *Prayer.*

3. *Quorum Check.* The by-laws should state the number required for a quorum; if not, then a majority of membership is determined by a silent count of members in a small group or by roll call or door check in a large group.

4. *Reading of Minutes.* "The recording secretary will now read the minutes of the last regular meeting (or minutes of . . . giving date)." If several sets of minutes are to be approved, they are handled in chronological order. The chairperson asks: "Are there any corrections?" If not, he adds, "The minutes are approved." If corrected, however, he says, "The minutes are approved as corrected."

5. *Correspondence by Correspondence Secretary.* If there is one, otherwise by recording secretary. To conserve time, motions arising out of correspondence may be handled at this time rather than to raise them again under new business.

6. *Treasurer's Financial Report.* The report is read. The chairperson says, "The treasurer's report will be filed."

7. *Reports of Other Officers.* (Usually these are given only at the annual meeting.)

8. *Reports of Standing Committees.* By-laws determine the sequence for committee order. The chairperson says of each report, "The report will be filed."

9. *Reports of Special Committees.*

10. *Unfinished Business.* (Remember: Use the word "unfinished," not "old" business.) Secretary advises the chairperson from previous minutes.

11. *New Business.* New business is introduced from previous items of business or proposed by members.

12. *Program.* Remember: The chairperson does not turn the meeting over to anyone, though the program may be introduced by a special person who is introduced by the Chair. The presiding officer, who is in "the Chair" throughout the meeting, continues to hold the gavel and maintain order.

13. *Announcements.* The chairperson always announces the date, time, and place of the next meeting.

14. The Chair leaves some brief inspiration with the members.

15. *Adjournment.* The chairperson may adjourn the meeting, if there is no further business, without requesting a motion to adjourn. "There being no further business to come before the assembly, the meeting is adjourned."

THE MECHANICS OF A MAIN MOTION

Rules for the Presiding Officer

1. A member secures the floor. The member rises, addresses you, and gives his name. You should recognize him by repeating the name and nodding to him.

2. A member introduces business. A member makes a motion. Another member must second it. If not at once you say, "Is there a second?" If there is no second you say, "For want of a second, the motion is not before the assembly." (Remember: At least two members must express the desire by motion and second to discuss a question.) If a motion is duly made and seconded you say, "It has been moved and seconded that (repeating the motion)." You then ask, "Is there any discussion?" The presiding officer must by a statement open the discussion, but he does not join the discussion unless he surrenders the Chair temporarily.

3. The Chair puts the question. You wait until there is no more discussion, then you put the vote, which you may preface by this statement: "There being no further discussion, the Chair will put the question to vote. Those in favor say 'Yes.' Those opposed say 'No.' The motion is carried (or lost)."

SOME FURTHER POINTS

A Motion to Amend

A motion to amend is in order only when a main motion is pending and paves the way for changing the main motion. Motions to amend are voted upon prior to the vote on the main motion in reverse order to proposal. There may be only one primary amendment pending to a main motion and one secondary to the primary at one time.

Ways to Amend. 1) By adding (at end only), 2) striking out, 3) inserting, 4) striking out and inserting, and 5) substituting.

Improving a Motion. If you need to perfect a motion and then amend it (if more thought is necessary), perhaps it should be referred to a committee or postponed to the next meeting.

Responsibilities of the Presiding Officer

The presiding officer must be addressed. He must recognize the member, accept the motion, hear a second, state the motion, open the motion to debate, take the vote, and announce the result.

Officers' Duties and Privileges

The duties of officers should be outlined by the by-laws or rules. The work of each committee should also be described in written form in the by-laws or standing rules. Officers and chairpersons must turn over promptly to their successors all files and information.

Appendix D—Model of Christian Leadership

Empathy: Luke 6:31; Hebrews 13:3; 1 Peter 3:8; 5:9; Galatians 6:1-2.

Competence: Exodus 35-36; Proverbs 12:27; 22:29; 31:10-31; 2 Timothy 2:15; 2 Peter 1:5-10.

Goal Achievement: Philippians 3:14; Ephesians 3:1, 10-11; 2 Timothy 3:10.

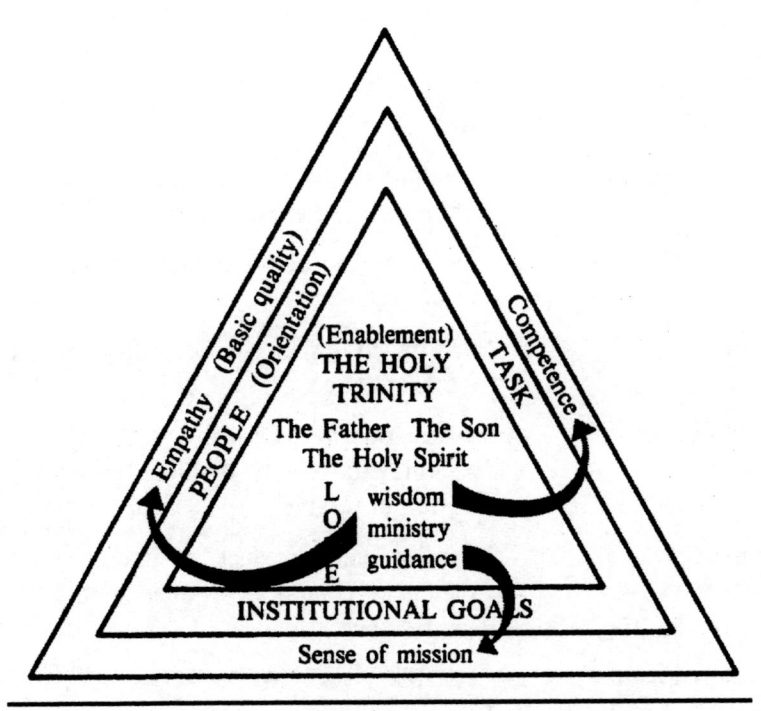

Empathy (Basic quality) — PEOPLE (Orientation)
Competence — TASK
(Enablement) THE HOLY TRINITY
The Father The Son The Holy Spirit
LOVE
wisdom
ministry
guidance
INSTITUTIONAL GOALS
Sense of mission

A Christian leader is a person who stimulates and develops the capacities of others and guides them in the attainment of Christian goals.

© Billie Davis, 1979

Glossary

The right-hand column lists the lesson in the independent-study textbook in which the word is first used.

			Lesson
abolished	—	destroyed; completely done away with	7
accountability	—	conditions, quality, fact, or instance of being responsible; dependability	4
administration	—	the managing of a business, office, or institution	1
allocated	—	distributed in shares or according to a plan; allotted	4
ambition	—	a strong desire for fame or success; seeking after high position, great power, or wealth	9
apathy	—	lack of emotion; lack of interest; listless condition, unconcern; indifference	9
appropriate	—	suitable; proper	2
assertive type	—	one who performs best when given a degree of independence and freedom to be creative; one who is positive and confident in a persistent way	5
assume	—	take for granted; suppose (something) to be a fact	2

Glossary

assumption	—	the act of assuming; supposition; presumption	2
assumptions	—	refers here to our beliefs about people; what we take for granted about them	2
attitudes	—	refers here to the thoughts and feelings that show one's disposition; opinion	1
authoritarian	—	believing in, relating to, or characterized by unquestioning obedience to authority as that of a dictator rather than individual freedom of judgment and action	6
authority	—	the power or right to give commands, enforce obedience, take action, or make final decisions	1

behaviors	—	ways of acting; conduct	1

capabilities	—	practical abilities; abilities, features not yet developed	1
casually	—	happening by chance; without definite or serious intention; apathetic; unconcerned; careless	4
centurion	—	the commander of a group of about 100 soldiers in the ancient Roman army	9
chants	—	words spoken monotonously or repetitiously; to utter, sing, or recite in the manner of a chant	9
characteristics	—	distinguishing traits, features, or qualities that are peculiar to, and help identify someone	1

circumcision	— a religious rite of the Jews (see Genesis 17:10-14)	3
climactic	— pertaining to or coming to a climax	4
competencies	— abilities; capacities	7
comprehend	— to grasp mentally; understand	3
compromise	— used here to mean a weakening, as of one's principles	9
conceited	— having too high an opinion of oneself; vain	4
confidant	— a close, trusted friend, to whom one confides intimate matters or secrets	6
consequences	— the results of actions, processes, etc.; outcomes; effects	6
consultant	— an expert who is called on for professional or technical advice or opinions	3
controversy	— discussion of a question in which opposing opinions clash; debate; disputation	3
courageous	— fearless; brave; full of courage	5
credibility	— quality of being believable; reliable	3
custody	— a guarding or keeping safe; care, protection, guardianship	9

defiance	— the act of defying; open, bold resistance to authority and refusing to recognize or obey it	7
depressed	— gloomy; dejected; sad	9

Glossary

depression(s)	—	a period or periods when one is low-spirited, dejected, and gloomy; emotional condition characterized by feelings of hopelessness and inadequacy	9
descriptive words	—	the artful selection of words which provide a feedback that is positive and encouraging	5
dimensions	—	here used as ideas or aspects	6
dire	—	calling for quick action; urgent	7
downtrodden	—	oppressed; subjugated; tyrannized over	6
dramatic	—	filled with action, emotion, or exciting qualities	3

empowered	—	having power or authority to	1
enchanted	—	to be under the spell of; bewitched	7
environment	—	surrounding things, conditions, or influences	9
equality	—	state or instance of being equal; like or alike in quality, degree, value; of the same rank, ability, merit	5
evaluative words	—	choice of words which view one's performance as measured against an accepted standard to demonstrate his lack of adequate performance	5
exemplary	—	serving as a model or example; worth imitating	1
exiles	—	those who are banished from their own country living for a prolonged period	7

exotic	— strange or different in a way that is striking or fascinating; strangely beautiful, enticing	7
expectations	— what is anticipated; one's beliefs about the probability of what will occur	2
faction	— group of persons who stand up for their side against the rest of a larger group; dissension	6
favoritism	— the showing of more kindness and indulgence to some person or persons than to others; having favorites; art of being unfairly partial	9
figurative meanings	— meanings not in their original, usual, literal, or exact sense or reference; for example, in "the *blaring* headlines" the word blaring is in a figurative sense	5
frustration	— state of being frustrated, checked, baffled; disappointment	2
Gentiles	— as used here, any persons not Jews	3
handicapped	— hindered, hampered; disadvantaged	4
harassing	— to trouble by repeated raids or attacks; also to trouble, worry, or torment	2
harmonize	— be in or bring into harmony, accord, or agreement	6
imminent	— likely to happen soon; about to occur	6
impulsive	— acting or likely to act on impulse; easily moved	2

Glossary

indulge	— to give way to one's own desires (because of a weak will or an amiable nature)	9
institutional	— of, pertaining to, or established by aninstitution	2
institutional goal	— the final or ultimate goal of the institution which is achieved by making and reaching other goals	7
internalize	— to make the leader's attitudes, ideas, norms, etc., a part of one's own patterns of thinking	9
intuitive	— having or perceiving by intuition; the learning or knowing of something without the conscious rise of reasoning; immediate apprehension or understanding	5
languid	— to be faint or listless; without vigor or vitality; drooping; weak; sluggish; dull; slow	9
magnificent	— exalted; exceptionally good; noble; sublime	4
manipulate	— to manage or control or by shrewd use of influence, often in an unfair way	2
martyr	— person who is put to death or is made to suffer greatly because of his religion or other beliefs	9
ministry	— the act of ministering or serving; ministration; refers to the collective ministries of believers in the New Testament church as seen in Romans 12:6-8; 1 Corinthians 12:28; Ephesians 4:11-16	1

morality	—	moral quality or character; the character of being in accord with the principles or standards of right conduct	9
morals	—	principles, standards, or habits with respect to right or wrong in conduct	9
motivated	—	being induced, incited, or impelled to action	2
motivation	—	the state or condition of being motivated	2
mystical symbols	—	spiritually significant messages or words beyond human comprehension; having magical power	9
operational goals	—	the objectives employed to help reach the institutional goal	7
operations	—	processes or actions that are parts of series in some works	1
oppressive	—	hard to put up with; cruelly overbearing; harsh; severe; unjust	1
organizations	—	the manner in which groups are organized or structured for some specific purpose	1
panic	—	a sudden, unreasoning, hysterical fear, often spreading quickly	9
perceptions	—	the act of perceiving or the ability to perceive; mental grasp of objects, qualities, etc., by means of the senses; awareness, comprehension; insight, intuition, or the faculty for these	5
perpetuate	—	to make perpetual; cause to continue or be remembered	8

Glossary

perpetuation	— carrying on; making perpetual	1
poise	— ease and dignity of manner; self-assurance; composure	9
policy	— a principle, plan, or course of action, as pursued by a government, organization, or individual	3
potentialities	— the possibilities or capabilities of becoming, developing	2
prejudice	— suspicion, intolerance, or irrational hatred of other races, creeds, religions, occupations, etc.	5
principle	— a fundamental truth, law, doctrine, or motivating force upon which others are based	1
privation	— lack of the comforts or of the necessities of life	7
professional	— pertaining or appropriate to a profession; here it refers to the scholarly study of leadership	3
psychology	— the science dealing with the mind and with mental and emotional processes	3

---

rank	— a relative position, usually in a scale classifying persons or things; grade; degree	9
rationally	— reasonably; sensibly	7
recognition	— the acknowledgment of achievement, service, merit in the form of some token of appreciation	2
recruitment	— the act or process of enlisting people for service	3

relations	—	the connections or dealings between or among persons in business or private affairs	2
relationships	—	connections, associations, or involvements among people	2
relevant	—	relating to the matter at hand; pertinent; to the point	4
remorse	—	deep, painful regret for having done wrong	8
reputation	—	what people think and say the character of a person is; character in the opinion of others	3
responsibility	—	condition, quality, fact, or instance of being responsible; obligation; accountability	1
responsible	—	expected or obliged to account for something to someone	1
responsive type	—	one who reacts easily or readily to suggestion or appeal; requires detailed instructions in order to perform task	5
ridicule	—	laugh at; make fun of	6
routine	—	a regular, more or less unvarying procedure; customary, prescribed, or habitual, as of business or daily life	6
scepter	—	the rod or staff carried by a ruler as a symbol of royal power or authority	7
self-concept	—	an individual's conception of himself and his own identity, abilities, worth	3
sensation	—	action of the senses; power to see, hear, feel, taste, smell	9

serene	—	peaceful; calm; tranquil; quiet	9
servitude	—	the condition of a slave, serf, or the like; subjection to a master	4
specific	—	something specially suited for a given use or purpose; definite, precise, particular	1
spontaneously	—	of one's own free will; natural; of itself	5
status	—	position; rank; standing; high position; prestige	7
strategy	—	skillful planning and management of anything	4
style	—	best defined here as the continuation of behaviors, or the tendency to act in a certain way	2
symptom	—	sign; indication	6
techniques	—	the method of procedure, or way of using basic skills, in accomplishing something	4
theory	—	a speculative idea or plan as to how something might be done	2
traits	—	the personal qualities of a leader	1
ultimate	—	greatest or highest possible; maximum	3
unique	—	rare; unusual	3
vaguely	—	not clearly, precisely, or definitely stated	5

Answers to Self-Tests

Lesson 1

1 c) has a specific way to accomplish His purpose.
2 b) people He chooses, directs, and empowers to accomplish His purpose.
3 a) knows beforehand His purpose and how He will move to achieve it.
4 d) Cultural expectations of able people and societal demands reveal the necessity for leadership.
5 b) follow other leaders, and all follow the Lord.
6 a) respect for authority and submission to God's will.
7 c) interest in and concern for other people.
8 c) Compassion, understanding of his part in God's plan, forgiveness, and love.
9 d) Patience and wisdom.
10 c) He reminded his brothers of his earlier dreams and predictions.
11 emotional stability.
12 Ability to share leadership.
13 empathy.
14 Consistency and dependability.
15 goal achievement.
16 group membership.
17 Competence.

Lesson 2

1 d) to be with him to help him.
2 c) He refused the Lord's call.
3 a) forget their initial enthusiasm.
4 b) should be shared with other leaders.
5 b) middle leaders who go to the battle.
6 d) trust others to share the vision.
7 c) Moses would survive and the people's needs would be met.
8 a) the potential for good in the people of God.

Answers to Self-Tests

9 b) God makes leaders responsible for His people.

10 d) "Expect more from your people."

11 d) his beliefs or assumptions about people.

12 c) People are essentially trust worthy and good.

13 b) High expectations.

14 You should have circled letters b) and c). Your evaluation may differ slightly from mine. I've noted that Mr. Land is running the risk of making people feel that they don't really count, that he is too bossy, that he doesn't trust them, and that it is his work, not the Lord's. He runs the risk of losing his support and not achieving his goals. His group will undoubtedly remain small-essentially, what he can handle. In addition, he may not be able to stand either the emotional or the physical strain.

15 You should have circled letters a) and d). Again, your evaluation may differ slightly from mine, but you probably noted that Mr. Murphy should see his vision extended as the goals are achieved His group should demonstrate real vitality and growth. A spirit of mutual trust should be apparent in group relationships. Fresh leadership talent will undoubtedly emerge. Mr. Murphy will not be over worked, and everyone concerned will be involved meaningfully in the tasks and working toward and achievement of the institutional goals.

16 autocratic style.

17 democratic style.

18 Theory X, autocratic style.

19 Theory Y.

20 recognition.

Lesson 3

1 b) help develop the capabilities of others.

2 c) different needs in the church require different kinds of leadership.

3 b) trained leaders who could multiply.

4 a) Personally instructs and advises.

5 b) was alert to leadership potential.

6 d) from the "call" a leader gains.

7 c) providing both the place and the environment.

8 d) the lives of others.

9 e) All of the above.

10 b) did not work very well.

11 d) is based on caring for people.

12 e) "Keep the strain of decision making as well as problems from your people."

13 b) Recognize the fact that the development of others enlarges your own effectiveness.

14 a) helps others and surrounds himself with competent workers.

15 d) share goals and decision-making so that you can say truly, "This is our work."

Lesson 4

1 False. (God knows all about our abilities and human re sources before we ever have the opportunity to demonstrate them. Our life experiences, however, provide valuable and practical background knowledge, which is a great asset in later leadership experiences.)

2 True.

3 False.

4 True

5 False.

6 False. (Without proper planning and organization the doing stage often fails.)

7 True.

8 True.

9 False. (Good leaders normally think through the task in the planning stage. Then they begin the actual execution of the plan.

10 False. (Planning is essential to any project regardless of the expense or number of people involved. It gives direction and purpose to the efforts. It is necessary to count the cost before beginning any task.)

11 False. (Planning is both thinking and writing, and planning that is a process usually requires a plan that is a written document.)

12 False.

13 True.

14 True.

15 False. (Such preparations will certainly help overall, but no plans are "perfect" and certain to bring success.)

16 True.

17 True.

18 True.

19 False. (He should refer the person to his immediate leader or invite the leader to take part in the discussion.)

20 True.

Lesson 5

1 c) He stressed obedience.

Answers to Self-Tests

2 d) records which communicate.

3 a) symbolic communication.

4 b) understand the meaning of the message exactly.

5 c) understand words in the same way.

6 d) communication has broken down.

7 c) perceived by the receiver.

8 b) whatever they say is understood by their hearers.

9 d) understood a message and put it in our mind's storage system.

10 c) Feedback enables the leader to judge.

11 a 7) Personality.
 b 6) Age and sex.
 c 1) Language.
 d 4) Prejudice.
 e 3) Customs.
 f 5) Status.
 g 2) Symbols.

12 a 2) Know your audience.
 b 4) Use precise language.
 c 5) Encourage response.
 d 3) Respect your audience.
 e 1) Know your material.

13 True.

14 True

15 True.

16 True.

17 False.

Lesson 6

1 True.

2 False.

3 True.

4 True.

5 False. ('n his actions we see evidence of very careful *organization*. Nothing was done by chance.)

6 True.

7 True.

8 True.

9 False. (It is possible that one might not define the problem correctly, choose the right solution, or carry out the action properly.)

10 False. (Members must leave knowing how the specific action steps are to be carried out. The leader must then implement the action and monitor it closely.)

11 True.

12 False. (The main difference is that decisions are required in many routine situations just to maintain the flow of work.)

13 True.

14 True.

15 False. (Group involvement varies according to the circumstances. However, the greater the group's competence, the greater the degree of responsibility it is given.)

16 False.

17 False.

18 True.

19 False.

20 False. (These elements describe the social dimension.)

21 True.

22 False. (Most groups agree on some basic ground rules for decision-making when they formally organize. At this initial point they usually discuss procedure and acceptable means for making decisions. If at a later date either their procedure or their decision-making method is found to be inadequate, means exist for revision. Many, many groups function well using the majority rule. Christian charity and wise leadership do much to ensure that it is used fairly for the good of all.)

23 False.

24 True.

25 False.

Lesson 7

1 c) emerging to meet a need.

2 b) Leaders must be willing to accept responsibility at any cost.

3 d) The leader, to act boldly and decisively.

4 a) institutional goal.

5 d) operational goals.

6 c) Setting objectives and goals is an easy task.

7 a) help get the work done.

8 b) responsibility.

9 c) reality thinking.

10 b) avoiding responsibility.

11 a 4) Leaders suffer loneliness.
   b 1) Leaders are servants, not masters.
   c 3) Leaders are criticized and blamed.
   d 5) Leaders suffer stress.
   e 2) Leaders have to work harder than those they lead.

Lesson 8

1 d) One must guard against overconfidence.

2 b) are to be used to help others.

3 b) personal humility.

Answers to Self-Tests

4 a) the people under a leader's care are God's people.

5 d) be continually conscious of the ultimate goal.

6 b) is an orderly way of looking at what goes on in an organization.

7 d) relate to each other and to the whole.

8 a) input, process, and outcome.

9 d) The needs of people are neglected because leaders do not care.

10 a) Determine the ultimate goal and set the objectives necessary to help reach the final goal.

11 a 4) Objectives.
    b 2) Relationships.
    c 6) Evaluation.
    d 1) A supreme goal.
    e 5) Tasks.
    f 3) Needs.

6 b) encourage or motivate them to keep their purpose in mind.

7 a) Christian workers are under-motivated.

8 c) the process behind the action.

9 b) need theories.

10 d) reward and punishment theory.

11 a) goal theory.

12 c) theories involving perception.

13 b) compliance.

14 d) identification.

15 d) internalization.

16 a 5) Power.
    b 2) Overconfidence.
    c 1) Ego-personal pride.
    d 3) Popularity and praise.
    e 4) Jealousy.

Lesson 9

1 a) Paul used every opportunity.

2 b) He offered practical advice.

3 d) Spirit-anointed and directed leadership.

4 c) Political turmoil and religious prejudice.

5 d) the basis of comparison with other people.

PEOPLE, TASKS, & GOALS

STUDIES IN CHRISTIAN LEADERSHIP

UNIT STUDENT REPORTS
AND
ANSWER SHEETS

People, Tasks, and Goals

DIRECTIONS

When you have completed your study of each unit, fill out the unit student report answer sheet for that unit. The following are directions how to indicate your answer to each question. There are two kinds of questions: TRUE-FALSE and MULTIPLE-CHOICE.

TRUE-FALSE QUESTION EXAMPLE

The following statement is either true or false. If the statement is
                TRUE, blacken space A.
                FALSE, blacken space B.

1 The Bible is God's message for us.

The above statement, *The Bible is God's message for us,* is TRUE, so you would blacken space A like this:

1 ■ | B | C | D

MULTIPLE CHOICE QUESTION EXAMPLE

There is one best answer for the following question. Blacken the space for the answer you have chosen.

2 To be born again means to
a) be young in age.
b) accept Jesus as Savior.
c) start a new year.
d) find a different church.

The correct answer is b) *accept Jesus as Savior,* so you would blacken space B like this:

2 | A | ■ | C | D

Student Report for Unit One

STUDENT REPORT FOR UNIT ONE

Answer all questions on Answer Sheet for Unit One. See the examples on the **DIRECTIONS** *page which show you how to mark your answers.*

PART 1—TRUE-FALSE QUESTIONS

The following statements are either true or false. If the statement is
TRUE, blacken space A.
FALSE, blacken space B.

1 I have carefully read all of the lessons in Unit One.

2 God has a certain, specific way to accomplish His purpose.

3 A great leadership asset is one's ability to see his people's potential for good.

4 Joseph's experience in prison indicates that a true leader develops his skills in isolation from the problems of others.

5 Theory X Assumptions are based upon a very positive view of people's potential for good.

6 Spiritual needs everywhere require the same kind of leadership.

7 Paul demonstrated his interest in developing leadership by looking out for potential leaders and helping them get started.

8 People achieve best when they are persuaded to do the will of the boss.

PART 2—MULTIPLE-CHOICE QUESTIONS

There is one best answer for each of the following questions. Blacken the space on your answer sheet for the answer you have chosen.

9 Biblical evidence demonstrates clearly that God has a plan. From this we can conclude correctly that
a) His purpose and ways are unchanging.
b) He knows in advance His purpose and how He will achieve it.
c) He is the victim of His purpose because of man's failure.

10 Two principles of effective leadership which Joseph demonstrated in the house of the government official were his
a) insistence that all subordinates respect and obey him.
b) efforts to preserve his position and to destroy the opposition.
c) desire to be popular with others and to please everybody.
d) respect of those in authority over him and his desire to do God's will.

11 Joseph's attitudes are an indication of the kind of attitudes a good leader must have. Which statement is NOT true of his attitudes?
a) He didn't seek revenge or boast about his achievements.
b) He saw his role as being God's instrument to bless others.
c) He reminded his brothers of his prophecies of ruling them.

12 Joseph's faith in God over the years, plus his sage advice to Pharaoh about Egypt's need to prepare for famine, reveal which leadership traits?
a) Patience and wisdom
b) Diligence and administrative skill
c) Submission to God and political resources

13 Moses recognized a principle about working with imperfect people:
a) Goals achieved through incapable people indicate great leadership.
b) People are a reservoir of strengths which can be developed.
c) People will fail but they are not necessarily failures.

14 When thirsty Israelites complained to Moses, he said, "What am I to do with these people?" God responded by telling him to
a) perform a miracle to impress the people with his authority.
b) share his ministry experiences with some of the elders.
c) walk alone in his hour of testing until he found a solution.

15 Dedicated leaders depend on the cooperation of people who are often less dedicated; therefore, they must develop leadership love which
a) enables them to accept lower standards of performance.
b) overlooks lack of commitment and human weakness.
c) trusts others to share the burden and help achieve goals.

16 Leadership studies indicate that how we act as leaders is a direct result of what we
a) perceive are the requirements of leadership.
b) assume are the expectations of society.
c) think our followers will approve.
d) believe about people.

17 Leaders who wish to have long-term effectiveness must
a) devote themselves fully to the development of others.
b) develop themselves and develop the talents of others.
c) give themselves fully to the development of their own ministries.

18 Older leaders and the church body can recognize the call of God on young leaders lives best by giving them opportunities
a) to learn under their supervision and to serve.
b) to be set apart and exalted as privileged persons.
c) providing the means for them to be formally trained.

People, Tasks, and Goals

19 When a leader surrounds himself with competent workers and helps others develop, he
a) makes his own position weaker.
b) may develop a strong personality-centered cult.
c) enhances his own influence and effectiveness.

20 The best policy for securing people's support for your goals is to
a) make all decisions and set goals because you are the leader.
b) share decision-making and goal-setting so that they are "our goals."
c) tell them of your love for them and then ask them to help you.

END OF REQUIREMENTS FOR UNIT ONE. Follow the remaining instructions on your answer sheet and return it to your GTN Instructor or office in your area, then begin your study of Unit Two.

Student Report for Unit Two

STUDENT REPORT FOR UNIT TWO

Answer all questions on Answer Sheet for Unit Two. See the examples on the **DIRECTIONS** *page which show you how to mark your answers.*

PART 1—TRUE-FALSE QUESTIONS

The following statements are either true or false. If the statement is
TRUE, blacken space A.
FALSE, blacken space B.

1 I have carefully read all of the lessons in Unit Two.

2 In the example of David we learn that the path to success in leadership is one of ease if one is truly God's choice.

3 Almost every task is done twice: once mentally, once in practice.

4 Feedback (receiver's response) mainly benefits the receiver.

5 Listening is a relatively simple process which demands little skill.

6 The purpose of the communication process is to have the receiver understand the meaning as it was intended by the source person.

7 Competent. experienced Christians should be encouraged to take more responsibility in making decisions.

8 Nehemiah's concern for Jerusalem, as well as the reproach he suffered, constituted his call to action.

People, Tasks, and Goals

PART 2—MULTIPLE-CHOICE QUESTIONS

There is one best answer for each of the following questions. Blacken the space on your answer sheet for the answer you have chosen.

9 Three of the following statements are principles which emerge from David's leadership methods. Which one is NOT?
a) He consistently sought God's will.
b) He recognized the need for excellence and competence.
e) He accepted tasks that helped him reach his goals.
d) He was loyal and considerate in relationships with everyone.

10 The major obstacles to effective planning can be overcome by prayer, maintaining an attitude of flexibility, and
a) developing a number of major plans instead of just one.
b) insisting that plans be simple, not detailed.
e) effective communication.
d) making contingency plans in case the main plan fails.

11 If a person bypasses his immediate leader and goes directly to the top leader with a problem, the top leader should ideally,
a) handle the matter himself.
b) refuse to hear the problem.
c) refer it to the middle leader or include him in the discussion.

12 Coordination, which is working the plan, includes all of the following but one. Which element does it NOT include?
a) Getting all components together in the most productive way
b) Getting followers to agree on a plan
c) Getting people and material to the right place at the right time

13 As political, military, and spiritual leader Joshua had to inform, encourage, give spiritual enlightenment, and also
a) issue firm orders which required implicit obedience.
b) provide a forum for discussion of his leadership strategies.
c) make sure that unity was not had at the price of uniformity.
d) to remember that unpopular leadership policies could ruin him.

Student Report for Unit Two

14 The listening process may be considered complete when
a) a message has been heard.
b) the message is remembered–stored in one's memory.
c) a message has been heard and attention given.

15 Barriers which interfere with effective communication may be defined best as
a) the attitudes which separate people.
b) the prejudices which blind people.
c) that which prevents the meaning intended by the source person from getting to the receiver.

16 Messages can be sent and received only if the sender and receiver
a) feel the same inclinations toward the subject.
b) share basic fields of experience.
c) hold similar ideals, prejudices, and world views.

17 Nehemiah motivated Jerusalem dwellers to arise and rebuild by
a) letting them see that his goal was their goal.
b) placing his burden before them.
c) convincing them of the divine nature of his call.

18 Group dynamics rests upon all the assumptions which follow but one. Which one does it NOT rest on?
a) People need each other and work better together as a group.
b) People influence one another as they work together.
c) The quality of group work is superior to that done by individuals.
d) Groups require less leadership to function well.

19 The first stage of the three-stage process of problem-solving is
a) analyzing the condition.
b) deciding if action is required.
c) defining the problem.
d) stating the problem.

20 Decision by consensus eliminates the possibility of there being a losing side and makes possible
a) true unity on the issues at stake.
b) an airing of the issues by those concerned.
c) deep loyalty in the group concerned.

END OF REQUIREMENTS FOR UNIT TWO. Follow the remaining instructions on your answer sheet and return it to your GTN instructor or office in your area, then begin your study of Unit Three.

Student Report for Unit Three

STUDENT REPORT FOR UNIT THREE

Answer all questions on Answer Sheet for Unit Three. See the examples on the **DIRECTIONS** *page which show you how to mark your answers.*

PART 1—TRUE-FALSE QUESTIONS

The following statements are either true or false. If the statement is
TRUE, blacken space A.
FALSE, blacken space B.

1 I have carefully read all of the lessons in Unit Three.

2 The ultimate goal toward which Esther worked, seeing her people saved, is referred to as an institutional goal.

3 Facing the ultimate crisis, Esther proved that a leader must stand alone.

4 To reach her ultimate goal, Esther had to initiate intermediate objectives which we call operational goals.

5 Probably the most neglected part of the Christian work system is needs assessment.

6 Most Christian leaders have little difficulty in determining the difference between objectives and activities.

7 Paul recognized that people can suffer burn-out even when they are doing good.

8 The highest response to leadership, which occurs when the worker sincerely claims the leader's goals as his own, is subordination.

People, Tasks, and Goals

PART 2—MULTIPLE-CHOICE QUESTIONS

There is one best answer for each of the following questions. Blacken the space on your answer sheet for the answer you have chosen.

9 Esther's response to the challenge of the leadership task, "If I perish, I perish," illustrates which leadership principle?
a) A good leader must be aroused easily by an emotional appeal.
b) A leader realistically adopts a negative attitude toward his tasks.
c) Good leaders see only themselves at fault if they fail.
d) Leaders must be willing to assume responsibility at any cost.

10 One of the most significant facts about good objectives is that
a) they make leaders function in a mechanical way.
b) they enable the Lord to work more easily in the church's program.
c) people work better and are happier when they have clear objectives.
d) people cease to have problems when they have clear objectives.

11 When people think in terms of the true purposes of the church and the objectives are made plain to them, they become willing to
a) make commitments and assume responsibility.
b) identify emotionally with a stated task.
c) cooperate when it is convenient for them to do so.
d) support the ministries of their church with morale and finances.

12 Professionals who have studied leadership principles in depth say that the only way to have a successful and productive life is to
a) recognize that some can be successful; others can't be.
b) understand that luck or chance is the key to success.
c) admit the facts and work with what one has; face reality.
d) realize that whatever will be will be; one can't change fate.

Student Report for Unit Three

13 The leader's personal experiences are intended primarily
a) as his educational stepping stones.
b) to help others.
c) to test his worthiness as a leader.
d) as his source of problem-solving guidelines.

14 All of the following solutions but one describe the Christian organizational system. Which one does NOT?
a) Every activity requires that something be started (input).
b) Every process is reviewed with the worker (feedback).
c) The activity begun goes through some kind of operation (process).
d) Something results from the operation (outcome).

15 The term management by objectives means to
a) identify objectives and handle work so they can be accomplished.
b) determine the goals you seek to achieve.
c) implement activities and expect to reach a goal.
d) develop a priority of objectives you would like to see accomplished.

16 Many organizations, especially churches, put in ideas and plan activities carefully, but they make the mistake of
a) planning the wrong activities for their particular groups.
b) copying the procedures of other equally uninformed organizations.
c) failing to state clearly in advance what action is expected.
d) trying to regiment the work of the Spirit.

17 People perform better when objectives are specific and when they fully understand and accept them, according to the
a) goal theory.
b) need theories.
c) theories involving perception.
d) reward and punishment theories.

18 We discern choice leadership principles in the accounts of Paul by means of
a) his speeches, published papers, and theology.
b) the evaluations of his contemporaries.
c) his own apologetics.
d) his bearing as a true leader as seen in his behavior in times of crisis.

19 We can explain best what the concept motivation means by saying that "motivation is the
a) set of beliefs or values which govern one's actions."
b) interest or eagerness expressed in doing a certain thing."
c) stated reason one gives for what he does."
d) reasoned approach one brings to the problem-solving task."

20 People do what brings them pleasure and avoid actions that bring them pain according to the
a) theories involving perception.
b) reward and punishment theories.
c) goal theory.
d) need theories.

END OF REQUIREMENTS FOR UNIT THREE. Follow the remaining instructions on your answer sheet and return it to your GTN instructor or office in your area. This completes your study of this course. Ask your GTN instructor to recommend another course of study for you.

PEOPLE, TASKS, AND GOALS

ANSWER SHEET FOR UNIT ONE

CS6261

Congratulations on finishing your study of the lessons in Unit One! Please fill in all the blanks below.

Your Name ....

Your GTN Student Number ....
    (Leave blank if you do not know what it is.)

Your Mailing Address ....

City .... Province or State ....

Country ....

Age .... Sex .... Occupation ....

Are you married? .... How many members are in your family? ......

How many years have you studied in school? ....

Are you a member of a church? ....

If so, what is the name of the church? ....

What responsibility do you have in your church? ....

....

How are you studying this course: Alone? ....

In a group? ....

What other ICI courses have you studied? ....

....

....

— Cut this page and send to your ICI instructor. —

ANSWER SHEET FOR UNIT ONE

Blacken the correct space for each numbered item. For all questions, be sure the number beside the spaces on the answer sheet is the same as the number of the question.

1	A	B	C	D		8	A	B	C	D		15	A	B	C	D
2	A	B	C	D		9	A	B	C	D		16	A	B	C	D
3	A	B	C	D		10	A	B	C	D		17	A	B	C	D
4	A	B	C	D		11	A	B	C	D		18	A	B	C	D
5	A	B	C	D		12	A	B	C	D		19	A	B	C	D
6	A	B	C	D		13	A	B	C	D		20	A	B	C	D
7	A	B	C	D		14	A	B	C	D						

Write below any questions you would like to ask your instructor about the lessons.

....

....

....

Now look over this student report answer sheet to be sure you have completed all the questions. Then return it to your GTN instructor or office in your area. The address should be stamped on the copyright page of your study guide.

For GTN Office Use Only

Date .... **Score** ....

Christian Service Program

PEOPLE, TASKS, AND GOALS

ANSWER SHEET FOR UNIT TWO

CS6261

We hope you have enjoyed your study of the lessons in Unit Two! Please fill in all the blanks below.

Your Name ....

Your GTN Student Number ....
       (Leave blank if you do not know what it is.)

Your Mailing Address ....

City .... Province or State ....

Country ....

---Cut this page and send to your ICI instructor.---

ANSWER SHEET FOR UNIT TWO

Blacken the correct space for each numbered item. For all questions, be sure the number beside the spaces on the answer sheet is the same as the number of the question.

1	A	B	C	D	8	A	B	C	D	15	A	B	C	D
2	A	B	C	D	9	A	B	C	D	16	A	B	C	D
3	A	B	C	D	10	A	B	C	D	17	A	B	C	D
4	A	B	C	D	11	A	B	C	D	18	A	B	C	D
5	A	B	C	D	12	A	B	C	D	19	A	B	C	D
6	A	B	C	D	13	A	B	C	D	20	A	B	C	D
7	A	B	C	D	14	A	B	C	D					

Write below any questions you would like to ask your instructor about the lessons.

....

....

....

Now look over this student report answer sheet to be sure you have completed all the questions. Then return it to your GTN instructor or office in your area. The address should be stamped on the copyright page of your study guide.

For GTN Office Use Only

Date .... **Score** ....

Christian Service Program

PEOPLE, TASKS, AND GOALS

ANSWER SHEET FOR UNIT THREE

CS6261

We hope you have enjoyed your study of the lessons in Unit Three! Please fill in all the blanks below.

Your Name ....

Your GTN Student Number ....
       (Leave blank if you do not know what it is.)

Your Mailing Address ....

City .... Province or State ....

Country ....

—Cut this page and send to your ICI instructor.

REQUEST FOR INFORMATION

The GTN office in your area will be happy to send you information about other GTN courses that are available and their cost. You may use the space below to ask for that information.

....

....

....

ANSWER SHEET FOR UNIT THREE

Blacken the correct space for each numbered item. For all questions, be sure the number beside the spaces on the answer sheet is the same as the number of the question.

	A	B	C	D		A	B	C	D		A	B	C	D
1	☐	☐	☐	☐	8	☐	☐	☐	☐	15	☐	☐	☐	☐
2	☐	☐	☐	☐	9	☐	☐	☐	☐	16	☐	☐	☐	☐
3	☐	☐	☐	☐	10	☐	☐	☐	☐	17	☐	☐	☐	☐
4	☐	☐	☐	☐	11	☐	☐	☐	☐	18	☐	☐	☐	☐
5	☐	☐	☐	☐	12	☐	☐	☐	☐	19	☐	☐	☐	☐
6	☐	☐	☐	☐	13	☐	☐	☐	☐	20	☐	☐	☐	☐
7	☐	☐	☐	☐	14	☐	☐	☐	☐					

Please write below one specific comment about the unit:

....

....

....

CONGRATULATIONS!

You have finished this Christian Service course. We have enjoyed having you as a student and hope you will study more courses with GTN. Return this unit student report answer sheet to your GTN instructor or office in your area. You will then receive your grade on a student score report form along with a certificate or seal for this course in your program of studies.

Please print your name below as you want it on your certificate.

Name ....

For GTN Office Use Only

Date .... **Score** ....

Christian Service Program